BUILDING WEALTH: PRIORITIES & PRACTICES

Biblical Principles and Wall Street Methods

Steve McCutcheon

Evergreen
PRESS

Building Wealth is a book of inspiration and instruction intended for individuals and to be general in nature and not intended for legal, tax, or individual investment advice. The investment model/strategy is intended for general educational purposes and the information may not be applicable or suitable for some individuals' purpose or usage. Investing is subject to economic and market risks, and the reader or any person acting on the content of this publication can lose money. Past performance does not guarantee future results.

There are many factors involved in investing success, the investor's judgment being the most important, and the author and/or publisher are not guaranteeing that any reader or user of the content of this publication will not lose money using this model on a short-term or long-term basis. Therefore, nothing contained in this publication should be construed to provide the reader or other user of the content of this publication with individual investment advice. Furthermore, the charts, figures, numbers, calculations, and other applicable information are drawn from sources believed to be accurate and reliable, and neither the author nor publisher is responsible for any mistakes in calculations, misrepresentations of factual material, errors or omissions, or for any reader's or other user's actions or results based on the information contained herein. The reader or any user of the content of this publication is solely responsible for the results of using the investment model or any other content of this publication.

ISBN 978-1-58169-344-7
For Worldwide Distribution
Printed in the U.S.A.
Evergreen Press • P.O. Box 191540 • Mobile, AL 36619 • 800-367-8203

To my grandson,
Austin Blake Dunlap

And in loving memory of my parents,
Reverend C.R. and Ophelia McCutcheon

My wife's parents,
George and Thelma Browning

And my sister-in-law,
Brenda Browning Wagner

Table of Contents

Foreword

My passion for over 30 years has been to help individuals and families integrate their faith into their financial decision-making. I believe that God's Word speaks with relevance to every financial decision that we make. I am often asked about how to deal with economic uncertainty and my answer always is, "Follow what God's Word says, period."

As I look back over my own career in the financial services world, I've experienced economic uncertainty, economic prosperity, good investments, and bad investments. It is my observation that every good financial recommendation and financial decision made will always have its roots in a biblical principle or in biblical wisdom. This book affirms my observation. Steve McCutcheon is an experienced and very successful financial decision-maker. He has written a book that has biblical principles as its cornerstone, but then shows how to work out those principles in a practical way.

What I particularly appreciate about this book is that it incorporates not only specific financial principles of finance but also, and just as importantly, the character issues of perspective, stewardship, diligence, humility, and discretion. Steve illustrates a value that he holds dear and one that I believe has made America great, and that is the spirit of entrepreneurship. Steve gives many illustrations of successful entrepreneurs. This makes the book readable and compelling.

Steve has written this book to his grandson offering him wisdom, education, and sound counsel. Because of this you will find this book to be of immense practical and spiritual value. It is a book that no doubt will be referred to frequently. It is a privilege for me to recommend and endorse this book .

Ron Blue, President
Kingdom Advisors

Acknowledgments

I want to thank several people for preparing me or helping me to write and publish this little book. My wife, Cynthia, researched and selected most of the Scriptures, and she was a valuable colleague in praying about and wording the biblical principles and theological notions that you will read. Also, she constantly encouraged me, helped me find time to write, and worked with me in the investment business since 1999.

Thanks to my daughter and son-in-law, Stephanie and Sammy Dunlap, and grandson, Austin, for your love, encouragement, and support.

I have many clients over the years that have supported SCM businesses, and I want to thank you for your patronage and affiliation over the last twenty-five years.

I have studied the works of many Christian and investment writers over the last forty years, and I thank each of you, who are too numerous to list, except two who have gone on to their rewards: Oswald Chambers and Derek Prince.

Thank you, Henry Blizzard, my friend and fraternity brother since 1958, for helping me get started in the investment business. Some of the ideas in Book Two were derived from our discussions. Dr. Jim and Barbara Prather read the first three chapters in the early stages of my writing and offered their encouragement and supported the investment business from the beginning. Thank you for your support and longstanding friendship.

I am indebted to the five entrepreneurs for allowing me to tell their stories: Ray Fulford, Bob Stone, Renee Keener, Aubrey Silvey, and Tommy Green. Thank you also Dr. Jack Crews, Rev. Gene Evans, Dr. Steve Davis, and Mr. Clarence Finleyson for the use of your stories.

Dr. Fisher Humphreys provided valuable insight into the history of early Christian theology, and I appreciate your help. George Mannes, senior editor of *Money*, thank you for allowing me to use your excellent article published July 2009.

Ron Blue, leader in Christian financial planning and noted author, you are very gracious to endorse *Building Wealth*—thank you very much. Dr. Carole Scott—thanks for your assistance with the points regarding the Federal Reserve. Millard Grimes, how can I thank you enough for asking me to write for *Georgia Trend?*

Thank you Keats Baldwin and David King, two research assistants, for your work to develop and test technology procedures and reports used in Book Two.

Dr. Don Adams and Dr. Debra Cobia, long time friends, advised me regarding the references and acquiring permissions. Don Hays gave me permission to use the Hays Advisory charts, which are strategic in Book Two. Also the Gaither Copyright Group advised me regarding the Elvis Presley at Notre Dame University story. Better Investing allowed me to use their *Stock Selection Guide*. Value Line Publishing gave permission for use of company reports from their *Investment Survey*.

Last but certainly not least, thank you Evergreen Press for taking a chance on an unknown author, and I appreciate Kerry Dierking's work in promoting *Building Wealth*.

To everybody mentioned and others, I appreciate your support and assistance at strategic points in bringing forth this book. God bless you.

Introduction

My grandson was born in July 2006, and he was one of those surprise blessings that I talk about in the following chapters. My wife and I did not think that we would be grandparents, but in January 2006, our daughter and son-in-law informed us that we were in for a big surprise. Soon after Austin was born, I calculated how old I would be when he reaches certain mileposts in his life. It shocked me to realize that I will be almost ninety years old when he graduates from college. I certainly will try to talk with him about investing and more importantly about life lessons when he gets a little older than he is now, but I am not deluded about any lasting breakthrough in that venture. Therefore, I decided to add to my pool of notes written over the years and to pass along in writing anything that might be useful to Austin. My notes have turned into a book because, even before Austin was born, I planned to write my stewardship testimony, reporting how God has blessed my family and me, and to pass on my ideas about how to make money by investing in stocks and managing one's own portfolio.

One of the subjects that I want to discuss with Austin is what the Bible says about money. I certainly do not want him to grow up thinking that trying to make money is evil, as long as he has his priorities in the appropriate order. Also, I want him to learn how to sacrifice to get ahead financially, save his money, consider starting his own business, and be a faithful steward of God's blessings on him.

Years before Austin's birth, I began a study of what the Bible says about money. I did this for two main reasons. First, some people still teach that seeking God's blessings on our finances is not biblical. They focus on three Scriptures:

You cannot serve both God and Money (Matt. 6:24).

The love of money is a root of all kinds of evil (1 Tim. 6:10).

It is easier for a camel to go through the eye of a needle than for a rich man to enter the kingdom of God (Matt.19:24).

I must admit that I have thought about these Scriptures as a Christian and a professional money manager because my job is to increase clients' total wealth. Evidently, I have not been alone in my concerns because I have read in numerous publications that rich people often have misgivings about their wealth. Most who evidence this concern are self-made wealthy individuals who come from humble beginnings. As they survey the poverty and broken dreams of their childhood friends and career associates, some of them experience first-degree guilt. The most notable example of this guilt that I can think of is Elvis Presley, who did not understand why he was so blessed. You may remember the stories of his passing an automobile dealership and seeing a lone figure staring in the showroom window at a shiny new car. How many automobiles did Elvis buy spontaneously? To me, this is an outward manifestation of some of the unspoken guilt that he did not deserve all of his wealth and acclaim.

The second reason that I began the Bible study is to gain wisdom from the Scriptures regarding the use of money. I have been amazed at what the Holy Spirit has taught me about the entire spectrum of money matters as revealed in the Holy Scriptures. Out of that study grew the concept of biblical principles that should shape our practices regarding seeking God's financial blessings and managing the money that God entrusts to us.

This book is the confluence of all of these notions with the catalyst being the birth of our only grandchild. My objective is to instruct in a system of building wealth over a lifetime and the righteous use of wealth. My basic assumption is that you can manage your own investments and will do a better job with the task than mutual fund managers or investment advisors. Furthermore, God has financial blessings in story for you, and I want to direct you to His principles that will prepare you to receive these blessings-in-waiting.

From the start, you need to understand four guidelines. First, I am using the term Wall Street to include the universe of investment professionals, whether in New York, Chicago, or small-town Carrollton, Georgia. Next, I want to assure my clients and former clients that any illustration, feature, or story in the text that you identify with is purely coincidental. I obtained my concepts, statistics, and features from academic studies, journal articles, and media interviews. I have collected this illustrative information for more than two decades from sources that report data that are broad enough to form the basis for generalizations. Third, I have added my thoughts, as indicated in brackets, to complete or amplify a point. Fourth, as you probably realize, my reference to Austin is simply a way of addressing any reader who is diligently seeking God's guidance about finances and is willing to select and manage his or her own investments.

Building Wealth is separated into two sections. Book One addresses the biblical issues that you may have contemplated, and this section provides you with a framework for moving with confidence into Book Two, which is a plan for building wealth.

I hope that you will enjoy life, build wealth, and contribute to God's kingdom on the earth, with this book contributing in some way to your journey. I welcome your feedback.

BOOK ONE:

Biblical Principles

Command those who are rich in this present world not to be arrogant nor to put their hope in wealth, which is so uncertain, but to put their hope in God, who richly provides us with everything for our enjoyment. Command them to do good, to be rich in good deeds, and to be generous and willing to share. In this way they will lay up treasure for themselves as a firm foundation for the coming age, so that they may take hold of the life that is truly life (1 Tim. 6:17-19).

CHAPTER ONE

Wealth Perspective

Most Americans focus early in life on building wealth. This is a mindset that became paramount with the survivors of the Great Depression of the thirties, and financial independence has been taught to succeeding generations. World War II veterans took advantage of the GI Bill to leverage their parents' ambitions with post-secondary education. In later generations, when most of us settle into our first jobs, we focus on buying a house, building an emergency fund, saving for the education of our children, and investing for a comfortable retirement. If the head of a household succeeds in all of these, he or she might be considered wealthy. Some Americans pursue wealth in order to enjoy a lifestyle of luxury.

Wealth is associated with security, independence, and comfort. Yet, just like beauty, wealth is in the eye of the beholder; and that which makes one person secure and comfortable may fall far short for another. Furthermore, the wealth perception disparities widen further across cultural lines, and the intrigue of American wealth is what draws thousands of immigrants to this country each year. For example, a villager in a Third World country probably views all Americans as wealthy because we have adequate housing, clean water and decent sanitation, motorized transportation, and numerous material possessions not in abundance in emerging nations.

In the United States and the other developed countries, we define true wealth in terms of total net worth. Each individual has his or her own benchmarks for appraising wealth. I will discuss my wealth benchmarks in chapter 6; but for now, let us define wealth as *net assets that provide financial independence*. Certainly, you should apply your own definition and benchmarks because you will need to set goals and measurements as you seek to improve your financial standing.

Wealth Perspective

I learned at an early age that wealth is relative to the person defining the term. When I was nine years old, my parents moved the family to southwest Georgia in order for my father to enroll in a Baptist college. He served as minister of two churches during the six years that we lived in Colquitt and Thomas counties. When I was eleven years old, my father decided that it was time for me to learn how to work, so he asked a church member and neighbor if he had any work on his farm that I could do. That started "indentured servitude" for me for five summers. I arose before daybreak and worked all day to help gather tobacco, beans, peanuts, cucumbers, squash, and watermelons. I helped feed and water the livestock and learned to work a G model John Deere tractor as well as Farmall and Ford Cub tractors. I also worked side by side with the sharecropper families and the day workers who helped with the produce harvests. I learned a lot about the hard scrabble life, heard a lot of curse words, and learned what these farm workers thought about wealth because they talked, indeed dreamed out loud, about improving themselves financially.

The sharecropper thought that the farmer was wealthy because he owned his house, land, and herds of livestock; had running water in his house; drove a late model pickup truck; and sent his children to the agriculture junior college in the next county. The day laborers thought that the sharecropper was wealthy because he had a permanent house and a steady job; dressed in a white shirt and tie on Sundays; sent his children to school on a school bus; and owned a decent pickup truck, although all the children had to ride in the open-air cargo flat. Now get this. The farmer thought the banker from whom he borrowed money to plant a crop was wealthy. The banker wore a shirt and tie to work, worked behind a desk from 9:00 a.m. to 4:00 p.m., took off on Wednesday afternoons, drove a Cadillac, attended the Methodist church, and sent his giddy daughter to the university.

I also learned at an early age that most people measure wealth by material possessions, houses and cars being at the top of the list. However, how many people have you known who incurred big debts to finance their expensive lifestyles? Of course, material possessions are the most obvious indicators people use to show their wealth and others to assess one's wealth. In biblical times, the phrase "livestock, silver and gold" (Gen. 13:2) was a common expression of wealth. Evidently, human beings have not changed in our perception of wealth over the course of human history. However, in consideration of the perils of easy debt, material possessions obviously are not an adequate measure of wealth.

Man's perception of wealth is relative, but God's definition of wealth is absolute. Jesus defined wealth as that which we store up in heaven and that which results in eternal blessings. He also said for us not to store up treasures on earth that can be corrupted and taken from us (Matt. 6:19-21). He ended this sermon with the words, "You cannot serve both God and Money" (Matt. 6:24). Obviously, there is an apparent conflict between the relative and the absolute regarding wealth, which I will address later.

Purpose of the Book

The purpose of this book is to teach you a method of building wealth by using an uncomplicated system of investing in stocks that I have developed over twenty-five years of investing professionally. I have read literally hundreds of books and articles on investing, but I have never read a book with the practical nuts and bolts that I am going to describe to you. I have used parts of this method for nearly forty years of my investing lifetime, and the total system has evolved over many bull and bear markets.

Who needs another investment book and why should you study this one? The bear market of 2007-2009 and the performance of most mutual funds are proof that most investors need to gain more control of their investments, and this book provides a complete course of action. Also, the times are different now from even a decade ago in personal financial planning. Millions of Americans born after World War II reached the early retirement age of sixty-two in 2008 and that cohort increased by 34 percent in 2009.

An inordinate number of retirees will receive lump-sum payouts from corporate pension plans over the next ten years, and later another retirement bubble will occur when the children of "boomers'" begin to retire. Furthermore, the trend in corporate retirement plans is the 401(k), whereby the employee manages his or her own investments, and in 2008, forty-eight million Americans owned 401(k) plans. The trend is in place: individuals are finding it necessary to manage their investments. Hopefully, this investment system that I recommend will assist you to become your own investment manager.

Aside from the retirement planning, most Americans seek ways to improve their quality of life, and many do this by investing in a portfolio of stocks or stock mutual funds. The number of investors will continue to grow; therefore, this book is timely and relevant for the modern household.

Why is this publication different from other investment books? Most investment volumes discuss strategy and leave it up to you to design and implement your methods. I am providing you with the methods to implement your strategy in a step by step process. By the time that you read this book, some of the free Internet sites might have changed, but that should be the only adjustment that you will have to make. This is an investment course with lab sessions that you can practice at home.

I will address in Book One the apparent conflict between what Jesus said about money and seeking wealth and the earthly wealth-building methods that I explain in Book Two. Here is the theme of the reconciliation of the two ways of building wealth: if we satisfy a set of priorities based on God's Word, no conflict exists between building eternal wealth and earthly wealth. As maturing Christians, we must go through a process that pleases God and allows for a return on investment in heaven and on earth.

Many Christians never receive all the financial blessings that God has in store for them because they never ask God to bless their finances and/or they do not satisfy the priorities God set forth for blessings. James, the brother of Jesus, said in James 4:2-3, "You do not have, because you do not ask God. When you ask, you do not receive, because you ask with wrong motives, that you may spend what you get on your pleasures." My objective is to set forth the several priorities that the Bible says will satisfy God's conditions for blessing His people.

In his book, *The Prayer of Jabez*, Bruce Wilkinson said, "God favors those who ask" for His blessings, as Jabez did (1 Chron. 4:10). Wilkinson said that God offers His love for all and that is why He sent Jesus to seek and save the lost unto salvation; but He "favors those who ask" if they do so in accordance with His will.[1]

The top priority in my method of investing and managing money is that we must live in accordance with God's will and purpose for our lives, including the righteous use of our money. Jesus said to seek first the kingdom of heaven and righteousness, and God will provide the necessities for life to us (Matt. 6:33). The next priority is to seek eternal rewards with the resources God has entrusted to us now and in the future, and to subordinate seeking earthly wealth for our own welfare and pleasure (Matt. 6:20-21). These are just two examples of the biblical principles I employ to lay a framework for teaching my investment model and discussing other financial matters.

Scriptures show that God blesses those who are obedient to His commands and fulfill certain prerequisites that He clearly sets forth in His Word for financial blessings. I focus on those scriptural principles to help you prepare yourself to fulfill God's conditions for each promised blessing. God loves us, He knows us better than we know ourselves, and He has a plan for our lives, which includes prospering us. These premises are in accord with His Word. For example, consider the promise God spoke through the prophet Jeremiah to the children of Israel as He declared their release from captivity in Babylon. God declared to the people that He had plans for them, "plans to prosper you and not to harm you, plans to give you hope and a future" (Jeremiah 29:11). Certainly, God's laws, principles, and promises of the Old Testament are applicable to us in the twenty-first century and beyond.

I need to define how I use the term *God's principles*, and I want to do that by contrasting *principles* with the *laws*. God's laws are the sovereign and unchangeable commands that He established, which govern the natural order of everything in existence ranging from the vast universe to the singular individual. Gravity and the Ten Commandments were established as immutable laws to govern nature and human behavior, respectively. God's principles set forth divine promises that can be fulfilled only following our accomplishment of predetermined conditions. For example, in Malachi 3:10, God said if we give back to Him a portion (tithe) of what He has entrusted to us (condition), He will reward us financially (promise).

Who can profit most from *Building Wealth?* Individuals who are seeking divine guidance for their finances and realize the long-term benefits of investing in stocks will benefit the most from this publication. If you have tried investing in stocks and have been humiliated, I believe you will find inspiration and instruction to try investing again. If you are participating in a 401(k) or 403(b) plan or IRA, as you manage your retirement funds, you certainly will find help from my investment strategy. If you are an experienced investor and have relied on a financial advisor or mutual funds, but you would like to manage your money yourself, the uncomplicated method described in this book should be appealing to you. Let me assure you that you do not have to be a sophisticated investor to profit from this practical approach to improving your financial well-being. Furthermore, if you have never studied the biblical principles that address managing your money, Book One of this text should be enlightening.

Comments from my adult students and research reports over the years have made it clear to me that many market watchers are perplexed about the workings of the stock market. Many mutual fund investors and participants in company 401(k) plans do not really understand the terminology and methodology of investing in commons stocks. Nonetheless, I have always maintained that the owner of an investment account is the best manager of his or her money, as long as the individual understands the basics of investing and has a system that will work for profit over time. I attempt to dispel much of the mystery of participating in financial markets and to lead you into the development of an investment strategy that will minimize risk and maximize return over a lifetime of investing.

Investment strategy is simply the process of establishing long-term investment goals; identifying appropriate investment instruments for your risk tolerance; and developing a system for finding, analyzing, and managing these investment instruments. I walk you through my methods of finding and analyzing stocks and managing a portfolio of stocks and other investment instruments.

My investment approach is uncomplicated, not requiring higher mathematics or any complex techniques. In fact, simple arithmetic is all that is necessary to do the computations that are useful in helping you understand the value and fair price of a stock. Mathematics that is more complex is involved in some of the methods, but these calculations are made by the software and websites that I identify. I certainly do not intend to lead you into day trading or discuss the techniques of hedge fund managers, which does not suggest that I completely understand myself what these traders do.

I frequently cite Bible verses that focus on God's principles for the use of money, and I explain the unimpeachable guidance that is available to us from the Holy Scriptures regarding money matters. I also express how you can bless others with your wealth and financial knowledge. I can see you helping others by imparting God's principles of financial blessings and the basic investment methods that I am going to teach you in Book Two. I hope that you will develop a course to teach in your church or Bible study and join me in teaching these biblical priorities and investment methods to all who are interested.

If you are a more experienced investor, what is in this book for you? First, I do not think one ever ceases to learn about investing; I certainly study methods and strategies as a regular practice. However, the discipline of this uncomplicated system might conserve your time and provide a more complete flow of information that will help you make decisions about the stocks you buy and sell, and when you buy or sell them.

What's Ahead

The second chapter begins with an admonition to begin or enhance your financial strategy with a commitment to a lifetime stewardship plan. It might seem counterproductive to start an investment book by talking about giving away money, but this step is important as you cultivate the attitude and practices that will be pleasing to God in your quest to improve your financial independence. While the culmination of what I discuss through this volume is substantially to improve your financial well-being, the overriding theme is investing in yourself and in the practices that ultimately will fulfill your spiritual goals, lead you as you prepare yourself to approach wealth building with righteous motives, and teach you to fulfill God's plan for your money. The subject of chapter 3 is the three personal characteristics one must demonstrate, according to Holy Scriptures, in order to receive and retain financial blessings and eternal rewards related to our use of the money that God entrusts to us.

Chapter 4 is my stewardship testimony, which includes the mistakes, difficulties, and disappointments that are part of life and that should not deter us from our goals. I review the principles that I recommend to you that I learned from Scripture and good teachers, including my parents.

In chapter 5, I discuss starting or buying a business as the ends and the means to financial success. Entrepreneurship is the most powerful force in the long-term growth of the US economy and the most productive way to become financially independent. Starting a business or buying a business can be a daunting task; therefore, my main focus in this chapter is motivational, although I do make some suggestions for how you might want to proceed if owning your own business appeals to you. Thousands of new businesses are initiated each year in the US, and many do not succeed. I will address that issue and offer some advice based on my own experiences and that of the five profiled entrepreneurs. I tell the stories of five Christian role models in my community who have been very successful in starting and running privately held corporations. Each of these individuals is a committed Christian, four of whom I have known personally for forty years. They tell how God has blessed them in business and how they recommend starting or buying a business.

Book Two begins with chapter 6, and I discuss the role of God-given vision in establishing your spiritual and financial goals, the nature of wealth, and the benchmarks of wealth that you can use to establish your financial goals.

In the next four chapters, I address the investment markets in general and focus on the systems and methods that I have developed for investing. I confine the discussion to common stock analysis and to building a portfolio of stocks. It is impossible to be all things to all people; therefore, I do not address any hedging techniques or other trading methods. I review the terminology and fundamentals of the investment world because we need a common language and understanding to enable our moving forward together. Furthermore, I advise you of different tools that are available on the Internet, publications that you need to buy and use as constant references, and computer software that will make analyzing and managing a great volume of data easier. Several chapters are devoted to this instruction section. After you study these chapters, you will be able to analyze a stock and determine if or when to buy it. Also, you will know what to look for to determine when to sell and preserve your gains. The systems and methods taught in Book Two are all you need to be a successful investor.

In chapter 10, I have included the common mistakes that investors make and the emotional aspect of investing, acknowledging certainly that professionals make mistakes and get uptight also. My intent is to help you improve your investment performance and total return by avoiding these pitfalls, and probably more importantly, control your emotions and strengthen your resolve in the inevitable times when your investments are not performing well.

I have included a chapter that synthesizes the investment methods into a suggested investing checklist to help you develop a routine to perfect your investment strategy. Then it is up to you, with God's guidance, to develop and implement your own investment plan. You will need to set your own financial goals and develop your own discipline to achieve those goals. Of course, no human being can give you a precise blueprint for becoming a high net worth individual. You will need to write down your own plan and address the ways to achieve each step.

Be careful about asking successful people for their ideas for and evaluations of your investment plan. I have found that successful people have been eager to share their knowledge and experiences with me, and I have received some good ideas and directions, particularly about starting a business. But you have to be in control and know how you are going to proceed under divine leadership, and others might not understand your scriptural approach to achieving your goals and following the investment system that I am going to teach to you.

Throughout the book, I draw on personal experiences to make points of good and bad incidences and behavior that may help you as you develop your investment strategy and train your emotions to cope with the swings in market sentiment. I certainly do not hold myself out as a perfect pattern for someone to emulate. What I discuss is based on the bumps and bruises of life, with specific reference to my life as a steward, investor, and entrepreneur, which may suggest to you what to avoid and what to pursue as you develop the best approach to investing in yourself and investing in securities as your investment plan unfolds.

Disclosures and Assumptions

I did not conceive this investment book originally to be based on a religious perspective. However, I did plan eventually to write a brief autobiography about my life as a steward and to discuss the scriptural basis for financial blessings. But one day, I received the inspiration to combine the scriptural teaching and testimony with the investment methods. I developed the outline for a book, reflected on my Bible study of stewardship, and thought about my own experiences. That process was a powerful witness that Scriptures about money are the immutable principles for financial success, and the righteous use of our money is a strategic element in fulfilling our purpose in life as Christians.

Readers who follow other religions may be concerned that I have shaped this scriptural text with the focus on a Christian concept at the apparent exclusion of other religions. As you will see from the quotes and conclusions that I make, much of the text is from the Old Testament. Of course, the concept of tithing originated with the teachings set forth for the people that God called His chosen nation. I could have expressed each Old Testament notion as Judeo-Christian theology, but I decided that I do not understand Judaism or other religions well enough to include them. Therefore, I address my fellow Christians as well as everybody who might be seeking spiritual answers and wants to learn more about Christianity and the plan of salvation through Jesus Christ.

Wealth Perspective

I want to address my friends who do not profess a faith in Jesus Christ. God instituted wealth-building principles and general standards for success that are available to all people, regardless of their faith or lack of profession of faith. All successful people apply these methods in some form, even though they may not communicate a faith in God and the divine formation of the fundamentals that they follow in achieving their wealth. God's perfect plan, however, is for all to come to Him through Jesus Christ, and He favors only those who believe in Him and seek His blessings. Nonetheless, the book has something for everybody, and I will review these principles of wealth building in great detail throughout the book because these principles are fundamental to your success in investing.

Some Christians may be concerned that I have presented a conservative interpretation of the Scriptures. I assure you that I understand that God allows different forms of worship and practice of our faith, and you do not have to be an evangelical Christian to receive His blessings in wealth building. He requires us to fulfill His Great Commission, but that fulfillment may be achieved in many ways. Likewise, many people who are not bold about their faith still have a strong and abiding commitment to Christianity that often is demonstrated in a reserved manner. One of my very best friends and I never discuss religion, because it is just not an issue when we meet. But I know that he is faithful and generous to his church. Also, one day he confided in me that he provided a golf club initiation fee and paid the dues and fees for a retired minister for as long as the minister was able to play golf. That act of kindness and other consistent acts of generosity demonstrate that his heart is turned toward God and that he hears the "still small voice" of divine direction. Actions are the best testimony of our faith.

Everybody has to settle his or her own relationship with the Almighty and the application of the Holy Scriptures to that individual's life. However, I do recommend that you study the Scriptures that I have cited, pray about and meditate on each verse, and see how the Holy Spirit instructs you regarding the issues that I have raised. My objective is simply to review the Scriptures related to establishing one's faith and receiving financial blessings and report the plan that has been successful for my family and me. I declare that this book chronicles the powerful evidence in my own life of unquestionable divine leadership in my finances and in discovering my purpose in life.

As stated previously, this book is two books in one. First, it is a spiritual treatise on giving, rewards, and withholding of rewards as well as eternal life; and second, it is a securities investing manual. To the pundit, the two may appear worlds apart. But the marriage of the two is perfectly clear to me and hopefully will be to you as you progress through the chapters. The theme is that the result and the means of building wealth is a spiritual matter ordained by God to honor Him, promote the spiritual growth and eternal and earthly rewards of the righteous, and advance His kingdom on this earth.

I acknowledge also that as a Christian layman, I may not appear qualified to address these spiritual issues as would be a minister or anointed and experienced Bible teacher. Nonetheless, I have drawn from some anointed teachers such as Derek Prince, particularly his book, *God's Plan For Your Money,*[2] which I recommend for a more literate and thorough discussion of the spiritual issues that I have tried to discuss in the chapter on stewardship that follows. I admit that I am thoroughly indoctrinated by Prince's treatise and that of other great teachers, such as Oswald Chambers, and I really cannot separate my own thoughts from all my reading and studying over the years. On the other hand, God has shown me independently through His Scriptures some very exciting views of His meaning about our finances that may not have been revealed in the more popular texts.

I must also give my late father and mother as well as my wife credit for their teachings over the years. My father was a scholarly minister, and my wife is a lifelong Bible student. Perhaps it will give you some comfort knowing that Book One is a compendium of inspired teachings from these family members, many great teachers over the years, and more importantly, the divine inspiration that I have experienced in bringing forth this book.

Let me assure you that this commentary is not a treatise on a quick remedy to your financial situation, in the sense of offering $10 and getting $1000 from heaven sometime in the near future. That is not to suggest that God will not do that, but patchwork remedies are not His normal manner of financial blessings. He is looking for us to conform to a lifestyle that He has set forth in His Word, and then He blesses us with success and prosperity throughout our lives. The doctrine set forth throughout this book emphatically states that expecting financial blessings must be preceded by holy motives and attitudes along with a righteous relationship with our Lord over a lifetime. I am advocating a lifestyle that will result in one's maturing spiritually over the years, being blessed with prosperity, and blessing others with one's wealth. The process is more important and rewarding than the ultimate prosperity. Our purpose in life is not to get rich but to enrich our lives by contributing into the kingdom. Based on divine principles, this benevolent attitude will result in financial blessings in our lives.

To conclude this chapter, I assume that I am addressing mainly Christian readers who are diligent in their Christian walk and committed to growing spiritually. If you are not a Christian or if you might doubt your relationship with God, you may accept the grace of God by acknowledging Jesus Christ as God incarnate on this earth. Jesus said, "I am the way and the truth and the life. No one comes to the Father [enters into heaven] except through me" (John 14:6). Jesus came, lived, and died as the sacrifice for our sin of iniquity brought on mankind by the judgment God pronounced on Adam and Eve and their posterity for all ages.

Adam and Eve were disobedient to God's ultimate command that they rely on Him and not seek to be independent of Him by eating of the Tree of Life, the symbol of rebellion (Gen. 2:9, 16-17; 3:1-7). God's creations sought to be like Him and to rule themselves. God sentenced mankind to eternal spiritual death because of this rebellion, and that is why we all need a Savior who satisfied God's judgment of mankind. God mercifully planned a perfect, sinless sacrifice that would satisfy Him. So after Adam's fall, God prepared to send His only Son, who would be in the form of a human being, because the redemption of mankind would require a human sacrifice. The Deity is eternal and could not die and serve as a sacrifice. Also, the sacrifice would have to be sinless in order to satisfy God's rule of atonement. As a dying sacrifice, Jesus vicariously assumed the sin of the world for a brief time, and He was separated from His heavenly Father because God could not look favorably upon sin in any form (Rom. 8:3).

Many people think that Jesus pled with His heavenly Father to spare Him from the torture and pain of the ignominious death on the Roman cross. But I do not believe that the pain and torture made Jesus sweat drops of blood. Rather, this was caused by the prospect of being separated from God Almighty and having His Father turn His back on Him because of this miracle of assuming sin for all mankind for all ages. Jesus was Divine, and the gravity of sin in His life drove Him to despair. Perhaps we can more nearly grasp the despair of Jesus in the garden of Gethsemane if we apply our personal experiences of despair. Have you ever been rejected by someone whom you loved and you thought loved you? Have you ever rejected someone and seen the pitiful hurt etched in that person's face and the remorseful pain in that individual's eyes? Have you ever hurt your parents or someone else you loved deeply? Do you remember seeing the hurt on his or her face? Do you remember the awful anguish that you felt? Multiply that anguish by an infinite number, and you can begin to imagine how Jesus felt. This pain was even more pronounced for Jesus because He was facing spiritual death.

Jesus actually was cast out from God's presence for a while, but He was restored and preached to the dead before His resurrection (1 Peter 3:19), but that is another story. For a Divine Being to become sinful was a gripping and wrenching experience to which only Jesus can attest. That sacrifice of the Messiah saves us from spiritual death if we will believe that Jesus Christ is the Son of God, and we live out our lives worshipping Him and obeying our heavenly Father.

That is the story of mankind's fall from God's grace and why every human being must have a Savior. Jesus Christ, the Messiah, offers us restoration if we believe in Jesus as Savior and allow Him to be Lord of our lives. The pardon and fulfillment of this act of divine grace requires a deliberate and completely voluntary decision on our part to accept Jesus as God's Son and the Savior from sin and perdition. Furthermore, salvation or redemption requires us to act out our faith in complete discipleship with Jesus Christ throughout our lives. Participating only in group rituals or catechisms required by custom or parents and/or relying on good works and compassionate deeds will not result in salvation and eternal life. Salvation comes from the cognitive acts of avowing that Jesus Christ is the Son of God and Messiah, confession of a sinful nature, and a commitment to following Jesus' commands. Salvation is evidenced by a complete lifestyle change.

Many who profess to be Christians and whose lives do not evidence Christianity may be unaccepted before Christ during the final judgment. Christianity is a commitment requiring separation from the ways of the world. Jesus said, "If anyone would come after me, he must deny himself and take up his cross and follow me" (Mark 8:34, Matt. 16:24). That means that we must follow Jesus and keep our commitment to Him, regardless of what life throws at us or what people of a sinful culture inflict on us. Thank God we have the nurturance of the Holy Spirit to direct, enable, and protect us.

If you have not made this deliberate decision to accept Jesus as Messiah and Lord, made the commitment to follow Him regardless of the consequences, and have not otherwise had a change in your life, you can make that decision now. You must acknowledge that you were born in sin, need a Savior, and are hopelessly separated for eternity from God without a Redeemer. Then you ask Jesus to come into your heart and birth within you a new person. You may accept Jesus by praying this prayer:

> Dear God, I know that I was born a sinner and that I am in need of a Savior. I believe that you sent Your only Son, Jesus, to live among us without sin. I believe that Jesus took the sin of all human beings for all time, and He served as a sacrifice to atone for the sin brought on mankind by the judgment of Adam and Eve. I accept Jesus as my Savior and make Him Lord of my life. I ask you to cover my sins for all time with the blood of Jesus, and I will follow Him and be obedient to Him all the days of my life. Please accept me into Your kingdom and fill me with your Holy Spirit, that I might serve You in holiness and ministry to my fellowman. Amen.

Bless you, my friend. You are now a Christian. Now find a Bible teaching church and join a spiritual membership. Be baptized. Get to work in the kingdom and begin by sharing your testimony of the saving grace that you have experienced.

Now I can confidently assume that we are on the same page, and we share the same belief about who we are in Jesus Christ and His reconciling us to the Father God. In the unlikely case that you have not yet made your confession of faith or reaffirmed your discipleship, at least you know the framework in which I am addressing the subject of stewardship and other steps along the path to financial blessings in your life. Now we can move through the steps in getting to the method of wealth building, beginning with the first step of righteous stewardship.

CHAPTER TWO

Stewardship

The key to unlocking God's favor is stewardship. God loves a cheerful giver (2 Cor. 9:7), and He has established a plan for rewarding faithful stewards. Stewardship is the righteous use of the financial resources that God has entrusted to us, and it is the fundamental action that satisfies God's condition for financial blessing. God's favor is available to all of us who do His will and seek His blessings.

Here is how His favor unfolds: if we are in a right relationship with Him, He will give us a vision for our financial success and give us a means of underwriting the vision. Our task as Christians is to seek His direction for the use of the money that He has entrusted to us now, make sure that we are in a right relationship with our heavenly Father by being obedient to His commands, be open to His direction in money matters, and keep in a right relationship with Him when the financial increase comes to us. These steps assure that we progress toward and are prepared for receiving the abundance of His blessings as we keep our commitments to Him. Keeping our commitments means being obedient to His every command and having a righteous heart and attitude when we receive financial increase.

The first step in this path of stewardship of our Lord's blessings is to declare in writing that you are a good steward of everything that God has entrusted to you and that you will keep that commitment regardless of how much or how little He provides in the future. The apostle Paul declared whether his blessing was much or was little, whatsoever state he was in, he would be satisfied (Phil. 4:11-12). This declaration of stewardship should be written, signed, and dated. A good place to write this declaration is in a blank page in your Bible. If you are married, I recommend that your spouse sign also, thereby creating a tight bond of unity, which maximizes the effect of your declaration. God honors unity. He said if two of you agree on any-thing that you ask for, He will grant your petition (Matt. 18:19-20). In fact, if a married couple is not unified, one partner will have difficulty imple-menting the declaration. Assuming that each marriage partner is com-mitted to the declaration and signs it, you should keep the document for the rest of your life.

Truett Cathy, the founder of Chick-fil-A, was interviewed on Georgia Public Television, and he told about a declaration that he and his board of directors, mainly family members, signed and have displayed in brass over one of the doors at corporate headquarters in metro Atlanta. The essence of the declaration is that the company pledges to be the best steward possible of the resources and mission that God has given the Cathy family and Chick-fil-A.[1] Certainly, your business or other enterprise should enter into a stewardship covenant for the righteous use of the resources that God has made available to you. I did that in the beginning when I first registered an investment management business with the Securities and Exchange Commission in 1986.

The word *steward* is derived from the root words *warden* and *house*. A steward oversees a large estate, keeps an accounting of the estate's business affairs, and manages a rich family's holdings. Therefore, stewardship is the oversight and management of someone else's money and property. This de-finition is consistent with the Judeo-Christian concept of stewardship and tithing. We are entrusted with a portion of God's ownership of all physical assets used by the earth's inhabitants, and we are commanded to be good and faithful custodians of that portion of His kingdom.

God commanded that we honor Him with a portion of our income and wealth. In the very beginning of time as recorded in Exodus 23:15-16, God established the law that no one is to appear before Him (in worship) empty-handed. He said further that we are to bring before Him as an of-fering of the "first fruits" of our harvest. In modern parlance, I see that as our writing the first checks each pay period for our tithes and offerings. From these Scriptures, we can conclude that stewardship is an act of wor-shiping God and positioning ourselves in a proper relationship with our heavenly Father. Leviticus 27:30 records that a tithe from the land belongs to the Lord, and the tithe is holy to the Lord. If we are obedient with the offering of our first fruits, this opens up a right relationship with our Lord and marks us as trustworthy stewards, eligible for abundant financial bless-ings (Prov. 3:9-10).

Serve God and Rebuke the Bondage of Mammon

In past generations, some Christians viewed having money and seeking wealth as evil. This view was based on Matthew 6:24: "You cannot serve both God and Money [mammon]." They feared that the use of money would be for evil purposes and eternally doom the rich person. According to Matthew 19:24, "It is easier for a camel to go through the eye of a needle than for a rich man to enter the kingdom of God." Incidentally, the eye of a needle was a narrow slit in the wall of a city, which was common in city-states of ancient and medieval periods in world history. Therefore, the passage in and out of this narrow gate in the city wall is difficult, but it is not impossible.

Paul wrote (1 Tim. 6:10) to Timothy and told him that the love of money is the beginning of all evil. Paul's emphasis on the *love of money* being the root of all evil certainly clarifies the issue and prompts those of us who seek financial increase in our lives to discipline ourselves to avoid falling into bondage to mammon. I define the phrase, "the love of mammon" as the selfish pursuit of riches with no consideration for the righteous uses of that fortune.

Dr. Fisher Humphreys, who taught Christian theology at Samford University until his retirement in 2008, says that "the Bible contains at least two sets of teachings about wealth. One is that wealth is a blessing from God. The other is that wealth is a source of temptation and can become an idol. Some people find it difficult to understand how both of these things can be true."

The latter doctrine—wealth can be evil—probably predates the Protestant Reformation and is not more characteristic of one Protestant group than another, according to Dr. Humphreys. He says that the doctrine probably was in evidence among the early believers who fled the corruption and hedonism of the Roman civilization as early as the third century. In any event, the doctrine was brought to America and preached by some founding church leaders who focused on Paul's writing in the sentence that follows the scripture cited above. Paul said: "Some people, eager for money, have wandered from the faith and pierced themselves with many griefs" (1 Tim. 6:10b). I think that it is reasonable to conclude that for centuries many Christians have just focused on the downside of seeking financial gain: It is too big of a risk to spiritual welfare to justify the pursuit of wealth.

I will focus on the teaching that God has a plan for us to prosper. As Dr. Humphreys said, the Bible teaches that "wealth is a blessing from God."

Obviously, many Scriptures do not support the position that wealth is always evil. Old Testament and New Testament Scriptures make it clear that God wants us to prosper, and in fact, God is the One who gives us the ability to gain riches (Deut. 8:17-18). God actually gave Abraham great riches and reinstated Job's wealth, and John the apostle's teachings made it clear that our Lord wishes for us to prosper and be healthy (3 John 1:2 KJV).

George Mannes, Senior Writer of *Money* magazine, wrote an article that discusses the religious aversion to seeking wealth, and I recommend that you read it (http://money.cnn.com). He interviewed three married couples who are devoted to their faiths: Christian, Jewish, and Muslim. Each couple struggled financially while holding fast to their perception of the teachings of their faith. The Christian couple tithed and expected God to take care of their needs, but they avoided seeking to build wealth based on the teachings during their youth. Their needs were met; but they had no excess funds, for example, to contribute to a retirement plan. After years of tithing and pursuing Christian vocations, the couple made steps of faith to seek higher earnings, and thus improved their family income from $30,000 to $117,000 annually. They concluded that even devout Christians have to exert some initiative to improve their income and just not be passive in the process of taking care of their financial needs.[2]

As we develop the discipline in our lives to avert the bondage of mammon as would be evidenced by unbridled avarice and undisciplined lust for money, the key phrase for us to focus on is "the love of money." Lust for money is shown by a myopic focus on gaining wealth for power, dominion, and self-indulgence. I am not referring to having drive and determination in our projects to improve our finances. Certainly, we must have a passion for our work and investing to be successful. But discipline must be part of our lives regarding seeking financial increase, somewhat like a gyroscope helps balance an airplane and keeps it on course. Developing a stewardship plan and implementing it is a major step in keeping ourselves on the righteous course.

Unfortunately, we have heard many stories about people who realized fortunes but have been arrogant, self-indulgent, and manipulative. In many cases, the pursuit of riches has become the driving force in their lives. In these cases, these people probably have fallen into the bondage of mammon, and riches have become their god. The key for us as we seek financial increase is to build in a spiritual deterrent against the unrighteous aspects of building wealth from taking control. We must not allow investing or any wealth-building measures to become our god and elevate our worldly pride or become our bondage to mammon.

The spiritual deterrent is the fear of the Lord. The answer to this deterrent to pride is to become fully informed about what God commanded about judging our own pride. Judging ourselves is scriptural (Lam.3:40, 1 Cor. 11:31, 2 Cor. 13:5) and is a good daily practice in finances and all of our endeavors. Scripture is clear that if we are truly redeemed, we will know in our human spirit that God is an awesome God, and likewise that the fear of the Lord is the beginning of knowledge (Prov. 1:7).

The fear of the Lord is not the type of fear that makes us wake up at night in a cold sweat, although I have heard a few stories about people who have had a nightmare that convicted them of unrighteousness and jerked them back to a righteous relationship with God. On the other hand, the fear of the Lord makes us sleep better at night because we have killed our personal pride and ambition, submitted our lives to His control, and received the peace that passes all understanding (Phil. 4:7 KJV). He gave us freedom to determine what we will do with our lives, but we recognize His omnipresence and His awesome power, and we submit to His gentle grace and direction for our lives. This act of submission is what salvation is all about and is the evidence of our redemption, along with our compassion and love for our fellowman (Col. 3:12-13, Mark 12:31-32). If we walk in that commitment and do not withdraw our submission, then we are walking in the fear of the Lord. This yielding will play out properly for the righteous use of our money.

The fear of the Lord serves as a human gyroscope for self-discipline regarding our motives, deeds, and purpose. It works like this: we examine our heart and actions, and confess our sins daily, which are the transgressions against the sacred purpose and laws that God has given for our lives. This act of judging ourselves in addition to daily confession of our sins keeps our lives in a right relationship with our heavenly Father, and this process defeats the bondage of mammon.

Are you aware that Christians will be judged in eternity by Jesus, who will expose our deeds, thoughts, motives, and stewardship? This lesson was repeatedly preached in evangelical churches in previous generations. Christ's judgment will determine how we will live in eternity. Rewards will be given and assignments will be made that will last throughout eternity. Of course, as Christians, our salvation is secured because the "blood of Jesus, his Son, purifies us from all sin" (1 John 1:7). This reference is to the unrighteousness associated with the iniquity passed on by Adam into which we were born. Also, His blood covers our periodic sins if we confess our sins. If we confess our sins, He is just and able to forgive us of our sins and cleanse us of all unrighteousness (1 John 1:9). Romans 14:10, 12 and 2 Corinthians 5:10-11 describe Christians fearing the Lord, judging ourselves, and giving an account before Jesus Christ.

John Bevere, in his book *Driven by Eternity*, addresses the issue of unholy motives, purposes, and deeds. My understanding of his point is that regardless of the image that we try to establish by our works and deeds, if we are motivated by envy, greed, and selfishness, we are building an unholy foundation that will not be rewarded in eternity.[3]

On the other hand, Jesus says that those who have properly stewarded God's assets on earth will be granted ownership of assets in heaven. Jesus said that by parting with treasures (money, property) on earth, we invest them in heaven, where they will be waiting for us when we arrive (Matt. 6:20). These treasures, with significant capital gains, dividends, and interest, will be passed out at the judgment seat of Christ. I should point out that those who do not know the Lord as their personal Savior will be judged at the great white throne judgment. This is the time when Jesus casts into outer darkness (hell) those who have rejected Jesus Christ as the Son of God and those who profess only with their mouths and have no change of heart and "do not deny themselves and take up the cross and follow Jesus daily" (Matt. 16:24). Bevere has an excellent description of the great white throne judgment.

The fear of the Lord is completed in us by a thorough understanding of what will happen at the judgment seat of Christ and the great white throne judgment for the unredeemed. As we judge ourselves as Christians and discipline our motives and conduct, we can rest assured of the rewards for our stewardship on earth and at the judgment seat of Christ.

A stewardship declaration sets in motion a powerful spiritual guard, which combats worldly pride overtaking you. Your declaration says that you will be faithful in the kingdom with your tithes and offerings and that you are ready for your faithfulness to be tested. To be sure, you will be tested. Satan will form a sustained attack against your resolution, but remember that you have spiritual armor and God's Word to fend off the attacks of Satan (Eph. 6:10-18). Your declaration of stewardship can take several forms, but the one that my wife and I followed was a sacrificial pledge to a budding ministry. I will discuss the pledge and the testing in more detail in the testimony chapter that follows.

As you follow through with your commitment when your stewardship is being tested, you will establish before God and man that you can be trusted to fulfill your commitment. Thereafter, at some point in time, you will begin to experience financial blessings that you can only explain as the hand of God moving on your behalf (Ps. 1:1-3). As you give God honor and praise with these financial resources, this act of humbling yourself completes an act of sanctification, as in sealing you from worldly pride, and releases you from the bondage associated with serving money.

Stewardship and greed cannot coexist. Greed is the antithesis of stewardship. They repel each other. Stewardship is a fast-working antidote for greed infestation. Here is the way a stewardship commitment works. When we establish ourselves as stewards, the Holy Spirit recalibrates our moral compasses to point us in His direction all the time. Then unselfishness and compassion rule our lives, and avarice and greed die.

The Joy of Giving

A commitment to a life of stewardship sets you up for a progression of spiritual benchmarks that will change your outlook on life and help you realize God's purpose for you. As you establish yourself as generous and compassionate, this act of obedience to God's command defeats the bondage of mammon. Thereafter, you will experience a tremendous spiritual breakthrough regarding your quest for financial increase. You will begin to reap the joy of giving and a tremendous unity with the Lord because of your obedience in money matters.

God understands how critical we view our financial security. Certainly, He is the One who kicked Adam and Eve out of the garden of Eden and set mankind on a lifetime of earning his living by the "sweat of your brow" (Gen. 3:19). God knows that we have to sustain ourselves; for that reason, He chose money as a measure to judge a believer's putting God first in his or her life. "The purpose of tithing is to teach you always to put God first in your lives" (Deut. 14:23 TLB). Therefore, it is clear from the Holy Scriptures that God uses money as the ballot placed before us as Christians to determine where God ranks in our priorities and consequently how we will spend eternity, whether heaped with rewards and assigned a ruling position or making it in with only the crown of life and limited assignments.

My pastor, Dr. Steve Davis, delivered a sermon from Luke 18 and 19 in which he talked about how Jesus addressed the issue of prioritizing wealth in our lives. He compared the decisions made by two wealthy men, the rich young ruler and Zacchaeus, and the role wealth played in their lives after they met Jesus. As you recall, the rich young man, who had kept all the commandments, asked Jesus what he needed to do to "inherit eternal life" (Luke 18:18). Jesus told him to sell all his possessions, give the proceeds to the poor, and follow Him. The young man decided to keep his wealth. On the other hand, Zacchaeus, the wealthy and repentant Roman tax collector, sought Jesus and later entertained Him in his home, volunteering to give half of his wealth to the poor and restore four times the amount he had overcharged any citizen (Luke 19:8). Dr. Davis concluded, "Jesus touched his [Zacchaeus'] heart and changed him. He has an encounter with Jesus that changed his life, and he knows who he is. Jesus now has his heart and thus his money, and Zacchaeus becomes a generous man. The word to Zacchaeus was, "It's okay to be wealthy." The wealthy young man, on the other hand, was defined by his wealth. He trusted in his wealth to tell him who he was. Perhaps he wanted [more than anything else] to be defined by his wealth." Dr. Davis concluded, "It's all about who or what has your heart." [4]

We show evidence of our salvation in the way that we use our money, and church members who profess Christianity but do not have the faith to step out and make any effort to tithe are not being obedient to God. Certainly, declaring and fulfilling our stewardship is a formidable step in acting out our faith, and those who do not should be concerned about giving an account before Jesus Christ in the final judgment of their lives. I know this sounds severe, but the Scriptures are clear on this issue.

I have studied the Scriptures and the teachings of Bible scholars who acknowledge they are writing as directed by the Holy Spirit, and I have come to realize that stewardship of our financial resources is not optional in the kingdom. If we are truly Christians and have our names in the Lamb's

Book of Life, we are commanded to give up a dedicated portion of our financial resources. Malachi 3:8-9 says, "Will a man rob God? Yet you rob me. But you ask, 'How do we rob you?' In tithes and offerings. You are under a curse—the whole nation of you—because you are robbing me." This Scripture is a strong indictment of those individuals and nations that withhold tithes and offerings. Not only are these people not blessed, but also they are cursed by God Almighty. They have no recourse except to get in the will of God regarding tithes and offerings.

This indictment is one reason that I say to Christians that your tithes and offerings are a means of worshiping God and evidencing your right standing before Him. If you do not get anything else out of this book, at least take this with you forever: God does not take lightly withholding His portion of the blessings that He has bestowed on us, and He will reclaim His portion and more from those who do (Mal. 3:9, Hag. 1:7-11). In effect, we break our spiritual covering on financial matters when we do not render unto God the portion that He has set aside for our tithe, and we will give up in extraneous expenses and missed blessings at least the amount that we normally would have tithed in obedience.

Can you see now how strategic that our stewardship is in the course of our seeking the committed life? Can you see that stewardship is an act of worship and a measure of obedience to our heavenly Father? Do you understand that righteous stewardship is pivotal in our satisfying God's conditions for financial blessings? The good news is that our heavenly Father is eager to bless us, and He pours out His blessings—indeed opens the very windows of heaven to bless us—in fulfillment of His promises for our obedience and righteous use of our money. Our God loves a cheerful giver, and He gives us great peace and joy deep in our human spirits that sustains us in difficult times, as we honor Him and bless others.

As you reap the joy of giving, you will focus more on giving than hoarding. The Holy Spirit takes over the human spirit because you have made a righteous choice. Consequently, you become immersed in the spirit of giving, and certain good causes become passions that will mark the basis of your life on earth for the remainder of the time that God gives you. You will experience a powerful renaissance as you experience firsthand the joy of "lay[ing] up for yourselves treasures in heaven, where neither moth nor rust destroys" (Matt. 6:20 NKJV). This powerful transition in your view of money signifies a maturing Christian, because "where your treasure is, there will your heart be also" (Matt. 6:21 KJV).

Your stewardship over a period of time establishes your trustworthiness, and you then are prepared to be trusted with even more of God's storehouse of blessings and placed in a more elevated position of service. Your heart changes regarding your objective of striving for financial increase, and God can use you in a greater work and bless you more than you ever imagined. He gives out unspeakable joy in our hearts when we give bountifully from the resources that God has entrusted to us.

As I was preparing this chapter, I opened my copy of the *Atlanta Journal-Constitution on* a Saturday morning, and there was a front-page story on Rosalynn Carter as she celebrated her eightieth birthday. The title of the story was, "I Have Been Blessed." The former First Lady said that she "would like to slow down. But the world keeps calling. Every year we say we've got to cut back, but I still don't want to miss anything. You go somewhere and see these people, who have lived with Guinea-worm, and now those villages have no Guinea-worm(s), and the people are joyful and dancing. I don't want to miss it."[5] Regardless of what you think about President Jimmy Carter's politics, you have to admit that the former President and First Lady are contributors more than takers, and they probably will continue experiencing the joy of giving as long as they live. Many of us cannot go to foreign countries as the Carters do, but we can give so others can go and minister. Our joy and our heavenly rewards are not diminished because of our method of ministering.

One of the first experiences in heaven that I look forward to is meeting the people who received salvation and have gone to heaven because of the stewardship of the McCutcheon family. In your stewardship, you will have this exhilarating joy also. Just imagine the numerous scenarios that will occur because of your tithe to your church's outreach efforts, such as backyard Bible studies. Then think about the offerings you made for Bible translations, the Jesus Film Project, and water provisions, food distribution, and Christian television around the world. What a joy it will be to hear "I would not be here if it were not for you." Another might say thank you for the Bible you made possible in his native language. He might tell you that he read the New Testament and accepted Jesus, and his life was never the same. He might tell you that his entire family is here because of one Bible. I can see young people come up to you and say that their lives were spared because you made fresh water or food available to them, and the message of the people who gave them water ministered to their souls. Hallelujah, this reunion and celebration with brothers and sisters in Christ will go on for eternity.

God's Benchmarks

My favorite Scripture about stewardship is from the Old Testament. God admonishes us in Malachi 3:10 to "'Bring the whole tithe into the storehouse, that there may be food in my house. Test me in this,' says the Lord Almighty, 'and see if I will not throw open the floodgates of heaven and pour out so much blessing that you will not have room enough for it.'" God will certainly bless any gift and even more so the tithe, which of course is the Hebrew equivalent of 10 percent. The tithe fulfills God's condition for putting Him first in our lives and for His pouring out blessings on His children. Therefore, the key to unlocking God's favor in finances is sustained tithing by a humbled steward who consistently puts God first and consequently has come to the point of not really caring if he or she accumulates any wealth for personal use.

This wonderful passage in Malachi 3:10 introduces the concept of the tithe as a benchmark regarding how much to give back to your Master and Lord. The tithe has been universally interpreted to mean one tenth of your income. You may ask, "Ten percent of what?" You will need to settle that with the Lord in the quiet time of your daily prayers, reading of God's Word, and listening to Him speaking to you.

My wife and I have always given 10 percent of our gross income from all sources, and since I have owned businesses, I have given at least 10 percent of the profits from each business before income taxes. Remember that Jesus said, "Give to Caesar what is Caesar's, and to God what is God's" (Matt. 22:21). This says to me that we pay income taxes after deductions on our personal tax return and business expenses, but we tithe on the first fruits of the total harvest, which is gross personal income and business profits.

Ten percent is the obligatory tithe. But the breakthrough tithe—when you declare yourself as a steward and lay out a stewardship plan—will be more than 10 percent. The Old Testament Scriptures are clear on believers giving to the poor, hungry, and forgotten people and even being generous beyond the tithe. Deuteronomy 14:27-29 (TLB) says,

Don't forget to share your income with the Levites in your community, for they have no property or crops as you do. Every third year you are to use your entire tithe for local welfare programs: Give it to the Levites who have no inheritance among you [poor], *or to foreigners* [missions], *or to widows and orphans within your city* [hungry/forgotten], *so that they can eat and be satisfied; then Jehovah your God will bless you and your work.*

I think of this spiritual and financial key as sacrificial giving or giving until it hurts and puts you in a financial bind. It takes this kind of giving to defeat the bondage of mammon and to establish you as trustworthy in financial matters. It gets God's attention and says that I am bringing to You, dear God, a sacrificial gift as a symbol of my commitment in money matters. Now, dear God, use me in service. See, dear God, I have a heart of compassion, and I am willing to be taught even more compassion. I am faithful with these financial resources that You have entrusted to me.

Our tithes and offerings, gifts beyond the tithe or sacrificial giving, build up spiritual capital that we can draw on for our own financial blessings. When we give to the poor, hungry, destitute (homeless), alone, and forgotten of our brethren, we actually buy debt securities from God's storehouse. Proverbs 19:17 says, "He who is kind to the poor lends to the Lord, and he will reward him for what he has done." Sacrificial giving to the needy is a risk-free investment that is systemic and can be leveraged into staggering spiritual, physical, emotional, and financial blessings.

The principle that I am invoking in forming this opinion about the sacrificial gift is based on Jesus' reaction to the widow and her gift into the temple treasury. Remember the story of the widow's mite? The rich gave their large gifts, but a poor widow put in two coins as her tithe, and Jesus knew her heart and her financial condition. He said, "This poor widow has put in more than all the others. All these people gave their gifts out of their wealth; but she out of her poverty put in all she had to live on" (Luke 21:3-4). Talk about a sacrifice! Jesus noticed her and had compassion on her. Of course, He noticed the rich, who gave also, and observed the small percent that they offered of their wealth. The story ends with Jesus' observation of the widow's sacrifice, but knowing our Lord's principles of giving, I dare say the poor widow never wanted for anything the rest of her life. Furthermore, she laid up vast rewards in heaven.

I remember my late father loved to tell the story of R. G. LeTourneau, who is credited with the title "Father of Heavy Equipment." LeTourneau, inventor of the heavy-duty tractor and lift, ran his business on godly principles. He started tithing the customary 10 percent from his business, but he gradually increased the gifts to 90 percent in his mature years, keeping for himself only 10 percent.

Another wealthy business entrepreneur, Henry Parson Crowell, founder of Quaker Oats, gave away 65 percent of his earnings for over forty years. He served on the board of directors of the Moody Bible Institute and gave generously to that institution. Also, he was a man of integrity and Christian influence on other business people representing numerous industries.[6]

My favorite story about stewardship is about an English aristocrat who was born into great wealth. Selena Shirley Hastings, an English noblewoman known as Lady Huntingdon, accepted Jesus Christ during the great eighteenth century revival and the rise of Methodism in England, lead by John Wesley and George Whitfield. Lady Huntingdon used her fortune to support financially these evangelists, build sixty-four chapels for converts coming out of the great revival that spread over decades in England, and build Chestnut College and a seminary. Chestnut College later merged with Cambridge University. She reportedly gave £100,000, which equals $350 million in 2010 dollars, for religious causes in the mid-1700s.[7]

Regardless of the size of our gifts, God looks at what we have left, just as Jesus did with the widow's mite as she brought every coin in her treasury into the temple. He rewards us according to the measure of our unselfishness as we contribute into the kingdom's work. To use an agricultural metaphor, if we sow sparingly, we will reap sparingly. But if we sow bountifully, we will reap bountifully (2 Cor. 9:6). This reaping is not limited to financial increase, and it is typically the increase of one hundred fold (*times*) the offering. It seems evident from the Scriptures that the bountifulness of reaping is dependent on the amount we have left for ourselves after the sum of our gifts. The lesser that remains, the greater is the increase. The reaping comes also spiritually, physically, mentally, and emotionally. The joy of giving provides healing to our bodies and uplifting of our spirits. King Solomon said, "A cheerful heart [joy of giving] is good medicine" (Prov. 17:22).

Stay the Course

Let me warn you that when you declare yourself a steward and follow my recommendation of making sacrificial gifts that will require a year or more to pay out, you likely will have second thoughts about what you have done. It is likely that there will be a lag period before you see the evidence of God moving in your finances. Also, you can expect that Satan will pounce on your trepidation and will torment you if you allow it. Just stay the course and engage in spiritual warfare with the adversary, and Satan will flee. Remember the Scripture: "Greater is he that is in you, than he that is in the world" (1 John 4:4 KJV).

The purpose of this book is not to give a lesson in the weapons of spiritual warfare. Many good books on this subject are available. Nevertheless, here are some Scriptures that will frame the issue for you if this is a new concept to you. Bringing this matter to your attention is important because Satan is like an enraged lion, roaming about and attempting to destroy us (1 Peter 5:8 KJV). Certainly, when you or I step out in faith to do anything aggressive in the kingdom, Satan will confront us with force. God allows Satan to have some latitude with us but no power over us if we use the spiritual weapons that God has provided (Eph. 6:10-18).

Reading the Word of God, prayer, righteous living, and speaking boldly and without fear about your expected financial increase are the key weapons you should use in any spiritual battle. Reading or quoting Scripture to the enemy is a powerful force in destroying any token resistance that Satan brings against you. Remember that Jesus used Scripture to defeat Satan when the Evil One tempted Him in the wilderness. Satan made three temptations, and Jesus answered with three Scriptures (Matt. 4: 4-10). This perseverance principle is another good reason to have a mastery of the Holy Scriptures, particularly those verses that will address issues in your life, including finances.

When hardships come during your period of sacrificial giving, tithing, or offerings beyond the tithe, recognize that this is a time of testing and learn to deal with satanic attacks. Satan has no dominion over God's anointed children, and we are able to defeat the enemy by simply persevering in our sacrificial giving and using the spiritual weapons available to us.

Keep your focus on Jesus and on your stewardship plan, and do not waver about what you are doing. Doubting the method and expected outcome when you commit to any worthwhile project is what I call the Peter Principal. (The spelling of principal is correct, because the focus is on the person.) Remember the story of Peter the apostle when he was on the Sea of Galilee fishing, and Jesus appeared in a boat in the distance (Matt. 14:23-32). Jesus began walking on the water toward Peter's boat. Peter recognized his Lord, and he called to Jesus and asked that he might walk to Him on the water. When Jesus said for him to come, in a burst of enthusiasm, Peter began his walk and did fine as long as he kept his eyes on Jesus, not questioning that he could actually walk on water as Jesus had bid him to do. When Peter began to look at the waves and question his own right to walk on water as Jesus did, he sank. Jesus had to rescue him.

If you begin to be uncertain that you can fulfill our Lord's admonition that you should give the tithe and that you should establish yourself as a committed steward, you will probably give up in your mission. But if you believe that you are commissioned to be a righteous steward of God's blessings and hold to His promises of blessings and sustenance, you can overcome any of the forces of evil that will ever come against you. Doubt, negative thoughts that rule your life, and whining about your conditions set up the formula for failure in any enterprise. God does not bless whiners, doubters, and scared Christians. God said, "I will never leave you or forsake you" (Deut. 31: 6; Heb.13:5). He is your partner in any enterprise, large or small, that is within His divine will.

We have established already that tithing and sacrificial giving are not just within His divine will, but tithing is commanded and freewill offerings are encouraged and blessed in proportion to the amount and frequency of the gifts (Prov. 11:24-25; Luke 6:38) and the cheerfulness of the giver (2 Cor. 9: 6-7).

If you still have reservations about committing to a life of stewardship, you might want to start with a small giving project. Just ask God to give you more faith to step out and begin to stretch yourself, even with a small pledge. The big step is the first step.

If you are a person who has to have everything worked out in your mind before taking the first step in a project, you probably will be miserable in a process that requires faith. Try this. Make a pledge that makes you sacrifice for one calendar quarter. You will survive, and probably in a few months, you will not miss the offering. Then rest a quarter and pledge for a six-month period. Keep doing this until you see the results of your stewardship. I believe that God will honor your small effort in the beginning and will build your faith as you continue to stretch yourself. He created us and knows us better than we know ourselves. Knowing us so intimately is why He wants to see us grow in faith, and as a result of our optimized faith, He can bless us in proportion. Remember, Jesus said if you are faithful in small things, He will put you in charge of many and greater things (Matt. 25:21). This parable means that He is eager to bless us with expanded spiritual and financial opportunities.

Over the years I have transitioned into being a risk taker. I have taken unpopular stands on matters conflicting with my religious beliefs and have spoken boldly about issues that concerned me, without fear of what others thought of me—even fifty years ago in college and graduate school. I credit much of these personality traits to my life as a steward. Here is the scenario: stewardship reaps blessings; blessings build faith; faith strengthens confidence; confidence yields boldness; boldness fosters risk taking; risk taking results in achievements.

This sequence of events does not mean that I have avoided all physical and emotional evidence of fear. It does mean that I fought through the fear and trepidation by concentrating on the blessings of stewardship, and I let positive thoughts flow through my mind. I tried to speak positively and not spew out defeatism. Also, I reminded the Lord what He said in His Word if I stepped out in faith. You can talk frankly to God, as long as you are respectful.

I can remember saying to God, "You lead me here, now where do we go from here? You said in Your Word that You would never leave me or forsake me. I know that You always come through, and that is why I put myself in the condition that I am in now. Now the problem is Yours. Let me know what You want me to do; otherwise, I am going on with my life as usual." He has always come through, and I have always given Him the praise and glory for what He has done.

I am engaged now in another venture that you are witnessing as you read. I am writing this book because I feel that God gave me the idea. The first few days of writing were like pulling the proverbial eye tooth. However, after I took the first steps, God gave me the inspiration—even though I still had to work at the craft. Now that the book is completed, it is up to Him where it is distributed. That is the way new ventures begin and how we leave matters that are in His will in His hands. Later, I am going to share about businesses that friends of mine have developed. These people are remarkable entrepreneurs, and we can learn a lot from them about stepping out in faith, working hard, and being good stewards.

God knows that you have more in you, and there is more in life for you than you realize. He is waiting for you to step out, work hard at the task, and stay the course.

The Great Commission

Stewardship serves as a means as well as an end. I have offered you an abundance of Scriptures and commentary about how sowing as a good steward with a righteous purpose can lay the spiritual foundation for you to reap financial increase from the very hand of God. Now please consider with me how stewardship allows you to fulfill one of Jesus' commands, which turned the world upside down for Christianity. This command was so awesome in the litany of Christianity that it is called the Great Commission.

We can fulfill Jesus' Great Commission through our giving of tithes and offerings. Jesus says in Matthew 28:19-20 (NIV), "Therefore go and make disciples of all nations, baptizing them in the name of the Father and the Son and of the Holy Spirit, and teaching them to obey everything I have commanded you. And surely I am with you always, to the very end of the age." The disciples were stand-ins for you and me, as they received this commission from Jesus Christ while He was on earth.

The Great Commission is a direct command to all believers everywhere, an obligation that we all come under when we become Christians. It means simply that we are to evangelize the entire world, from our front doorsteps to all around the world and back. You probably have heard the term "evangelical Christians," and I ask what other kind of Christian is there? Sometimes the term is even used derisively. But all Christians have mandates to share the gospel of Jesus Christ and to bring into discipleship our fellowmen wherever they may be if they do not know Jesus Christ as Savior and Lord of their lives.

We can tell others about Christ in our own way, but my experience is that the Holy Spirit has to create the conditions and prepare the heart of the person to whom you will tell the story of Jesus. In his book, *Prayer of Jabez*, Bruce Wilkinson says that he prayed for his ministry to be expanded, and he says that our platform for greater service can be broadened too if we are willing. In a personal example, Wilkinson shared the story of his praying for the Holy Spirit to bring someone into his path for ministry during an airplane trip from the Atlanta airport. As he sat in the terminal waiting for his plane to board, a young woman, dressed very professionally and sitting near him, appeared under great stress. He spoke to her and prompted her to talk about why she was making the flight. She was meeting her husband and lawyers to finalize a divorce. Her husband had been unfaithful, but he had confessed and asked her to forgive him. He also begged for reconciliation with her to preserve the marriage. She was heart-broken and did not feel that she wanted to reconcile and go on with the marriage.

Wilkinson told her about how Jesus can change the worst of us and can heal her heart and resurrect the troubled marriage. She accepted Jesus and pledged to drop the divorce suit and to work to restore the marriage. A life and a marriage were saved because a humble servant sought to be faithful to the command of our Lord to bear a witness.[8]

My ventures in the area of witnessing have been mainly dropping a word about the Lord and/or inviting someone to church. Even in modest efforts such as mine, Satan will tell Christians that they are not good enough to bear a witness for Christ. Although all have sinned and fallen short of the glory of God (Rom. 3:23), God does not require that only saints can do His work. He is looking for redeemed sinners who are obedient now and who are willing to bear His witness. You never know whom God has directed to you to hear His Word. Just remember that a brief encounter over a cup of coffee might be the only or last time this person hears about Jesus Christ and the way to eternal life.

We do whatever we can personally and through our businesses and professions to evangelize, but to reach around the world as in the Great Commission, we are going to need some help. By our acts of stewardship, we can send others around the world and into places in the US that we cannot go or would be unable to communicate due to a language barrier. Hundreds of willing ministries, probably in addition to your own church, will represent you and your faith. Before you sow into these ministries, check them out carefully regarding their doctrines, administrative policies, and procedure to make sure they are efficient, accountable, and honest.

Although Satan has corrupted the air waves with lasciviousness, violence, and greed, God has raised up some great ministries that spread the gospel throughout the world by television. Billy Graham used television to reach thousands of unchurched and otherwise unredeemed souls. Unfortunately, some television ministries have abused their sacred trust; and these preachers, teachers, and evangelists will have to stand in judgment for their untruthfulness and greed. But let us not condemn the process of reaching souls through the mass media because of those who have disgraced the Lord's work. Also, let us not condemn those whose message or manner does not fit our tastes in worship if their message is the atoning work of Jesus Christ as Messiah and Lord.

I am not suggesting that you divert financial support from your local church, as long as that church is preaching the gospel, ministering to the oppressed and hungry, and supporting missionary and other evangelism efforts. Your church may be meeting the preaching and ministry functions but not addressing the evangelism mission, both domestically and worldwide. I urge you to find an outlet to fulfill the Great Commission because we will all have to give an account of our efforts in Christian evangelism. I can hear Jesus, as our judge, saying, "Whom did you bring with you?"

All of this brings me to the subject of the development of a stewardship plan. You might be thinking, *Why do I need a detailed plan for where I am going to give my money? I only have a few hundred dollars, and I am going to give that to my church.* Or, *I cannot even come near giving a tithe to my church right now. How can I give to evangelistic ministries?* You may have every penny already spent on home mortgage, car payment, day care for children, transportation to work, or a myriad of other vital demands.

In each of these cases, just pray that God will help you become a tither. Tell Him that you are committing to Him to be a steward, and ask Him to help you to do so. You might find that you have to take a second job for a few hours each week so that you can make a sacrificial gift to get started on your stewardship plan. People take second jobs all the time to buy nice automobiles or to provide braces for the children. Work extra to make an investment in the kingdom and validate your stewardship. God will honor this sacrifice even more than tithing out of abundance.

Regardless of your financial condition now, write down where you can contribute or where you would like to give your tithe and offerings. Write down the ministry or type of ministry and the percentage of your gross income that you would like to give. Do not forget to give your church your first consideration in your plan. Also, the tithe is the Lord's, and it is the "first fruits" of your giving; therefore, you give in your tithe before you pay anything else. Remember also that offerings are above the tithe, and these contributions should be made to Christian and humane endeavors after you have given your tithe into the "storehouse," as commanded in Malachi 3:10.

More about the stewardship plan follows later. But for now, stewardship facilitates fulfilling our Lord's Great Commission, and you should remember that your ministry and rewards are not diminished in any part because it is accomplished through financial support.

Confidence

Confidence in financial matters is a progressive outcome from a life of consistent stewardship. Confidence is the mental state evidenced by assurance in yourself during any undertaking. A confident person sees a positive outcome from a set of non-routine activities. Once again, the progression from stewardship though confidence to achievement is listed below:

- Stewardship reaps blessings.
- Blessings build faith.
- Faith undergirds confidence.
- Confidence yields boldness.
- Boldness fosters risk taking.
- Risk taking results in achievements.

Our mental state and verbal communication are the most important dimensions in the process of undertaking new ventures. If we proceed confidently and speak positively in new ventures, we can be optimistic about a positive outcome. Pastor Gene Evans, Bible teacher extraordinaire and repentant CPA (just kidding CPAs), told about a client of his CPA practice whose mobile home business was distressed in 1979 when interest rates increased to 20 percent. The owner expected to file bankruptcy because of a dramatic reduction in sales. Gene read Mark 11:23 to him and asked the owner if he believed Jesus' words about faith and commanding the mountain to be cast into the sea. The owner, a non-Christian, said of course, "Everybody believes the Bible." Gene told him to speak positively about the future of his business. The owner heeded the direction, ordered all his employees to do so or they would be fired, and printed signs to remind all about speaking positively. The first month afterward, the business sold quota, increased from there every month, and continued to prosper. The owner later asked Gene to lead him in becoming a Christian. Our attitudes and words can make us or break us when we are invoking God's favor, and confident people speak boldly about the intended outcome of our steps of faith.

Confidence overcomes the inevitable fears that develop when we find ourselves in an unfamiliar environment, such as in the investment arena. Confidence helps us speak boldly about the outcome of our new ventures, and the mind and human spirit feed on the expressions from our mouth. Confidence gives us the emotional energy to study and learn, to keep trying after temporary setbacks, and to deal with the critics and negative people who normally would discourage us.

Let me assure you of the power of confidence and your words. Your belief in yourself, based on God's promises if you are in His will and a good steward, will fortify you against the fear-of-failure syndrome. How many people have you talked to who have been victims of the fear of failing? You can hear their remorse when they say what they would have liked to have done in life. What kept them from pursuing their dream? Probably the fear of failing more than lack of money, time, or cooperation of others.

Failure embarrasses us and inflicts a blow to our self-concept if we allow these normal reactions to control us. However, when we have confidence that stems from God's promises, we do not care what people say, and we can not be embarrassed or humiliated. We know that if we confront barriers, God will work them out or will use obstacles to turn us in His intended direction. The principle is that if we are faithful in our stewardship and obedience, God is faithful to His Word and will make a way for us to succeed. I can look back on life and see many times that I have had blessings that I can only explain by God's direct intervention after my wife and I have taken a step of faith. Life is a constant process of taking steps of faith, and the confidence that grows from a life of stewardship will fortify you also as you will take those steps of faith. More about exercising confidence is included in chapter 4.

Conclusion

Stewardship is a powerful force in the kingdom of God. It is both a law, commanded by God as a means and measure of worship, and a principle set forth by God as a condition of blessing. Practically, our stewardship helps spread the gospel of Jesus Christ, but it also is a means of putting God first in our lives and partnering with Him as we step out in faith to advance His work, fulfill His purpose in our lives, and claim the blessings that He has intended for those who meet His conditions.

Stewardship builds *spiritual capital* that will bank your efforts to improve your financial conditions. God established the promise and the conditions, and if you do not believe that He did or that the system works, it will not work for you unless God overrides your misjudgment for some purpose that He only knows. God expects you to evidence your belief in His way by stepping out in faith and testing His plan for your finances. To reject His plan overtly or by neglect is to mock God's Word at worst or to fail miserably at least in fulfilling His purpose and plans for your life.

As you practice stewardship, you will receive rewards that you probably never imagined. You will realize over time the joy of giving, and stewardship will transition you from seeking wealth for your purposes to seeking wealth for the good it can achieve in the kingdom.

CHAPTER THREE

Diligence, Humility, and Discretion

In previous chapters, I have addressed the nature and provisions of obedience, stewardship, and blessings. I have attempted to make the point that the objectives of accumulating wealth over a lifetime are, of course, to provide for your financial security but more importantly, to contribute to the kingdom. Our first objective should be to make a difference in the lives of those who need help.

Randall Jones, in his study of the 100 richest men in town, found that the common theme among these mega-rich was seeking first to serve. Jones reported, "If you seek money strictly for the sake of becoming rich, most likely you will never achieve true financial freedom. Ironically, great wealth most often comes to those who seek it least." [1] Jones also found that unimpeachable character is a high calling of the wealthy people that he interviewed. He reported under the heading of Moral Moorings that each interviewee felt that his or her reputation rules in the conduct of business.[2] He cited the downfall of former heads of Enron, Tyco, and WorldCom and wrote, "Their fate shows that fortunes without a moral foundation are nothing more than mirages destined to disappear faster than they were created." [3]

The biblical principles that I have identified also focus on the work ethic and personal characteristics that are indispensible for a lifestyle that is worthy of a good report and, most importantly, God's continuous favor. Here are the three personal characteristics that are scriptural and must be evidenced in our lives as we follow the biblical stewardship path to financial increase. Each characteristic is a grouping of traits and functions.

Diligence

I hope I have not lead you to believe that because of your stewardship, God will drop wads of money and great comfort in your life without your diligence to produce wealth. Of course, God is sovereign, and He will do whatever He desires; indeed, I have heard of a few cases where someone found money in a mailbox or had an otherwise unexplainable change in his financial condition. I do not doubt the origin of these surprise blessings. However, these were cases involving an impending emergency, and no lasting resupply of money mysteriously accrued to the beneficiaries. God's plan is for us to be diligent, resourceful, and productive. He expects us to work for a living and be productive in our jobs. Also, He promises to reward our stepping out in faith to create and produce. We need to give God something to bless.

Benjamin Franklin's homily, "God helps those who help themselves," has reached almost biblical reverence. In fact, I have heard it quoted as a Proverb. Nevertheless, that saying certainly sums up my belief in the fact that God established diligence as a condition of blessing in financial matters. Diligence is the well-planned and unrelenting pursuit of a goal. Diligence means vision, planning, study, work, perseverance, and optimism.

God installed the function of work when He expelled Adam and Eve from the garden of Eden. God cursed the ground and told Adam that because of his sin, he and mankind to follow would earn his living by the sweat of his brow (Gen. 3:19). The expulsion from Eden and assignment to work in an uncooperative soil was at first a punishment, but God in His mercy installed principles that were designed to make work productive and to reward us for our diligence. He said that by applying these principles, we can be successful in our work and rewarded in the kingdom. God's Word also says that a lazy man in mind or body will not rise above his mediocre conditions, but a diligent man will realize wealth (Prov. 10:4).

Diligence is consistent with the principle of stewardship as a working doctrine to measure our worship of Him and dedication to advancing His kingdom on earth. He set up the conditions for blessings on earth and rewards in heaven accruing from our diligence as the pathway for showing mercy to our fellowman and using the abilities that He gave all of us.

God gave each person certain talents and gifts, which He imparted before we were born. "We have different gifts, according to the grace given us" (Rom. 12:6). God's plan was that we would honor Him with these talents and gifts and use them in our work. He also intends for us to develop a friendship with Him and take Him as a partner in our work. Basically, He had to uphold His sentence on mankind to live "by the sweat of his brow," but God still desired the fellowship with His creation that He had with Adam before that fateful day for Adam and all mankind.

Even now, God reaches out to us for fellowship and partnership in our work. Evidently, many people reject an alliance with God, judging by the nature and outcome of their work; but they get to keep the talents and gifts that God imparted to them. Paul said, "For God's gifts and his call are irrevocable" (Rom. 11:29). Furthermore, God is committed to the laws and principles that He set forth, many of which apply to our work. These laws and principles will not fail, regardless of who applies them, unless God has mandated a special restriction on the user. Because of the talents and gifts given to all of us and laws and principles that God has set forth, everyone can succeed in life's work.

Dr. Pat Robertson, founder and chairman of the Christian Broadcasting Network and a prolific writer on Christian issues, has done an inspired and scholarly work of summarizing ten of the basic and immutable laws of God. (See Appendix A.) At least seven of these ten laws apply directly to our work.

People who do not profess Christ as Messiah and Lord but are very successful in business or a profession use these basic principles, although I doubt that few have any idea where they originated. Also, very wealthy people often give away money to charities, calling it philanthropy and perhaps not acknowledging it as Christian stewardship. Some even play a game with their charity by drawing great attention to themselves and trying to one-up other wealthy patrons in the self-aggrandizement sweepstakes. But regardless of these theatrics and self-serving roles, they cross into the boundaries of offerings; therefore, their gifts and offerings for a period are blessed on earth. Why? Because God is faithful to His laws and principles, and He holds out the expectation that all will come to Him, relinquish our independence, come under His authority, and rely on Him. He wishes for us to prosper by using His way (Job 22:21), through faithful stewardship, unfailing obedience, and persevering faith; and He yearns for all mankind to acknowledge Him as the Christ and follow His way (2 Peter 3:9).

Let me back up and address the issue that I raised about gala fundraisers. My point is that even a good and charitable activity can be misused by some, depending on the individual's attitude and motives. The Scriptures say that any such gifts to the poor or needy should not be done in vainglory; if such is the case, those that abuse this trust have all they are going to get on earth, and no such rewards are everlasting. Matthew 6:1-4 says to be careful not to do acts of righteousness before men to be seen of them. If you do, you will have no reward from your Father in heaven. I am not judging any individual or organization regarding their motives for charity; that is God's province. I am just addressing the issue to petition people to judge their own motives and assure that their works meet the standards of biblical stewardship. More attention will be given to this topic under the section entitled Discretion.

God always wishes for fellowship with mankind and for partnerships with His own family. God and Abraham had an optimal relationship. God even called Abraham the friend of God. That same relationship is available to us also. As was noted earlier, we do not have to be saints to fulfill God's purpose, but we do have to judge ourselves and repent of our sins. We should desire to draw close to God.

One of our primary purposes in life is to have an alliance with God that fosters a continuous relationship. How this fellowship develops will be a uniquely personal matter. Nonetheless, I can attest to the fact that God uses our work to bring about that alliance if we are willing, and it is rewarding to see how God can direct and prosper our work. I know that it must be a great pleasure for Him to see us grow in our work and to acknowledge Him in all our undertakings.

Diligence means more than the "rock-busting and gut-wrenching" toil that we all do in the routine of the work week. Diligence means seeking a vision of what God has planned for you and then planning your life around His plans. The Scriptures say that before a man builds a house (*or career or financial plan*), he sits down and counts the cost (Luke 14:28). In modern parlance, I believe that this simply means we order our steps according to the direction in which we perceive that God is leading us. It means conferring with your wife and family about the direction that you perceive, leading the family in praying about your perception, and coordinating family affairs to implement the plan.

My experience has been that God will not give you details in a road map fashion. Certainly, He could, but He wants you to use your brain, experiences, and most of all your faith. He wants you to take steps, and as you take steps, seek His guidance. He likes the affiliation and fellowship of a good career and financial journey with you. He does not want to give you the road map and then see you follow that course as if you do not need Him.

Do these laws and principles of diligence and stewardship always result in earthly prosperity for the believer? I have observed a few people over the years that have been diligent in their work, steady tithers, and faithful in their Christian service; but they still struggled financially. Usually, these obstacles are short-term while God is positioning the person or family for a greater calling and financial blessings. Although we might think of ourselves as spiritually mature, God may still be working out something in us to meet His standards or to prepare us for a new or expanded direction.

My wife and I went through a period of health problems and less income when I took early retirement, and then God fulfilled the vision He gave me of a business venture. Therefore, if the blessings have not been evident, just continue waiting and speaking positively; in God's time, He will be faithful to His promise. While you are waiting, ask God if you need to confess anything else or if you are following a path that needs redirection. You can expedite your financial renewal by being compliant with what God is working in you or following a new direction in which He is leading you.

I suppose that God does set aside some people who are good stewards for other work that does not include financial independence. All of the disciples, after Jesus' ascension, practiced the rules of stewardship, diligence, and humility; yet they lived in near poverty. However, I believe that such a person in our time is fully reconciled with his or her mission in life, and the matter of finances is never an issue. However, if the person complains of not having sufficient financial support, the problem probably is that the individual has never diligently sought a vision from God for financial increase and pursued the vision.

My mantra has been that we have to give God something to bless and to measure our faith in financial matters. Some people can have an abundance of faith for a healing, but do not have a vision and faith for stepping out in pursuit of financial increase.

Diligent people are energized by a vision of where they want to go. As a Christian, you should go to God in prayer and ask Him to give you a concept, a vision, of what He has for you regarding your finances and how you should proceed to realize that vision over a lifetime. Remember, the heavenly Father knows what you need before you ask, and He has set aside financial blessings until you ask and evidence diligence in pursuing His blessing. When God gives you an idea, begin meditating on that idea until it gets to be a mental picture of your operating in that idea from God. When you fully develop this idea in your mind, you are envisioning yourself as being financially successful. Ask God to show you how your wealth can be useful in His kingdom, and begin planning in your mind to fulfill that stewardship mission.

Keep pondering this vision until it gets down into your spirit, and you are virtually preoccupied with your vision. Share the vision with your spouse only at this point, and seek his or her commitment with you. Do not settle for, "Just do what you want to, honey." Get your spouse to pray about the vision and talk with him or her about the dedication that the vision will require. When your husband or wife agrees with you, write a description of the vision, and both of you sign and date the vision statement. Then discuss the matter with the children and seek their input and prayer. As they agree with you, have each child sign the vision statement with you. At that point, keep the vision within your family until God releases you to discuss it with others.

Keep your commitment to the vision and do not doubt its fulfillment. Keep praying for God to reveal to you the next steps; then step out in faith with eagerness and optimism. Never speak any doubt and always speak as if the vision were in place. Persevere in your pursuit of the vision, even when the barriers come against you. Remember the Scripture, "Whatever you ask for in prayer, believe that you have received it, and it will be yours" (Mark 11:24).

There is a theology labeled by its detractors as "Name it; claim it," which is framed as simply being a presto, instant fulfillment of a prayer or pronunciation. The label seems too simplistic to me. My experience has been that claiming a blessing is a journey. Sometimes it takes years to experience the vision that you get from the Lord. Therefore, leaving people with the impression that they are not having faith if their blessing does not come when they claim it is not wise. On the other hand, critics to laying claim to our blessings are not "seeing the forest for the trees." We cannot ignore or be skeptical of God's admonition to claim our blessings as stated, for example, in Mark's gospel. Claiming a blessing is simply verbally expressing your belief that what God spoke through the writer, Mark, is true.

As I indicated, my experience with claiming God's blessings has been an extended process. The following is the way the process worked for my wife and me, and I recommend it to you. After you get the vision of where God is taking you, you will need to make a brief written plan. This will be a concept plan that will paint the bold strokes for your enterprise that will lead you to improving your financial condition. This is a brief statement that seals your understanding of what God has revealed to you. It is not a step-by-step document because God will give you the steps, usually with significant time between revelations. Each person may have a different experience in that regard than I had. Randall Jones reported that the mega-rich whom he interviewed did not develop a business plan,[4] but I will bet that they had a concept that they probably wrote down or at least could recite verbatim.

If God leads you into a new career field, like starting a business or into investing in stocks, you will need to study to understand the field. Read books, take courses, talk to experienced people in the new field of work, and seek credentials in the new vocation. For example, if you decide to go into real estate, you obviously will need to take a series of courses and their corresponding tests. The same process is necessary with investment management. I studied for two years before I even started preparing for the three examinations that I took for certification. I see former members of my Sunday school class who were struggling financially but decided to study real estate and build careers in that field. Thirty years later, they are financially independent.

Studying in a new field is hard work. First, it is difficult to find time to put into researching, reading, and memorizing. Next, using every measure of energy and resourcefulness you possess is required. Typically, you will have to work late at night when everybody else in the family is asleep and on weekends when your friends are having a good time. I do not minimize the effort that you will need to make to prepare for a new venture. Even if you follow my method of investing that follows in Book Two, you will need to study to understand the concepts and processes, particularly if you are just beginning to invest in stocks and manage your own portfolio.

I relate all this from personal experience and from discussions with would-be investors who get excited whenever a bull market in stocks is the lead on the evening news. When the market is roaring ahead and people are talking about a bull market, I get calls from people who have never invested in stocks who tell me they want to "get into stocks." I usually ask them a few questions to measure their understanding, and most do not know anything about investing. Then I tell them they need to study investing before they even consider "getting into stocks." I give them a list of books and periodicals to get them started and suggest that they become familiar with *Value Line* at the public library. I refer them to a continuing education course on investing at the local university. In every case so far, a long pause hangs in the air before my caller responds, and then I get a hasty "thank you" before they hang up. I am left with the impression that they are thinking, *Thank you but no thanks; I'm not putting my time in on that stuff.*

I have another suggestion to facilitate your understanding of a new career field. Seek an internship or apprenticeship with a professional in the field. Offer to be a go-fer or to do other menial work without pay, just for the opportunity to soak up whatever you can in the workplace. This will take some resourcefulness if you are already working full-time; but it can be done, probably on the weekend or by using your vacation. In the meantime while you study and plan, continue to meditate on your vision of where you want to be. Pray, meditate, and speak positively about your new venture because this active process will build your faith and confidence.

At times you will need the fortification of a well-formed and solid dream that has convinced your inner spirit that you can see this vision become a reality. From the very beginning, barriers will confront you. Sometimes you will be overwhelmed with the magnitude of what you have to learn and the regulations that you have to satisfy. The five friends who started businesses whom I will profile in chapter 5 will attest to the barriers and discouragement that are inevitable in forging ahead in a financial venture.

A number of barriers are indigenous to entrepreneurship and other ventures, but the most daunting are Satan's tactics—such as fear and doubt—that attack you at every turn. Remember that God promised that He will never leave you or forsake you (Heb. 13:5; Deut. 31:6), and that promise certainly is applicable in times of conflicts and frustrations. Just remind God in your prayers of what He promised and seek His guidance about how to deal with the situation. Regarding the fears and doubts that come into your mind, just speak in confidence that the vision is done and that "No weapon forged against you will prevail" (Isa. 54:17). These barriers, fears, and doubts are just testing to see if you are committed. Persevere. Do not turn back or even let turning back linger in you mind. Begin speaking optimistically about your venture and even deciding how you are going to bless others as you break out in your finances. Remember God honors optimism, and your human spirit and emotions thrive on your own optimism. Furthermore, as you begin to break through and see some success in your venture, you will have less doubts and fears, and the barriers and obstacles will become just routine asides instead of the source of a major crisis.

Be diligent and be steadfast, and you will realize your vision of financial success.

Humility

Let me warn you that you probably will not escape some criticism and maybe even ridicule as you move forward in your stewardship plan and give testimony of God's blessing you for your stewardship. Some people will have a field day with your commitment and testimony. Other cynics might take the course of pointing out your weaknesses, and we all are vulnerable to criticism because of our natural man. If some of your critics think you are "holier than thou," you will hear about it sooner or later. Remember that all of this is a component of the testing of your commitment to stewardship; do not be drawn into a debate on the issue or return the criticism. Suffer quietly, but pray a prayer of forgiveness, release, and blessings on your detractors. Soon you will see some good things happen in those relationships. Pray for each critic or group by name and treat them with loving respect, and then stand back and watch the Holy Spirit work on your behalf. Remember this phase of your stewardship walk is predictable, understandable, and strengthening.

The winnowing process in this phase will work a good work in you and set you on a remarkable path to spiritual blessing and financial increase. Most of all your reaction in this declaration phase will glorify God and will allow a remarkable demonstration before your eyes of the efficacy of the Holy Spirit among us. If you have not witnessed the power of the Holy Spirit at work in human relations, you will when you declare yourself as a steward, experience the inevitable criticism, and forgive your critics. Nevertheless, keep to your stewardship plan and grow spiritually in the meantime.

The biblical principle that operates at any time that you are criticized and forgive your critics is what some Bible teachers call "binding and loosing." It is based on the verse, "Whatever you bind on earth will be bound in heaven, and whatever you loose on earth will be loosed in heaven" (Matt. 16:19; 18:18). That scripture must be coupled with God's maxim that "Vengeance is mine; I will repay, saith the Lord" (Rom. 12:19 KJV) to complete the principle of binding and loosing.

The connection between the two Scriptures is this: as human beings, we all have a spirit that will live forever. God also has a spirit that is the third being of the Trinity named the Holy Spirit. When we become Christians and acknowledge Jesus Christ as the "Lamb of God, who takes away the sin of the world" (John 1:29), we have born within us the Holy Spirit, who is our protector, teacher, and comforter as stated in John 16. This place of residence of the Holy Spirit in us is what Jesus was saying when He called our bodies His temple (1 Cor. 6:19; 3:16). Also, this birthing of the Holy Spirit in us is the origin of the much maligned term in some circles, "born-again Christian," which indeed is actually a badge of redemption. Because of our likeness with Jesus Christ, we have a spiritual connection with Him and to the very throne of God. This connection allows us constant communication with our heavenly Father God through Jesus Christ our Lord. Jesus has promised to protect us, defend us, comfort us in doing His will and in His service, and give us authority over satanic attacks.

God has promised that He will take vengeance on His adversaries in eternity, and He will do so on our behalf at the time of His choosing. Be sure to discipline your thoughts and actions because Scriptures make it clear that we will be accountable for not only our words but our very thoughts (see Matt. 12:36; Rom. 14:12). But He has given us the power to seek mercy and plead for restoration of ourselves and our brothers and sisters. Therefore, by the words of our mouths, the attitude of our hearts, and evidence of our behavior, we can loose any offender; and that offense will be unbound for that offender.

By this very act, the Holy Spirit can begin to convict the offender, rehabilitate the relationship, and set us free of any bondage. The forgiveness principle is vitally important in your business and personal relationships, and it is another step in your preparation for the righteous requirements of wealth-building according to godly principles. It is also pivotal in building up eternal rewards. God looks at the heart and evaluates our words, motives, and behavior. He blesses us unboundedly when we are obedient and trustworthy with the gifts and blessings that He bestows on us.

I read a very practical lesson in forgiveness in the sports section of the *Atlanta Journal Constitution* at the end of football season in 2007. Bobby Petrino had just resigned as head coach of the Atlanta Falcons before the end of the season to take the head coaching position at the University Arkansas. The Atlanta fans, sports writers, and broadcasters were vitriolic in their criticism of Coach Petrino. Several of the Falcons' players were harsh in their public quotes, and no doubt, much of their criticism stemmed from their feeling of neglect during a disappointing season. Distractions and disappointment surrounding quarterback Michael Vick's arrest and subsequent imprisonment were also contributing factors to poor team performance.

The Falcons' sixty-four-year-old defensive coordinator, Emmitt Thomas, was named interim coach. One of Thomas' first public statements addressed Petrino's leaving. Thomas said, "I think they've got to understand that they've got to take the high road on this. You never know all of the circumstances that happened with Coach Petrino's decision. What we have to do is wish him well and go on about our day-to-day activities and prepare for the other games and try to win some football games. "[5] This statement is essentially an expression of forgiveness or at least non-blame toward Coach Petrino. This is what we have to do in our own personal and business relationships in order to please God and move on in our conducting business God's way. The Falcons continued to struggle, but they did win the last game of the season; Coach Thomas' attitude did a lot to stabilize the Falcons' upheaval. Coach Thomas evidenced, as Shakespeare said, that "he believes that right make might; (*and*) his strength is the strength of ten (*men*) because his heart was pure." [6]

Forgiveness is the most powerful evidence to ourselves that we are in the process of humbling ourselves before God. But one can forgive and still be impatient with others and with God and even not show the most rudimentary kindness to others. How many times does the Holy Scriptures tell us to "love our neighbors as we love ourselves" (Matt. 19:19)? Love for others is the supreme act of humility because we are putting others first and striking a blow to our own selfishness. Likewise, God wants us to have patience, which is the ultimate act of prostrating ourselves before Him and killing our natural humanistic predisposition. Why is this? Because, when we accept Christ as our Savior, we must still make Him the Lord of our lives, which means we still need to kill the Adamic nature of trying to control everything in our lives. God is looking for evidence that we have given control back to Him. When we can wait on God to act on our behalf, we evidence what the Almighty is looking for in order to bless us.

The ancient patriarch Job is the most notable patient man with God and his circumstances. Remember the story of Satan's getting permission from God to try the patience of Job. Job lost his fortune and some of his family. His body was tortured with sores and excruciating pain. His best friends observed his fall from God's favor for a season, and Job's wife admonished him to curse God and end it all (Job 2:9). Then Job gave us that great retort and basic theological lesson when he answered his detractors with: "Though he slay me, yet will I trust in him" (Job 13:15 KJV).

Of course, Job at times mourned his condition, but he never blamed God or failed to be subservient before God. In that regard, Job taught us another lesson in humility, which is resignation. Job asked if we would accept the blessings from God but blame Him in our time of trouble (Job 2:10). Job did not rail against his circumstances because he knew that God was in control, and he made sure that he did not offend God. So often, I believe that we sin against God because we try to manage every circumstance, and we rail against God for our hardships. We may not directly address God, but we do so against authority figures, such as parents, teachers, or employers. Here is the lesson that we can learn from Job, and this lesson reflects on the failing of Adam. Adam wanted to be like God and control his own destiny. Job relinquished control of his life, took what God allowed in his life, and stayed the course until every circumstance turned in Job's favor. And turn they did, because God not only healed Job, but He restored and multiplied Job's fortune (Job 42:12).

What do you think would have happened to Job if he had been impatient with God, cursed his circumstances, and demanded that God restore him because of his faithfulness to God all his life? Based on the Holy Scriptures, I believe the story would have been quite different. Job's redemption would have been delayed or even denied, depending on how long it would have taken him to learn patience and resignation.

I read a good story recently that illustrates what I believe that God is looking for in order to make sure that we have learned the lessons that we need to master to qualify for God's blessings. The story is about Frank Wren, General Manager of the Atlanta Braves. He told the story to a reporter for the *Atlanta Journal Constitution* about his resignation to being Assistant General Manager of the Braves at the age of 49, only to be appointed GM three days after he and his wife made a resignation declaration. To go back a decade, Wren was appointed GM of the Baltimore Orioles but was fired after one year, although he had a three-year contract. Then the opportunity opened for him to join the Braves, where he found a good life with family and community friends who shared his Christian values. Yet he yearned to be a GM again, and although he had a chance to do so with the Pittsburgh Pirates, he declined in order to stay with the Braves and the good life he, his wife, and sons had forged in metro Atlanta. Yet the desire for the top GM position continued to challenge him. He said that after the 2007 season, he and his wife had a rare opportunity to have a Saturday night date, and over dinner, the conversation turned to where his career was going. Was this the highest he would go in baseball? Wren concluded that since he was forty-nine years old, he needed something to happen in a few years. The question he and wife, Terri, discussed is whether they would be happy if there were no further advancements. They agreed that they could be happy even if he had reached a dead end. Three days later, Braves GM, John Schuerholz, moved up to president of the Braves organization, and the Board of Directors appointed Frank Wren.[7]

You may question if Wren's resignation to his present condition was what triggered the promotion. Would the promotion have happened if Wren and his wife had not submitted to the present conditions? No, it probably would not have occurred if Wren and wife had needed to learn more humility, but their lives had evidenced learning these lessons, and the Saturday-night date decision was just the punctuation of a life story of learning God's lessons of grace and humility. Job 22:21 states this case for submission clearly: "Submit to God and be at peace with Him; in this way prosperity will come to you." If your 401 (k) has been depleted during the 2000-2009 market flaying, you know somewhat how Job felt. Can you and I see God in our circumstances? Do we think that God even concerns himself with our 401 (k)? Do the lessons from Job have any application to us in our losses? (Answers: Yes, Yes, and Yes!)

The story of Job provides us with the keys to realizing the fullness of God's blessings in any endeavor, including our vision regarding financial matters. However, to understand the full meaning of submission, learn more about meekness, which is the mindset that leads to the act of submission. You should understand the Old Testament and the New Testament uses of this powerful little word, *meekness*. Job was imbued with meekness. Certainly, he was helpless to improve himself after he lost his family, fortune, and health, which characterize the typical profile of meekness. In addition to the word *helpless*, the other characteristics used to describe a meek person are mild, gentle, and even impoverished.

In Jesus' sermon on the Beatitudes (Matt 5:5), He blessed the meek and said that they would inherit the earth. The noun form of the Greek word (New Testament), *praotes*, meaning meekness or the meek, has a much fuller and more poignant meaning than the Hebrew form of the word, meekness, in describing Job. The Greek noun form sets forth something that happens in the soul of the redeemed person that manifests itself in the characteristics often ascribed to meekness but describes also how we accept God's dealing with us.

It is more than resignation to earthly conditions; it is the change of heart when one encounters the awesomeness and majesty of God Almighty. This change is reflected in the absence of redeemed person's contending with God as God chastens and purifies His own and elects His own to service in the cause of His kingdom on earth. A well-known biblical example of Jesus' election is the conversion of Saul of Tarsus, who because Paul the apostle and evangelized the Greek and Roman kingdoms (Acts 9).

God uses periods of financial distress, health issues, and evil attacks to bring about the transformation of His elect to do the work that He has set us to do, which includes the realization of the vision He gives us. These struggles with financial issues, health problems, and evil attacks are the headwinds of life; but they help us to understand the awesomeness and majesty of God, which is a function of the Holy Spirit building meekness in us during these times of travail. Certainly, Job recognized what was happening, and he did not struggle with what God was doing in his life. He passed the test and grew in grace, wisdom, and earthly blessings. Colossians 3:12 (KJV) says that the meek become God's elect (*favored, blessed*).

Meekness is acknowledging the Deity, awesomeness, and majesty of God Almighty. Meekness is not fighting God or struggling with our conditions in life. Meekness is the form of humility that bonds our human spirit with the Holy Spirit and that works God's awesome blessings in our lives. As I quoted earlier, Jesus said that the "meek shall inherit the earth," and James the apostle said, "Humble yourselves before the Lord, and he will lift you up" (James 4:10). It is the meekness of humility that God rewards with generous blessings, and more often than not, it includes financial blessings and acclaim.

Meek people do not use God's name in vain, as in swearing to damn someone, and they do not use God's name frivolously. Any use of God's name to punctuate a sentence is unholy, and such usage subjects the speaker to judgment by the Deity, as set forth in the third of the Ten Commandments.

Using God's name in vain or frivolously brings judgment on the speaker. The character "Higgins" on Magnum PI of 1980s television started using God's name the first time, as I recall, on television to punctuate a sentence. Now it is common usage on television, but it is irreverent and woe to those who are profane. Networks that persist in this wickedness will continue to suffer financially, and their influence will atrophy further over time. Irreverence is the opposite of meekness.

How do we realize this meekness before the Lord? Meekness is the transforming work of the Holy Spirit in our human spirit, and this transformation of our inner man manifests itself in our view of others and ourselves. It works a gentleness and self-control in us, as Paul the apostle stated it (Eph. 4:2; Gal. 5:22-23). This transformation begins with our total reverence of God Almighty and His Son, Jesus Christ. It means praising and honoring Him in every way possible in our lives. Then we invite the Holy Spirit into our hearts and lives to immerse our human spirit and serve as our guide and the conveyer of our daily meditation and worship of God Almighty.

The effect of the Holy Spirit controlling our lives is that we then confess our sins daily and purpose to turn from our sins and transgressions. As this transformation develops, we realize that we are not struggling with life and blaming God for our conditions, but we recognize that God is doing something in our lives to bring us into the person He is looking for in order to bless us and to use us in His kingdom. If we learn to pray the prayer of acceptance of where we are in life and to acknowledge that God is doing a good work in us, we are well on our way to the level of humility that the Scriptures call meekness.

There is one more lesson from Job that is embodied in the characteristic of humility. Job was grateful to God for his blessings. Job acknowledged that God had given him everything he had in life: wonderful family, good friends, and the abundance of land and crops. He said that the Lord God had given him everything. Gratitude is the antithesis of self-sufficiency and pride. Gratitude is the recognition and public acknowledgement that all talents and successes come from God through His undeniable blessings in our lives. Job said the "Lord gave and the Lord has taken away; may the name of the Lord be praised" (Job 1:21). This act of subjugating ourselves and exalting God is further evidence that we have humbled ourselves before the Lord, so that He can lift us up (James 4:10).

Gratitude and publicly exalting God are probably more difficult for entrepreneurs than any other group of achievers. Talented people with athletic and artistic skills are more likely to recognize that their abilities are God-given. Either you have athletic talent or good musical skills or you do not. You do not have to be a skilled musician to recognize a gifted instrumentalist or singer. An ordinary person can hear the difference. Athletes demonstrate the same results. You can see even on the playground who is going to be part of the next generation of skilled athletes, based on players' coordination, foot speed, and agility.

With entrepreneurs, however, they are often not the most brilliant people in their class or otherwise demonstrate early in life a special skill that identifies them as achievers in starting a successful business. No entrepreneurial gene exists, nor does a fool-proof profile of human skills and characteristics that assures success in creating and running a new business. Certainly, entrepreneurs are generally very intelligent, although they may not be scholarly. But they have a vision; they know how to provide services and products to improve lives. They also are persistent.

New businesses evolve over years and usually after many struggles on the part of the founders. Many entrepreneurs were average students, and some even are dyslexic. I saw a television report of a brilliant real estate entrepreneur in Texas who was dyslexic and could not read the detailed documents germane to his business. However, he found a way to work around his impediments and pursue his vision. Thus the title, "self-made man (or woman)," is often applied to those people who have carved out businesses from nothing. Therefore, it takes a spiritually well-grounded person to resist the accolades and self-aggrandizement that sometimes accompanies success after years of struggles in a new business.

But in all fairness, many entrepreneurs recognize that opportunities occurred at strategic times in their lives that could not be explained in any other way except that divine intervention made something pivotal happen. God relishes the partnership with an entrepreneur, and the Almighty is owed the public gratitude for the successes that come to us in carrying out the vision that God gives us. The Scriptures say that God inhabits the praise of His people (Ps. 22:3 KJV); we are admonished to acknowledge (praise, honor) Him, and He will direct our steps in all our undertakings (Prov. 3:6 KJV).

The more that I read and hear about Elvis Presley from those close to him, the more I respect his humility. He was not perfect, but that is probably one reason I understand him. From every indication, he acknowledged that God gave him talent and set him on an unprecedented career in entertainment. He often said that he did not understand why God had given him such talent and had chosen him for such success.

Presley gave God the honor and glory owed only to Him, as indicated by this story from one of his tours. At a concert at Notre Dame University, several girls seated in the center section stood with placards spelling: "Elvis, You Are the King." Presley stopped his performance, pointed to the girls and said: "No, there is only one King, and that is Jesus Christ." [8]

Elvis was courteous to all and generous to a fault. He was respectful of his parents and never blamed them (as a substitute for God) for his impoverished upbringing. He evidenced the salient characteristics of meekness. He was not accepted as a teenager and was subjected to ridicule and abuse from his peers. One story is that the football bullies at Hume High School in Memphis tried to hold him down and shave his hair, but he was rescued by a nominal acquaintance. Nevertheless, he never seemed to be unforgiving or unkind. Elvis' story of success as an entertainer is legend. He has surely been one of the most acclaimed people in entertainment throughout the world. Humility in all its facets is a powerful characteristic for your good and the glory of God.

Discretion

Discretion is an old English word that appears frequently in the King James Version of the Old Testament. Bible dictionaries and commentaries use numerous synonyms for discretion, but judgment, reason, prudence, self-discipline, and wisdom fit best in the context of this discussion. When the kingdom was divided into Judah and Israel, God spoke to the people of Judah in a parable about a farmer who prepares the land for planting (Isaiah 28:23-29). The parable relates that God sometimes allows hardships in our lives to prepare our hearts for His work, much like a farmer tills the soil to make a crop. The farmer tills the soil to prepare within the season for a later harvest. Isaiah 28:26 (KJV) says, "For his God doth instruct him to discretion [self-discipline], and doth teach him." God teaches us how to discipline our lives to make the best use of the money that remains after we have given Him our tithes and offerings. He does this by tempering our human spirits with His Holy Spirit.

God expects us to discipline ourselves, learn from Him to use good judgment, and demonstrate reason, prudence, and wisdom. In the context of our topic of realizing and retaining wealth, discretion is the judgment we make to restrain ourselves from calling attention to ourselves with the use of our money, whether it is for personal use or charitable or religious gifts. Discretion is the evidence of our humility as we make the practical judgment to guard against the natural tendencies for self-aggrandizement.

Does this mean that when you realize an improvement in your financial conditions that you are to deny yourself a nice house, a better vehicle, or even a second home? I do not believe that you are expected to live in the same conditions as before you began to prosper, but if you are in partnership with God to use your finances to serve Him, you should seek God's guidance in each use of your new-found wealth. I would not even think about making a major purchase without praying about the matter. I think we need to seek His approval of the venture and rely on His guidance in the purchase. This act serves two purposes: first, you make sure that you are in God's will and secondly, you seek His guidance in opening up the doors for you.

My wife and I recently wanted to buy a lot next to our daughter's house and property in the mountains. The purchase of the land would square off our daughter's jagged lot, which barely complied with the septic-system codes, and the additional land would protect the view from her house. She had tried for three years to buy the lot, and her aunt, who previously owned the house until her untimely death, had tried to make the purchase for more than a year. My wife and I prayed for months about buying the land for our daughter, if it were in God's will, and if so, we asked for favor with the owner of the property.

After a few months, we contacted a real estate agent and asked him to broker the deal. We prayed that if this were God's will that He would bring about the deal at a reasonable price, and we resigned ourselves that we would be satisfied with whatever the outcome. We offered the owner the appraised value as recorded on the county tax index. After one exchange of negotiating, the owner accepted our offer. We continue to thank God for blessing us and for teaching us how to proceed in these matters.

Discretion is a kindred spirit with humility in materialistic matters. Opulence, showiness, and boasting are the antitheses of discretion. Entertainers, athletes and tycoons who live in mansions and stock their garages with more cars than the week has days are not practicing discretion. Frivolous and demonstrable use of wealth is just not consistent with the disciplined life that God expects of those who are seeking His blessing on their finances. TV evangelists and other Christian leaders need to go the extra mile in demonstrating discretion in the use of the money entrusted to them.

Recently the story broke about Senator Charles Grassley's seeking income tax records and other financial information from several prominent ministers and teachers who appear on television each week. People who are avowed Christians and are in the public eye, such as television ministers, are sometimes unwarrantedly suspected if their material possessions are above the ordinary. Some examples of fraud and excess have drawn media attention and rightly so. Those who are honest and forthright need to build in protection.

Billy Graham dealt with this issue early in his ministry. He set up a board of directors, requested and received a flat salary, and lived a modest life in the mountains of western North Carolina. The point is that God does not overlook imprudence in His people and holds ministers and teachers to an even higher standard (James 3:1). Christians who seek God's blessings on their finances and vow to honor God with tithes and offerings are held to the same standards as ministers and teachers.

Thomas J. Stanley and William D. Danko in their book, *The Millionaire Next Door,* discuss the frugality and the very conservative lifestyles of these unassuming millionaires who have accumulated their fortunes over a lifetime. Most of these wealthy people have made their money in a business that they either started or bought and remade. They buy off-the-rack clothing, drive older vehicles that they probably bought from a previous owner, and live in the house, maybe with additions and remodeling, which they bought soon after they married their one and only spouse.[9] Granted, these wealthy are not as rich as the RMIT reported by Randy Jones in his book.

I do not think that the next-door millionaire lifestyle of frugality is a prerequisite to satisfying God's standard of discretion; but probably more often than not, humble people are likely to fit that description. The criterion for discretion for use of the money after you have given God the tithe and any offerings is simply to seek God's review of your plans and to submit to what you feel that He is leading you to do. Study the Bible in this matter and be open to hearing from God through His Word and other ways He speaks to you.

God opens doors for new ventures and grand improvements in your comfort and pleasure without your making any special effort to bring these about. The heavenly Father knows what pleases you and will make things happen to make you happy. Have you ever bought your child a nice automobile or sent her on a trip to Hawaii or Europe? Maybe you have bought her a new bedroom suite or done something expensive that she had not asked for and certainly was not expecting. Do you remember how much fun it was to shop or plan for the surprise gift? Do you remember how excited you were on the day that you presented the surprise? You were probably just as excited as she was. Do you remember how much you enjoyed the hugs and gratitude that she expressed to you for weeks afterward? God is like that with us. God inhabits (lives in, lives for) the praise of His people (Ps. 22:3 KJV), and He likes to surprise us as obedient sons and daughters when we have learned our lessons of humility and discretion and have been generous in blessing others.

I received a grand surprise gift years ago that still amazes me. First, I have to confess that I have a weakness for high-performance automobiles. Contrast this with the fact that my wife and I live in the house that we built in 1969 and in which we raised our only child. It has eight-foot ceilings and is small and otherwise modest by today's standards. But over the years, I have loved Mercedes automobiles and SUVs. I rode in an MB for the first time when a friend of ours shipped one back to the US when his tour of duty in Germany with the Army ended. I rode with him in it in the mid-1960s and really got hooked on the ride and the safety features. In 1972, when our daughter was three years old, I became exasperated with the fragility of the Ford sedan that I was driving, and my wife and I really worried about the safety of the family when we took long trips. We prayed about what we should do. Soon after that, I was talking with my friend who owned a Mercedes, and he told me about a man who wanted to sell his 1968 Mercedes sedan. I bought the four-year-old, low mileage MB and sold the Ford.

We drove that Mercedes around town and on long trips, including a trip to Colorado. After the trip to Colorado in 1974, I began thinking about getting a later model automobile and conceded that we would need to look for a lesser expensive domestic vehicle. We decided to go shopping for a small Buick or Pontiac, and I heard about a dealership across the state line in Alabama that almost wholesaled new cars. So we decided to drive to Gadsden, Alabama, on a Saturday morning in October 1974 and shop for a General Motors product.

When we arrived at the dealership, in addition to the symbols displayed for the GM vehicles, a big three-point encircled star of the Mercedes Benz logo was displayed over the dealer's showroom. This dealer had a franchise to sell and service MB's, in addition to his GM franchises. I turned my little 1968 maroon Mercedes into a parking place in front of the dealership, and promptly a salesman came outside to greet us. Naturally, he thought we were interested in buying another Mercedes. Rather sheepishly, I had to tell him that we were looking for something much less expensive.

We started looking at domestic cars, but somehow the discussion drifted again to talking about the Mercedes products that he had on the lot. He asked me if I would be interested in a slightly used Mercedes 280, which was the mid-line sedan in those days. I told him that I would look at it. Much to my surprise, the slightly used sedan was almost new because it had about two thousand miles on it and even smelled brand new. He told me that an older man had bought the car for his younger wife. She had driven it six weeks and brought it back to the dealer, replacing it with a Pontiac sports car. He offered me an unbelievable deal with the trade-in of my 1968 sedan. My wife and I drove off in an almost new Mercedes, knowing that God had just given us a surprise party. I drove that car almost twenty years and enjoyed it immensely. I am still amazed at that deal and am convinced that the heavenly Father sent us over to Gadsden to collect His surprise gift.

My recently retired family physician, Dr. Jack Crews, a humble and soft-spoken Christian, told a similar story about how he acquired his vacation home in the western North Carolina mountains. He said that he bought it when he was in his internship following graduation from medical college. At the time, he had no savings and a modest salary of only $400 a month. He found the cottage when he and his wife, Carolyn, were taking a much needed weekend in the mountains to rest after many long days working through his residency.

They had driven by the house and were struck by the beauty of the small house framed against the mountains and rushing creek. Almost hidden in the weeds was a "For Sale by Owner" sign. He and Carolyn walked the property and fell in love with the place. They went back the next day and met the owner, a retired minister who was moving to Florida. Dr. Crews told the minister that he did not have much money, and the minister said he was not asking much for the house. So they struck a deal: $1,500 down and $35 a month mailed to the minister and wife in sunny Florida. Dr. Crews had to rush back home to borrow $1,500 to cover his check for the down payment. He and Carolyn built another house on the property several years ago, but they still marvel at how surprised they were to stumble on their little piece of heaven in the Smokey Mountains.

Our Lord requires our discretion, not only in use of money or material things, but also in our contributions for charitable and religious purposes. We are required to keep from drawing attention to ourselves in giving our tithes to the Lord and offerings to charities. Jesus said that if we draw attention to ourselves, we receive no heavenly reward. That is a costly indictment for succumbing to pride.

Read the words of Jesus in Matthew 6:1-4,

Be careful not to do your 'acts of righteousness' before men, to be seen by them. If you do, you will have no reward from your Father in heaven. So when you give to the needy, do not announce it with trumpets, as the hypocrites do in the synagogues and on the streets, to be honored by men. I tell you the truth, they have received their reward in full. But when you give to the needy, do not let your left hand know what your right hand is doing, so that your giving may be in secret. Then your Father, who sees what is done in secret, will reward you [openly].

Do you see why I was so hard in chapter 2 on a few sponsors of charity events? Our indiscretion can rob us of such great rewards, and indiscretion is not limited to outward appearances. We can be just as vain while feigning humility. God knows our attitudes and the insincerity that we might carry in our hearts. How do we deal with this issue? Inviting the Holy Spirit to do a work in us is the only way to assure a transformation from Adamic pride to meekness of spirit. Even then, the transformation is not sudden, but while we are sincerely striving to be like Jesus in these matters, God honors our attitude and our submission to Him for transforming our lives. The Scriptures are clear on this issue: Do not seek public recognition for your good works; let recognition come to you unbidden.

A respectable profession has as its mantra: *doing good and telling everybody about it.* Public relations is promoting a company's image or in the case of a publicist for a celebrity, promoting the good side of the client. I believe that devising a good work simply to draw attention to a company or individual is an indiscretion. But in fairness, many companies and celebrities have never flaunted their good works. But these good works may be uncovered; and in these cases, if someone else such as the media publicizes the good deed, the company or the celebrity loses control of the publicity and has not violated his or her discretion. Here again God is the judge, but we need to make sure that our heart is set on doing good and not on attracting attention.

While I was writing this chapter, my pastor told me that he and the trustees of our church wanted to have a brief recognition ceremony after Sunday worship for families who had made endowment gifts to our church. This included my wife and me because we had established a scholarship fund in memory of my parents, who also had been members of our church.

This story bears out how important our words and pronouncements are before God. We have to guard against being critical and need to monitor our conversations and pronouncements. The psalmist said, "May the words of my mouth and the meditation of my heart be pleasing in your sight, O Lord, my Rock and my Redeemer" (Ps. 19:14). I am sure that ministers and Bible teachers are tested constantly against their sermons and lessons.

I balked at the idea of being called in front of the church sanctuary after an 11:00 a.m. service to be recognized for a financial gift. We took days of praying about what to do to have any peace about the matter. Finally, I emailed the pastor that I would cooperate because he had said that the purpose was to inspire others to set up endowments and to attract contributions to our family scholarship fund. I trust that I made the right decision, but I must admit that I was not comfortable with the attention. That discomfort represents a real work in me over the years, because a few years ago, while I was striving to move up the corporate (university) ladder, I would have relished the acclaim.

Conclusion

God expects us to work within the confines of the vision that He gives us for our lives. If you are unhappy and unfilled in your occupation, conduct a spiritual check to see if you are working at what God intends for you. Seek His vision for your life, success, happiness, and prosperity.

Our happiness and success in our occupation and our lives in general are greatly dependent on how closely we synchronize with the will of God and accept what He is doing in our lives. God orders circumstances and events to make us more like Jesus. The two personal characteristics that evidence our becoming more like Jesus are humility and discretion. Humility begins with forgiveness, proceeds through meekness, and ends with faithful gratitude to God and constant reverence for His name and holiness.

We act out our being more Christ-like by our discretion, our self-control. When we proceed through this pilgrimage of consciously committing to being more like Jesus, the Holy Spirit begins a monumental work in us, and we give our lives for the Holy Spirit to effect our self-discipline mechanism. We do not have to work out our transformation ourselves. When we commit to the work of the Holy Spirit in our lives, the Holy Spirit orders circumstances that bring about the changes in our attitudes and conduct that make us not even recognize the old self. As we move through this walk, we begin to realize blessings that can only come from the very hand of God.

CHAPTER FOUR

Adventures in Stewardship

My first recollection of attending church involved a stewardship lesson from my mother at Mercer Avenue Baptist Church in College Park, Georgia. As was the case with most neighborhood Baptist churches of that era, everyone met in the sanctuary for an assembly program before breaking out to Sunday school classrooms. Just before I was dismissed to Mrs. Lily Coleman's Beginners Class, my mother placed a nickel coin in my hand, closed her hand around mine, and said, "Here is your gift to Jesus. When you make your own money, don't forget to give Jesus a tithe before you spend anything on yourself." I did not know what a tithe was, but that fact did not deter mother. She repeated that little homily before Sunday school for the next five years.

My parents accepted Jesus Christ and committed to Christianity as teenagers in College Park in the 1920s, and they married in 1932, in the midst of the Great Depression. Both parents had to drop out of high school in their senior year to help with the family incomes. Mother was one of eleven children, and my father was the sole supporter for his mother and two younger brothers after his father died prematurely. When my parents married, my father worked several jobs to make a living, including operating a barber shop. He learned the trade from my grandfather who owned a five-chair shop in the West End of Atlanta in the early 1900s.

Not long after my parents married, my father became very ill with scarlet fever, and he was bedridden for many months. During that time, he studied the Bible and Bible commentaries searching for direction for his life. Based on his study of the Bible, he and mother pledged that they would begin tithing from their meager income, and they followed through on that pledge and continued their tithing until they died in their nineties.

After I was born in 1939, my father began selling life insurance with American National Life Insurance Company. In those days, insurance representatives also collected door to door from their customers in what was known as a "debit." Evidently, he was very productive because he progressed through the ranks in the Atlanta office until he was appointed sales manager in the early 1940s. When he was thirty-five years old, his draft board called him for a physical examination, but he was never inducted into the armed services. My parents told stories for years about the hardships of war-time rationing of certain foods and commodities.

I remember the fear and depression that permeated both sides of our family and also our church family during the war years. I was very young, but I will not forget the prayer meetings at church and the family gatherings when prayers were offered for my three uncles who were in war zones and for all the troops. I recall vividly the announcements that the Germans had surrendered and later that the US had dropped the atomic bomb in three large cities in Japan. I remember our excitement during an evening radio broadcast in August 1945, when H. V. Kaltenborn, the famous radio commentator, announced that Japan had surrendered and that World War II was over. The celebrations in the streets and the thanksgiving prayer meetings will be etched in my memory forever.

After WW II was over, my father was promoted to deputy superintendent of the Atlanta District of his insurance company. Those were the halcyon days of Atlanta, before the boom-town atmosphere that surrounded the city a few decades later. Business people and shoppers could parallel park their automobiles on Peachtree Street in front of their office buildings or the department stores. Inside the Healy Building, we rode to father's office floor in a gated elevator driven by a splendidly uniformed operator who knew everybody in the building and performed his duties with the zest of a corporate executive and the aplomb of an Old South aristocrat.

I enjoyed the occasional Sunday afternoon trips with my father to his office and the lunches at Leb's and Ship Ahoy restaurants. Life was pretty good for the family as seen through the eyes of an elementary school boy. I was at peace with my family and with God because I had accepted Jesus as Lord and had committed myself to Christianity and was baptized when I was eight years old.

Mother was a stay-at-home mom after I was born. Her interests mainly centered on her church and taking care of a rambunctious son. She did not dispense corporal punishment herself, but she was more like a prosecuting attorney when my father held court after returning from one of his occasional business trips. Mother taught some good lessons to a boy who observed more than he heard, and she demonstrated a life of unselfishness and giving to others in need. She started a lifelong ministry of cooking food and raising flowers to share with countless sick and lonely people. She also prepared surprise meals for those who favored her or her family in some special way or who just needed to know that someone cared for them.

My father served as a deacon, Sunday school teacher, and choir director in our church, and he began serving from time to time as a lay speaker at other churches. He was known as the "Sunday school boy" around his office until he was promoted to a district level office, and then he was known as Mister. He told me years later that his heart was not in the insurance business, and he realized after a period of time that he was called into the ministry. Everything came to a decision point when a community church in College Park asked him to serve as their pastor in an interim capacity. After much prayer and consultation with my mother and me, he accepted the call as pastor, and the church ordained him into the ministry in 1946. He served as a bi-vocational pastor for two years, but he realized that he needed more education. Therefore, he applied for admission to Norman College, a Baptist college in south Georgia, and a pastor friend arranged for father to serve as pastor of a rural Baptist church twenty miles from the college. In late July 1948, we packed and moved to Norman Park, Georgia. Mother was the key to that move because she supported the venture and drew on their spiritual capital built up over many years of investing in the kingdom.

The Move to Southwest Georgia

When we arrived in Norman Park, father had some disappointing news. The admissions officer told him that he could not be admitted for the fall term because he was not a high school graduate and did not have a GED. Father asked when he could take the GED, and the admission director told him the schedule and gave him a list of GED prep courses that the college provided. He saw that the next exam was the following Saturday, so he said he wanted to sign up for the Saturday exam. The admissions officer told him that he would not have a chance to pass the examination without proper preparation. Nevertheless, father prevailed, took the examination, passed with a high grade, and was admitted for the fall term. He finished his academic and Bible course work in record time, graduated with honors, and was president of the ministerial association and honor society.

I can see my father now studying in a corner of our living room at his desk equipped with a fluorescent lamp that projected over his books from a long double-jointed arm off its base that hummed constantly. He loved the literature courses, and I helped him memorize passages from Robert Burns, Alfred Lord Tennyson, the Brownings, and Robert Frost. I still remember most of the Burns' passages even now and much of Tennyson's lessons. Those literary sessions provided me with the first exposure to good literature, which in later years was renewed as I read a series of the classics. Also, in later years, I drew on that experience with father to shape my own theory of good writing: good prose is beautiful music set to words. Good writing has rhythm, a beat if you please, that the reader feels deep within the soul and subconscious.

A good writer has that rhythm in his mind and in his spirit, and he can select words and join phrases to match the meter, the rhythm that he hears. For example, a series of three tiny phrases have more rhythm than simply two words or two phrases joined by a conjunction. Three in a series builds energy like a good piece of music. The reader feels exhilaration from the well-written prose. Often the rhythm is more enjoyable than the narrative.

The lesson that I learned at a young age is that children absorb lasting feelings and wisdom during sessions with parents. I was blessed to have had such parents who took the time with me and were willing to let me explore ideas and concerns. I had rather have had their time and interest even in our humble setting than all the money and luxuries that other children might have received. This parental love and guidance certainly offset the hardships of a growing boy's adjusting to being a preacher's kid and any financial depravation that was inherent in the life of an adult student and his family.

My parents sacrificed to buy me baseball spikes, glove, bat, and Keds basketball shoes. A big boy broke my new bat during a pick-up game, and father said if I would take it back to the sporting goods store and ask for a refund that he would buy me a new bat if the manager refused. I agonized over that matter for weeks, but finally my desire for new bat overcame my fear of this confrontation. Of course, the manager refused, and father kept his word and bought me a new bat. Certainly, the bat has been long gone, but the lesson continues to be applied regularly.

For three and a half years, we drove forty miles round trip each Wednesday night and Sunday to Big Creek Baptist Church in Thomas County. Also, in the summers for three months, we lived near the church while father and I were out of school. It was a wonderful break for the entire family, although I really enjoyed my school. I played basketball and baseball on the elementary school teams that competed with other schools in Colquitt County. Nevertheless, living in the country during those summers was an idyllic life for a ten- to twelve-year-old boy. I swam in the creeks and rivers in the community, learned to fish with a pole, set hooks and trot lines, and camped out to attend to our hooks as we waited for the mud-cats and channel catfish to hit our bait.

My first summer in the country was a lazy time, and I got bored often when my friends on the farms nearby were helping with farm work and the endless chores that were obligatory in the fields and barns. However, my father had a plan for me for the next summer, and he executed his plan well before we were dismissed from school after my completing the fifth grade. He asked one of the neighbors and a member of our church if he had any work that I could do on his farm. By this time, I was eleven years old and was very tall for my age. I eagerly awaited our return to the country house, owned by another church member, to begin working on the farm. At least I knew that I would not be bored.

My work that summer was mainly in gathering the tobacco crop. Tobacco leaves mature from the ground up; therefore, the harvest took five to six weeks. Five or six men "cropped" the lowest three to four leaves each week, and each cropping was hauled to the barn where "stringers" tied the tobacco leaves to five-foot wooden sticks, cut in a four-sided configuration. The stacks of tobacco were handed to the stringers in three and four leaves by the youngest members of the harvest team. I was a "hander" that first year for which I was paid $2.00 a day for my effort plus helping to load the barn with the sticks of tobacco leaves.

I remembered my mother's homilies in College Park to tithe first before I spent anything on myself. I think that my parents waited to see what I would do with my earnings because I do not remember any more short sermons on that issue. During tobacco season, I contributed for each day's work ten cents in Sunday school and ten cents when the offering plate was passed in the sanctuary each Sunday.

It took about four days to cure a load of tobacco by wood furnace in those uniquely shaped tobacco barns. When the drying by heat was finished, the crop was sufficiently aired and allowed to take up moisture. After a day or so, the sticks of tobacco had to be removed from the barn and stacked in a warehouse for the next curing process. I helped with the removal of the sticks from the barn and later with un-stringing the leaves from the sticks and storing the dried leaves in large round mounds stacked on burlap sheets. Later the cured tobacco sheets were transported to the tobacco auctions in Thomasville or Moultrie.

I was paid a little money for these duties, and I dutifully gave a tenth of each cash payment in the offering plate on Sunday. I felt good about my stewardship and never questioned the gift to Jesus nor longed to have all the money that I was paid for myself. Some may say that I was brainwashed by my mother's long indoctrination, but even at that age, I believe that the Holy Spirit was the teacher and mother was just the voice. I cheerfully accepted the training, and that simple beginning as a steward has made a major difference in my life.

By January 1952, father completed his coursework in college, and he accepted a call to another church, New Bethel in Colquitt County, located between Meigs and Moultrie. It was a large country church with members from the surrounding farms and small businesses in the community. I had to leave my basketball team in Norman Park in mid-season and a cute girl-friend. This was a tough move for a thirteen-year-old boy, although the country setting near the Little Ochlocknee River provided an exhilarating venue for a budding Tom Sawyer/Huckleberry Finn lifestyle. I rode the school bus six miles to Meigs School, but that transition did not go well. I did not like my teacher, and I was a nuisance in the classroom. I made it through five months of school, mainly because I had the afternoons to romp in the woods and go skinny dipping in the river and creeks near home. A large pasture bordered the back side of our house, and a couple of scruffy looking horses made their home among the scrub oaks dotting the grassland and sandy slope to the Little Ochlocknee River. I never saw anyone give those horses any attention, much less use them in farm work. So I began to feed and pet my broken down "neighbors." They soon learned to meet me when I got off the school bus. Eventually, I got the nerve to mount one of them with no bridle or saddle, but my "gallant steed" allowed me to sit comfortably on his back as he wandered all over the many acres in that semi-wooded tract. Eventually, depending on my patience, he dropped me off near one of the swimming holes in the river.

Once again, my enterprising father put out the word that his son was available for farm work. Therefore, that summer and two more summers, I worked in the fields along with my buddies from the church. I worked in tobacco and the produce crops from late May until early September. I learned to drive a tractor and do light jobs such as hauling tobacco out of the patch to the barn. My last summer there, I did some cropping during the tobacco harvest, for which I received $3.00 a day plus all I could eat at the farmhouse during the long lunch breaks, called dinner by the farmers.

We usually went to the fields by sunup in order to get most of the work done before the sun and little breeze made it too hot to work. By noon, all the croppers were exhausted and starving. Those farm families spread feasts the likes of which I have not seen since, although my mother was a wonderful cook. But it was the variety and volume of food that was almost overwhelming. Every meal entailed the obligatory southern sweet tea and apple cobbler. After a robust lunch and a nap on the front porch floor, about two o'clock, we hung the tobacco sticks in the barn and headed for the creek or river to go swimming. It was a miracle that no one had muscle cramps and drowned after all that exhausting work. Those were good times and provided a spirited entry into puberty.

I continued without reluctance to contribute my tithe each Sunday after collecting my cash wages from the different farmers for the two to three days of work each week. I did not identify any special improvement in my income, but my father did upgrade our family transportation by buying a maroon-colored 1949 Ford coupe to replace the worn-out 1941 Ford sedan that he bought at the end of World War II. I loved that coupe because it was "cool." I could see myself driving it for show and attracting girls in droves in three years. But no girls were in my life, except one on the school bus who constantly harassed me. In every new school, someone was eager to take on the preacher's kid. I had my share of fights and shoving matches. This was long before I learned the power of forgiveness, but I doubt that I would have been a willing student of the concept at that age.

My time at Meigs School came to an end after the eighth grade. By that time, I was almost six feet tall, and I had showed some promise in pickup basketball games at lunch time. However, I did not like the school. The teacher who was my nemesis in the seventh grade followed the class as our social studies teacher in the eighth grade. I visited the principal's office a few times because of clashes with my nemesis and was rightfully disciplined. However, I got along very well with the other teachers and the principal. In fact, the principal visited my house during the summer when he learned that I planned to transfer to Moultrie High in the ninth grade. He was a truly humble and decent man, and I am sure that he broke with precedent to visit me at home. He attempted to change my mind about transferring, and I regret to say that I lied to him. I told him I was still thinking about the move, and I tried to divert his attention to my buddy who planned to transfer also. I lied to him because I hated to see him disappointed and to feel any blame whatsoever that I was unhappy at Meigs. I never saw him again after that visit to apologize, and I was too immature or proud to write a letter of apology.

In September 1953, I enrolled at Moultrie High School as a freshman and rode the bus sixteen miles each way. Attending that one year in Moultrie was a good experience. I played "B" team basketball and joined the ninth-grade football team. I had never played football, except pickup touch games, but I quickly learned my offensive and defensive end positions. I had superior foot speed and quickness, and later during the next spring varsity practice season, the coaches switched me to quarterback.

In basketball, I played for a good coach, and I looked forward to varsity basketball to play for a legendary coach in Georgia high school sports, who was in his day, a standout college player at Georgia Tech. But that was not to happen because we moved to another town during the summer after my ninth grade at Moultrie High.

During my one school year at Moultrie, I worked as a clerk in a crossroads country store each Saturday. I pumped gas, swept the floors and concrete porch, and kept the cold drink box and cracker jars filled. The lady who ran the store had a son my age, and we tossed a football in dull periods and listened to Georgia Tech football games in the fall. I realize now that I did not do much work, but I was paid $2.00 a day from which I continued to contribute my tithe each Sunday.

I saved my money for strategic uses, since I had my eye on a pretty brunette in our church who had flirted with me on the bus. The problem was that she was two years older than I was, and she was ready for an experience with anyone who had a driver's license. That did not stop me from trying, and I carried out a daring and stupid feat to date my much admired girl friend. The scene opens in November 1953. Our social studies class had just seen the film at a local theater of the Coronation of Queen Elizabeth II. I was staying with a farm family in our church while my father and mother were in Atlanta. My father was hospitalized and Mother was constantly with him.

I worked on the family farm for the six weeks that I lived with this wonderful family, but I made an outrageous move that infuriated the farmer. I "stole" his truck to go to a church youth meeting one Saturday night to see my intended girlfriend. As I expected, she was delighted to allow me to drive her home, and this act of "manhood" started a brief courtship with an "older woman." But the move put me in the doghouse, rightly so, with my mentor because first, I did not have a driver's license and second, I did not ask to use the truck. I still wince when I think of that trick. The shadowy redeeming feature to that delinquency is the boldness in evidence that served me well in my entrepreneurial ventures many years later.

During the following spring, I joined the varsity in spring football practice at Moultrie High School. I often rode home with my friend and teammate who had transferred with me who, incidentally, did not have a driver's license. Maybe there is some poetic justice in my driver's license delinquency story. Nevertheless, when my friend stayed over to meet his girlfriend or missed school, I had to hitchhike on a lonely county blacktop road to my home. One such afternoon, it was misting rain, and I had not caught a ride in almost an hour. I was wet, cold, and desperate.

A farmer came along in a deuce and a half truck with stake bodies reaching above the roof line of the cab. At least four fat and grizzly-looking farm boys were stuffed in the front seat. One of them lowered the window and said that I could ride in the back if I could get in it. I was in no position to be picky. I climbed up and over and jumped onto the bed of the truck, backing up to the cab and squatting down. I was quite dry there and off we went. I looked up when I got seated, and there was a mid-size calf staring me in the face. I was not afraid of calves because I had been around them for years.

We rode on with the calf swaying side to side and pooping occasionally in his own corner of the truck bed. After about twenty minutes, the truck stopped, and the driver turned off the main road. He lowered the window and said that was as far as he could take me. I climbed out, thanked him, and set off down the road to catch another ride. Fortunately, the rain stopped and a long, black Chrysler sedan stopped for me. I walked to the passenger side, and the well-dressed driver told me that I was welcome to ride.

I should have checked myself after climbing out of the farmer's truck because I immediately began to smell an awful odor when I closed the door of the sedan. The driver and I chatted, but he soon rolled down his window, and I took off my letter jacket (which was still without a letter), folded it, and placed in the floor of the car. That did not help. I realized that I had backed into cow poop stuck to the side of the truck, and my jacket was smeared with the remnants from this white-face hamburger on the hoof. I told the driver to let me out because we both knew we could not take it much longer. I got out, thanked him, and walked several miles to the store where I had worked, and I waited for a friendly neighbor to drive me home after dark.

The following summer before we moved again, I worked in the fields two and sometimes three days a week. The other days I hitchhiked into Moultrie to play Babe Ruth league baseball. This was in the early days of the league, and I was excited to play on an organized team with uniforms and plenty of baseballs. We didn't have to worry about the game being stopped because someone fouled the ball into the woods.

I hitchhiked to the games because my father often was busy with his duties, although he often arranged his hospital visits in Moultrie to give me a ride to games. However, he did not go too far out of his way to accommodate me. His idea was to build in toughness and independence, even if it meant that his 15-year-old son missed a game because he could not catch a ride sixteen miles into Moultrie. I am disgusted when I hear the occasional modern-day brats drill their parents who are a few minutes late for a pickup.

On this particular day in June 1954, I caught a ride with a gentleman. I thought he was the only occupant of the vehicle, and the long swishing antenna on the back bumper did not give him away. As soon as I got into the car, I realized that I was in the presence of the county warden, and he had a prisoner caged in the back seat. Since I was in a baseball uniform, the warden knew where to deposit me.

Unfortunately, about halfway to Moultrie, he took a call on the radio that redirected him on a side trip. He stopped at a prisoner work site for what seemed like hours, and the backseat prisoner and I started talking. The prisoner was being transported to another prison for added penalties because he had tried to escape a work detail. He was either a talented con artist or he truly was touched by someone showing compassion. Father later confirmed the typical prisoner's split personality based on his years of jailhouse ministry. Eventually, the warden returned and drove me to the game, which had a couple of innings left to play. The coach substituted me into the game at first base, and I only got to bat once, but I was not disappointed. I figured that I did not have anything to complain about in comparison to the poor, wretched soul in the back-seat cage.

The Move to Greenville

In late July of 1954, we moved from Colquitt County to Greenville, located in west central Georgia. Greenville is the county seat of Meriwether County, which is best known for Warm Springs, where President Franklin D. Roosevelt maintained his Little White House. I missed Moultrie High with its many opportunities in athletics, but I was pleased to be within site of the high school buildings from our home at Greenville Baptist Church. I was relieved that I would not have to hitchhike any more nor arise before dawn to board a school bus at 6:45 a.m. for a sixteen-mile ride.

Greenville High participated in the lowest classification in athletics compared to Moultrie, which was in the highest classification. However, many notable people came out of Greenville High, and the little town was rich in tradition and southern charm. The main street was lined with beautiful antebellum homes, and the church members and city loyalists were well-educated and quite charming. I have never seen a place that had an endless lineup of pretty girls. I wish Garrison Keillor had observed what I saw in the lovelies of Meriwether County, and if so, surely he would have rewritten his slogan for the women of Lake Wobegon.

I dated several of the local lovelies when I was in high school, but one of them dumped me for a dude who had a driver's license and ready access to a car. My father only sparingly gave the keys to the family car when I reached sixteen years old. Little miss cheerleader was ready to be entertained in the big cities and could not wait for all-American boy to be trusted with the family car. I should have known that the sin of "stealing" the farmer's truck would come back to take its toll when I reached sixteen!

My stewardship story does not completely end in Greenville, but there is not much to tell until after my senior year because not many working opportunities were available for this teenage boy. Therefore, I asked for and received an allowance for a while, but I soon rejected that means of building my fortune. I much preferred to work. My friend and I cleaned the church sanctuary and Sunday school rooms for a few months, and I worked at a small grocery store during one Christmas season, but that was it until the summer of 1957. Of course, I contributed my tithe during the church services when I had money, but I did not have much money to use in dating and certainly no funds to buy gifts for girlfriends. However, I did receive gifts occasionally from girlfriends. One such gift ended a budding relationship after several months.

A really cute, slender blonde gave me a very nice set of sterling silver cuff links during the Christmas holidays. Of course, I did not wear cuff links, but such a gift is not for use but is a trophy that you admire and save for dates when you become a fraternity man. Nevertheless, I was embarrassed by her present because I did not produce a reciprocal, elegant gift and a romantic card.

However, since this gifting occurred about a week before Christmas, I could have recovered if I had a source of income. I am sure that I thought of bank robbery or more likely, lifting a ten dollar bill from the church offering. But seriously, my moral compass regarding money was well-fixed by that time, so I suffered the ignominy of being the only boy every to receive a gift from a girl and not return the generosity. I decided that this circumstance was not to be my legacy because she would probably do the same for Valentines, my March birthday, surely for next Christmas, and who knows what other occasions? I could see myself working for the rest of my life to pay back gifts to this girl who was too generous for our enduring relationship.

Those were the days before I learned to accept the grace of others. I could accept the grace of God by accepting Jesus Christ as my redeemer, but I could not accept a gift from anyone else without feeling that I had to return the favor. Many years later when I learned the heavenly rules of stewardship, I came to know that the good Lord favors us most times through other people. In some ways, it is an affront to God and to His emissary to refuse a gift that will be unreciprocated or to be anxious until we can reciprocate. Perfect peace includes being able to accept a gift knowing that we have been favored by the hand of God. Of course, God may use us then or later to bless someone else. When I receive a gift now, I look around and see who is in need of a blessing. I am amazed by what I learned from a failed relationship with a high school girlfriend even though it took almost the rest of my life to recognize the lesson.

Preparing for College

I learned another stewardship lesson while I was a senior in high school. First, I will have to admit that I was unsophisticated in the process of researching colleges and seeking admission to higher education. I did take the College Board Entrance Examination, but I cannot tell you my score because I doubt that I even cared about the results. However, I decided that I wanted to be a physician because I admired my home town doctor. He drove the biggest and best looking car in town and had attracted an intelligent, tall, and stately wife with a knockout figure. Of course, the fallacy here is that I concluded that money can buy a person complete comfort, love, and happiness.

My doctor-mentor advised me to major in pharmacy as a backup if I did not get admitted immediately to medical school. I made the decision to pursue medicine, although I did not take chemistry in high school, and the physics and biology that I took were hardly suitable preparation for college-level sciences.

My father did not want to discourage me, so he agreed to plan a trip to Birmingham to visit Howard College, a Baptist college that offered a degree in pharmacy. We made the trip, but I did not like Howard, mainly because it was located downtown and was a drab looking place. Later, the Board of Trustees changed the name to Samford University, and then built a beautiful campus in the woody suburb of Homewood. Nevertheless, I was too early for Samford and not impressed by Howard, so father suggested that we drive south to Auburn, Alabama, to visit Alabama Polytechnic Institute, commonly known and later officially designated as Auburn University.

I liked Auburn immediately. The university was positioned on a beautiful campus, was a member of the Southeastern Conference, offered a pharmacy degree, and boasted almost ten thousand students. The drawback was that the men to women ratio was three to one. My father did not care about the ratio; he was only concerned about paying the expenses, including the out-of-state fee. With that in mind, he drove directly to the athletic field house. He said that we needed to talk to the basketball coach about a scholarship. I was mortified at his boldness. I was a small high school athlete; and besides, it was March and I knew even at eighteen years old that the recruits for next year had already been signed. But my mild protestations did not deter the Reverend C. R. McCutcheon.

Clyde Ray McCutcheon, the Scot-Irishman who was named for the River Clyde in Scotland, was undoubtedly the boldest man I have ever known. He feared no person, circumstance, or situation. Much later in my life, and as I studied the principles of stewardship, I determined that his life as a steward and knowing who he was as a Christian gave him confidence to operate and boldness to speak confidently about the favor that he knew God had laid up for him and his charge, particularly on matters of finance.

I wish that I had known this fact as we charged into the field house at Auburn, although at eighteen years old, I doubt that insight would have placated me. We approached a receptionist, and he asked to see the head basketball coach. The sweet woman was not taken back by this intrusion, and she said that Coach Eaves was not in the office; would we be willing to talk with Coach Beard. We had never heard of Coach Beard, but father said that we would talk with him. Later we learned that Coach Beard was the athletic director.

When we entered Mr. Beard's office, he was very gracious but ready to talk business. Father told him that I was a good high school basketball player but from a small school that did not make the state tournament, so I did not have much visibility. He asked Mr. Beard if any scholarship money was available for me. Mr. Beard replied that all the scholarships had been promised and that only Coach Eaves and his staff made those decisions. But Mr. Beard said that during the first week of fall quarter, Coach Eaves and his staff would hold open tryouts and that I should try out for the freshman team. He said if I made the team, the coaches could see if I could play basketball at a higher level.

He then said something that gave me a first-time glimpse of the other side of stewardship. I think that up to that time I thought you only "paid" your tithe as a requirement as a Christian without my giving much consideration to the blessings that accumulate and flow eventually in significant multiples. He said he thought that Auburn had a policy of waiving out-of-state fees for ministers' children from any state. He called the Registrar's Office and verified the ministerial concession, and we went immediately to the Admissions Office to apply for the fall quarter and to the Registrar's Office to claim our waiver forms. That episode was the first time that I realized that stewardship is not an isolated command for obedience sake but is also a condition for blessing, and I believe the Holy Spirit taught me this lesson. On the way home, father expressed our gratefulness to the Almighty.

High school in Greenville was a pleasure, and I still have many friends from those days. I enjoyed playing basketball, baseball, as well as track and field. Also, my debate team won the state championship, and I won state medals in boys' oratory and in track and field. Life was good in high school, and it improved immediately after high school because I, along with four of my high school mates, obtained a job with the state highway department painting the centerline.

We traveled over northwest Georgia for twelve weeks each summer for four years with a crew that painted the centerline and sideline stripes on all state roads in our region. We stayed in cheap hotels and tourist homes Monday through Thursday each week and drove home on Fridays. The crew parked our support equipment in different central locations for about three weeks and worked out of these strategic points. Then we moved to another strategic location and worked throughout that region. The State Highway Department paid us about $150 a month plus $25 a week for subsistence. That was big money to a high school boy and later a college student, and I worked that job every summer for four years until my senior year in college.

It was hot and dirty work, but I did not mind at all because the job provided steady money that could be applied to college expenses and to dating and buying little gifts for girlfriends. Of course, I continued to contribute my tithe each pay period and deposited the remainder into a bank account for college expenses. I was amazed how that small college fund grew, and with some help from my parents and later financial assistance, we never had to borrow any money for college tuition and expenses.

I graduated from high school in May 1957, and after a senior trip to Washington, D.C., I began working with the centerline crew of the Georgia State Highway Department. That period was during the early days of rock and roll music, and I loved all those classics. My favorite Elvis Presley tune was "Don't Be Cruel," and my all-time favorite song is still "Unchained Melody." We enjoyed this good music at Friday night teen club dances just off the square in the city gym. Some charitable souls planned these events for local teenagers because it was a thirty-minute drive to a movie theater in Manchester, LaGrange, or Newnan, and otherwise nothing for teenagers to do. Gill's, the local barbecue restaurant, was another sure date-night stop because the food was good, cheap, and served in a dimly lit jukebox orchestrated dance hall.

We also drove during the summer to the Overlook on the top of Pine Mountain in adjacent Harris County as it peered over beautiful Callaway Gardens. Nothing could compare to a beautiful summer Saturday night on the patio dance floor that overlooked the valley as we danced, with every young woman leaning against the rock wall, to the silky voices of the Platters singing "Only You." I loved to dance, but I was not very good at fast dancing. I saved myself for the slow numbers and to keep my underarms fresh and my Aqua Velva in place while the "Speedos" had to vacate the floor to refresh themselves following more vigorous footwork.

My parents, who probably never danced a step in their lives nor tasted a drop of beer or wine, were not friendly toward the fine art of "rhythm and coordination," as practiced at such idyllic places otherwise referred to as "beer joints" by those uninitiated in these aesthetics. My parents and I did not discuss the fine art of dance, although father sometimes referred to its potential for evil in his sermons. This parent/teenager truce was the first time for the practice of *Don't Ask, Don't Tell*, which President Clinton later copied but did not give due credit in his doctrine regarding another form of conduct. My summers were defined and punctuated for years with this rock and roll culture until I met a beautiful Auburn student who became the love of my life and lifelong partner.

Off to College

I matriculated at Auburn in the fall of 1957. My parents and I had located a tiny basement room just off campus that I shared with a senior student. There were five men students in this underground arrangement that was cramped at best and stifling in the worst of times. The most notable character was Manouchehr "Mitch" Azmouhdeh, a brilliant chemical engineering student from Iran, who later became the head of the secret police under the Shah of Iran. I learned in later years that Mitch was tried and executed when the Shah was overthrown in 1979. The other members of the party were not as colorful or as notable as Mitch, and we peacefully coexisted for the full nine-month term until I moved into the fraternity house.

God provided mercifully for our finances during that time, although I did not get a basketball grant-in-aid. I tried out for the freshman team, made the squad, and played in some of our games, but I was not an SEC caliber player. I could run and jump with the players my size, but I could not shoot outside, nor did I have the hand speed of the other guards and small forwards. I also sustained some injuries that slowed me down, but I was not ever going to be a starter in the SEC. I did not answer the call for tryouts in my sophomore year. To complicate the situation, I suffered with strep throat in the early fall quarter, so that illness killed any lingering question about intercollegiate basketball. I pursued other interests. I was initiated into my fraternity, became interested in student government, spent a lot of time at the Baptist Student Union, and found a girlfriend, after a freshman year of grudgingly accepted "monasticism."

Throughout my four years at Auburn, my family and I did not have any significant financial problems. Of course, I did not have a car and otherwise lived modestly. I lived in the fraternity house because it had the best food on campus and pleasant quarters. Late in my junior year, I was elected president of the fraternity, which was an anomaly because I stood out like the proverbial sore thumb since I was the Sunday school boy, although not so-named to my face. During my senior year, I was further blessed financially.

The first blessing was one of those surprise blessings that I described in chapter 2. My father received a call one day from an attorney in my home town that an anonymous donor had provided a $1,000 scholarship for my senior year. Based on 1960 economics, this was a big gift. In fact, it turned out to be about all that I needed for college expenses that year. In later years, I found out that the gift came from a wealthy industrialist in Newnan, Georgia, whom we knew only from publicity in the area newspapers. The second blessing was in preparation during the spring quarter before I left campus for the summer. I made application to sell senior rings that the Balfour Company sold exclusively to our senior class. I was notified that I was selected as one of eight sales representatives chosen by Auburn University and Balfour.

I approached the sales rep job as if it were life or death. I mapped a strategy and set my sights as being the top salesperson. The university also aided my effort because the Student Union Manager set up a sales booth in the foyer of the Student Union Building where there was the most walking traffic on campus. Each sales rep was assigned a day to work the booth. I took my turn for several weeks, but after a month, I staked out the booth on Fridays to see if other reps showed up to sell; if not, I took their place. While Friday was not a good sales day, that effort led to a process. Late in the quarter, I did surveillance during the other days of the week, and filled in when there was a no-show by the designated rep. I kept this strategy going for the remainder of the year and into the summer because I had to attend summer school. I changed majors in my sophomore year and that plus flunking a couple of science courses caused me to have to take an over-load in the spring quarter of my senior year and attend summer school in order to graduate in August 1961. My future wife graduated in June and left the campus then to plan our September wedding.

By June of my senior year, I had a nice bank account. I had saved money from the previous summer, almost eliminated draws on my bank account because of the scholarship, and made more money than any other ring salesman. Of course, I faithfully contributed my tithe to my home church. I knew that I had been blessed.

All of this new found relative "wealth" allowed me to buy my fiancé a nice but modest engagement ring, but I still had another blessing in store. I bought the ring at Ware's Jewelry in Auburn, and Mr. Lamar Ware Jr. suggested that I keep my cash and just pay a down payment and send him the remainder over time without interest. We sealed the deal on a handshake. Twenty five years later, we added to that ring ensemble by dealing with Mr. Ware, who was just as humble and gracious as I remember, although his business had expanded to other locations in east Alabama.

Married, Military and Graduate Schools

We were blessed further because my new wife found a job teaching kindergarten in southwest Atlanta, but we only had a long Labor Day weekend and two vacation days to get married and take a short honeymoon. I promised her a European vacation when we would be permanently settled in our jobs.

Those were the days eligible young men had a compulsory military obligation. Unfortunately, I did not pursue my Air Force officer commission program after the sophomore year, which was one of the biggest mistakes that I ever made. I should have not settled for average grades in the

ROTC courses and planned on going for the commission. Consequently, when I graduated I had to deal with the military issue when looking for a job. Employers were reluctant to hire men before their military obligation was satisfied; however, again, we received another surprise blessing.

We were shopping in a new center in southwest Atlanta and wandered into a Belk's department store. We were greeted by a young man whom I recognized immediately. He was a fraternity brother who had graduated two years before me and had finished the obligatory two years as an army officer. At that time, he was assistant manager of the Belk's store. After some small talk, he offered me a job selling men's clothing, and he talked to me about entering the Belk's store manager program. I gladly took the job and sold men's clothing until I was called for basic training in the Army Reserves.

My wife and I made the decision before we married to tithe from day one of our married life. Our decision came easy for her because she learned about stewardship from her family. Her parents and grandparents were Christians and were faithful and generous to the Lord's work. Her father and grandfather were industrialists in northeast Alabama, having settled there from Chattanooga when they had problems with their plants. They contributed tithes to their church and offerings to missionary and charitable ventures. They sponsored a missionary family in Brazil in the 1950s and 1960s. Consequently, my wife brought to our marriage an equally strong commitment to tithing and a testimony of the grace of God toward good and faithful stewards.

We joined a community church in East Point, Georgia, about five miles from my ancestral home place in College Park. A friend in the church who was an officer in an Army Reserve unit asked me if I would join his detachment. I was pleased with the opportunity, and I joined the quartermaster detachment in April 1962. In the meantime, I decided to pursue a graduate degree in college student personnel administration, and I took the Graduate Record Examination about the time that I was inducted into the Army Reserves. Not long after my induction in the Reserve unit, I was called to active duty for basic training at Fort Jackson, South Carolina. My wife continued teaching kindergarten and living in our apartment in East Point.

Basic Training was a grueling eight weeks in every imaginable phase of combat training. For the first four weeks, recruits (the best of all name choices) were restricted to the post, but after the first thirty days, we were allowed a pass from Saturday noon to 1600 hours (4:00 p.m.) Sunday afternoon. I was able to visit my wife and parents after about five weeks on post, and I was able to make a trip home for two days after the eight weeks of Basic. During my trip home, I made application for the masters program at Florida State University and for graduate student housing owned by the university.

When I returned to Fort Jackson, my company was dispersed to the several installations on the post for Advanced Individual Training (AIT). Some troops went to infantry training, but most of us were college boys who enrolled in an administrative school across the post for eight more weeks of training. This program included field training and combat support, leadership training, and typing and records management. Since I had two years of ROTC, I was ordered to be a temporary platoon leader.

One of my jobs was to have the classrooms cleaned on Thursday nights, which I did faithfully except on one occasion. I went to the movies with a group, and I forgot to assign troops with demerits to clean two large classrooms. When I got back to the barracks about 2200, I realized what I had done. At that time, it was impossible to find my troop detail, so I had to spend about two hours cleaning the classrooms and waxing and buffing the floors. I never told that story to anybody on post!

In October 1962, the newspapers and airwaves were filled with the stories that the Soviet Union was constructing missile sites on the shores and inland of Cuba. Soon after the stories broke, all troop leaves were cancelled, and troops were confined to the post. Later, all discharges from service were suspended and all troop dismissal dates were extended indefinitely. The rumors on post were rife and spread like the proverbial wildfire. Of course, I was concerned about our country and the prospect for a nuclear showdown on the seas and possible invasion of Cuba. The reality of infantry action was elevated as we saw recent infantry AIT graduates being shipped to combat units at other posts. Outside communication with my wife and family was practically impossible because the few pay telephones on post were besieged with troops during every free moment well into the early morning hours.

The naval blockade stood down the Soviet ships, and Premier Nikita Khrushchev gave President Kennedy assurance that the Soviet Navy would not fire on the US vessels and would allow the US Navy officers to inspect

Soviet ships. Great relief spread throughout all the military as was readily apparent even to a troop in training, as well as the entire country. However, the suspended release/discharge policy was not rescinded for many weeks.

During the interim and after the Soviet pullback, the troop telephone traffic returned to normal, and I was able to telephone my wife. Of course, we had corresponded by mail during those weeks of travail, but it sure was good to talk in person. She told me during the conversation that the Florida State University Graduate Office and the Housing Office had both sent letters requiring payment of deposits and early fees. The total was several hundred dollars, but we were well able to pay the entire amount.

I was still under orders for service with an indefinite dismissal date, and we did not want to lose the money if I did not get out of service by the end of December. We talked and prayed about the matter and agreed that we should go ahead and send the money to FSU. That was the first time that we had to take a major step of faith and to draw on the spiritual capital that had been invested during a young life of stewardship. In late December, I was dismissed from training and transferred back to my Reserve unit, and we were free to implement our plans to move to Tallahassee and to enroll at FSU.

The 250-mile drive to Tallahassee, towing the smallest U-Haul trailer, was a trip of ecstasy and agony. We were excited about the new venture, but we were facing the reality that neither of us had a job, and we had only $700 in the bank and owed additional rent and enrollment fees. I remember praying and reminding God (as if He needed it) that we had tried to be good stewards and that we were stepping out in faith and depending on Him. By the time we arrived in Tallahassee, I was at peace with the situation.

After we moved into the married student housing and spent a few days unpacking and arranging, we drove downtown to buy a few items for the apartment. When I parked our Ford, I noticed a help-wanted sign on the glass door of an office complex that was in a converted retail space. The Leon County Extension Service was advertising a vacancy for an assistant home demonstration agent. They needed someone to coordinate the 4-H Clubs in the county and to provide other youth-oriented services. My wife had graduated from the School of Home Economics at Auburn, although with a major in early childhood education. Nevertheless, she qualified for the job, and she interviewed and was appointed to the position within only a few days. The appointment carried a twelve-month salary and exceptional health care benefits for her and me. The total income was considerably more than that of a public school teacher with comparable experience, but that was a moot point because the teaching jobs were awarded only to permanent residents of Leon County.

After a semester in graduate school, I was appointed to a graduate assistantship in the dean of men's office, and we were offered a two-bedroom apartment in a new men's residence hall at a nominal rental rate. I graduated with a master's degree in May 1963, and enrolled in doctoral courses for the next term. However, Wofford College offered me a job, and we moved to Spartanburg, South Carolina, in late July 1963, where I served as assistant dean of students and instructor in psychology. Before we moved from Tallahassee, we bought a new Ford and had considerable checking and savings account balances remaining. God had provided for our needs and added a measure of prosperity in accordance with our stewardship and courage in trusting Him to be faithful to His Word.

We spent two years in Spartanburg while I was on the faculty and administrative staff at Wofford. I received an entry level salary and an apartment in a men's residence hall the first year and a two-bedroom house on campus the second year. Also, after the first year, we "house and dog sat" in a beautiful country home for a couple who spent the summer in Europe. Country living on the banks of the Pacolet River in rural and historic Cowpens was an idyllic experience.

We could see God's hand working on our behalf financially at every turn during those two years, and during the second year at Wofford, we decided to step out again in faith to continue graduate school. Therefore, I applied for graduate school and a graduate assistantship at Indiana University, was admitted to the doctoral program and hired as an assistant director of a large undergraduate residence center, complete with an apartment in the men's residence tower.

We moved to Bloomington after I spent two weeks at Army Reserve summer camp with much more money than we had when we moved to Tallahassee, but we still needed a job for my wife to keep from spending our savings. Here again, God opened doors that amazed us. My wife applied for a kindergarten teaching position in late August, and she was hired and started work within a few days. (You see the pattern here: the first order of business is to find the wife a job.) The second year of graduate school, I received a graduate assistantship in the institutional research office, so we moved out of the residence hall apartment and into a two-bedroom house near her school.

In the summer of 1964, the Vietnam War was front page news, and many Army Reserve units were being called up for service. I had about eight months remaining on my commitment, and I was in a Public Affairs company in Bloomington. Our mission was to run military governments in occupied countries, but we did not get called up, so I completed my graduate program on time. I received job offers at two universities but decided to take an offer as assistant to the president from West Georgia College in Carrollton, which is about fifty miles west of Atlanta. We added to our savings account while we were in Bloomington, and we were very much aware that God had blessed us immeasurably as we had been stewards of the provisions that He had provided.

Finally a Permanent Job and Other Uncertainties

I began my duties at West Georgia College in July 1968, and within eighteen months, my wife and I built a house, vacationed in Europe, and had a beautiful baby girl. I enjoyed the work with the college president, a brilliant physicist and an adept planner and leader of this emerging institution. However, early in 1971, the president was offered a vice chancellor position at the Board of Regents' office in Atlanta, so the chancellor appointed an interim president. Within a year, the Regents elected a new president.

During the next two years, a good deal of friction developed among the faculty and staff, and West Georgia experienced its part of the wave of student unrest that was in evidence throughout the nation. This was the time that Newt Gingrich was a faculty member in the history department and was a self-appointed gadfly on campus, which was his terminology. Concurrently, the president reorganized the college and developed schools and divisions, and one such unit was the division of continuing education and public service, which in large part was run like a business on the proceeds from off-campus credit and non-credit courses. The president appointed me as director of that division and told me I had no choice but to take it or else. I felt like Br'er Rabbit when he was thrown in the briar patch.

I was glad to move on to a new challenge and a new office with a good staff and refreshing work with adult students. Years later the president apologized for moving me out of the president's office, thus acknowledging a conspiracy of sorts in his inner circle. I replied that it was a good move for me and that I had long ago forgiven everybody involved. I believe that forgiveness set me free and allowed God to continue blessing my family and me financially and otherwise.

I have already admitted my weakness for high performance automotive vehicles, and I shared the story about getting a big surprise in 1974 when my wife and I were shopping for a new automobile. We bought an almost new Mercedes 280 Sedan, and subsequently drove it almost twenty years. However, along the way we had major engine trouble, which brings me to another stewardship story.

In the autumn of 1979, an evangelical Christian organization contacted us and requested us to make a long-term commitment to underwrite a television ministry in the Middle East. This organization had acquired a television station in Lebanon, and the plan was to beam by satellite Christian programming to all the Middle East countries in the several languages. We were asked to contribute $5,000 a year to sustain the project.

I was shocked and my wife was nervous that we might make the pledge. We had never been solicited even for a total of $5,000. Nevertheless, we prayed about the matter, and we were not able to dismiss from our minds the urgency of the request and the nature of the mission. We somehow felt supernatural confidence that we could fulfill the pledge. We realized that this pledge paid quarterly would be an offering because we, as well as the organization, insisted on continuing our tithe to our local church. We signed the pledge and wrote our first installment check in March 1980. Soon after that was when the Mercedes comes back into the story.

The warranty on the Mercedes expired in October 1979, so I did not feel compelled to have the oil changed at a dealer in order to comply with the warranty. I decided to try a local service station for the next oil change in March because that was more convenient. I had been dealing with the owner of the local service station for years, and he seemed to be a competent mechanic. Also, a local parts dealer carried an oil filter that fit this make and model. My mechanic friend changed the oil and filter, and I picked the car up and drove it about two miles to our home.

That night, my wife had a Bible study meeting nearby, and I suggested that she drive the Mercedes. After the Bible study was over, she called me and said that something was wrong with the car because she could not start it. She said that there was "this oily fluid on the concrete driveway." The engine had locked up because of heat from losing all the engine oil. The mechanic had not properly secured the oil filter.

A local foreign car mechanic had rebuilt Mercedes engines, and I had my car towed to his shop the following morning. He estimated that the repair would be about $2,000, which was about one-fifth of the purchase price of the vehicle. I had to have the work done, but we never questioned our annual pledge and continued our tithe and contributions to our offering pledge. To condense the story, I knew I had to forgive and console the mechanic, who incidentally was humiliated about his malpractice. Within a few days, the mechanic's insurance agent called me and said that the insurance company was going to pay most of the cost of repair.

Then I had to deal with everyone who opined that a rebuilt engine would not endure like a factory-built product. That advice did not prove true because I drove that car another fifteen years. The lesson that I take from this episode is that Satan will take every opening to test our resolve. He cannot create hardships, but he has been allowed some facility to incite fear, doubt, and confusion to discourage us from our stewardship and other discipleship. However, God is in control. If we persevere, God will make a way for our escape, grow our faith and confidence, and add to our prosperity.

During the next five years, no major stewardship issues surfaced. We continued with our pledges and enjoyed our work and family time with our daughter, but I began to look for other occupational ventures. I completed two correspondence investment analysis courses, took the graduate securities analysis course at West Georgia College, and completed two courses for professional licensing. I had been an investor for many years, but I approached this study from a professional prospective. I later passed the examinations for broker and principal licensing and began teaching investment courses at West Georgia College for adults.

But as I was getting prepared for a new profession, my wife was told by her gynecologist that she had a tumor in her right breast and that she should have a biopsy. We were referred to Emory University Clinic for further tests, and her biopsy revealed that the tumor was malignant. She had surgery in April 1985, took chemotherapy at Emory Clinic in Atlanta, and had reconstruction surgery in February 1986. She lost some hair, but it came back thicker and more beautiful than ever. She had sufficient energy and was just as radiant and effervescent as ever. In fact, people remarked about her upbeat demeanor, radiant countenance, and energy. We prayed diligently, friends and family did the same, and I declare to you that we both heard in our minds God say, "Cynthia is going to be all right."

Some people, even some Christians, do not believe that God speaks to an individual in such dramatic fashion, but you will not convince me of any skepticism. During her surgery and chemotherapy, I embarked on further shoring up my life and dedicating myself to not wasting my time in pursuits that did not have usefulness in the kingdom. I also set about to seek further guidance regarding the purpose God intended for my life, and I felt after a time that it was not in college administration.

Before my wife's illness, one reason that I felt God was redirecting my occupation was that I had applied for a few positions that were ideal for my education, experience, and demonstrated abilities, but I was turned down. One time I received a rejection letter before I received the obligatory application acknowledgment letter. If this happens to you, my friend, step back and ask if you are being given a message. Sometimes God speaks to us profoundly by what He does not do. The blessing is the redirection that comes from the denial. In my case with the confluence of my wife's health issues and my own searching for what I was supposed to do, God began to show me that entrepreneurship was where I needed to direct my vision and planning, although the exact venture had not evolved.

Starting a Business and More Uncertainties

My wife's health was excellent after the surgery and chemotherapy, but we felt that we had to remain in the University System health insurance plan and focus on an early retirement date. Therefore, we developed a ten-year plan. Many people today cannot even wait one year for the fruition of their wants and self-determined needs. We are in a microwave society, and that impatience is very much reflected in the trading mentality in the stock market.

Nevertheless, I had a simple vision that God gave me to be an entrepreneur, and I waited for the Lord to confirm that I should start a business in investment management. That confirmation occurred when I started teaching investment analysis courses to adults. A couple of students asked me after class if I would help them with their investments. They said they understood the investment method that I was teaching but did not have the time to pursue the project continuously. I agree to help them, and I proceeded to form SCM Associates as a proprietorship and to register with the US Securities and Exchange Commission as an investment advisor.

I later formed a corporation, along with a good friend of many years, and added a few more accounts, including a couple of small corporate pension and profit sharing plans. I was fortunate to be employed in the academic community where outside consulting is encouraged as a public service, but I did not encroach on my normal duties during the work week.

In 1987, I formed Southern Capital Management Company to sell mutual funds. I hired three sales people in nearby towns to serve as sales representatives, in addition to managing separate accounts for clients. Before the stock market crashed in October 1987, I used a timing device that I will tell you about in chapter 8 to get out of the market ahead of the crash. However, the process of selling shares did not work efficiently. Therefore, my associate and I decided to register a mutual fund with the SEC and collapse all our investment accounts into a fund that would allow us to be more efficient and to add significantly more accounts while I was at the college and he was practicing law.

Up to that point, the registration fees and other expenses had been nominal, and I paid them out-of-pocket from monthly personal cash flow and modest investment management fees. However, when we decided to register a mutual fund, I made a significant financial commitment, although in the beginning it appeared that we could minimize the cost by registering the fund without help from a securities attorney. That did not turn out to be the case, and here is that story because I learned an important lesson I want to share with fellow entrepreneurs and those desiring to be good stewards.

The Road to Approval of the Mutual Fund

We read about a man who started and ran a small mutual fund without the help of expensive securities attorneys. Therefore, my associate and I made a trip to see this enigmatic mutual fund manager and to research the investment company (mutual fund) registration process in Washington, D.C. Within the next year, we wrote and submitted the registration application to the Securities and Exchange Commission, and within six weeks, we received a response that contained 38 exceptions to which we were compelled to respond. It became apparent that the SEC was not favorable to a couple of "rubes" from Georgia in the mutual fund world without an SEC practice attorney providing surveillance of a fledging investment company.

We took the hint and engaged a securities attorney and an SEC-practice auditor and in the process exceeded my personal $30,000 budget for the project. However, in February 1989, the SEC approved the registration and operation of the SCM Portfolio Fund, Inc. About two years later, the *Wall Street Journal* printed a story about us and a few other "bantam" mutual funds stating that we did not deserve to be registered and sit alongside the giants like Fidelity and Vanguard in the no-load fund arena.

We received a few other disparaging comments, but we were not dissuaded. The mutual fund allowed me to build an investment management practice while employed full-time elsewhere. However, out of this period of discouragement, and this is the way God works many times, *Georgia Trend* ran a story about mutual funds in Georgia and of course, included our fund. The story was factual and not editorial, and we were pleased with the fair and balanced approached by the publisher/editor.

Soon after that story ran, the publisher/editor called me and asked me to write a column about Georgia stocks for his monthly publication, which was mailed to 50,000 subscribers at that time. I agreed and for the next fifty issues, I wrote a one-page analysis and recommendation about a Georgia stock. This article gave me some visibility, provided a modicum of investment credibility, and attracted a few accounts. It is amazing that people who appear on television or in print can leverage that experience into a level of self-acclaimed expertise which may or may not be justified, and often, in my opinion, is not valid. In any event, it helped me get established at least statewide, but the most important feature of this monthly assignment is that I knew God was in the project and that investment management was my God-intended occupation. This project was a confirmation because I had prayed that God would give me a platform such as a newspaper or journal column.

In 1995, I owned three small corporations in the investment industry, all of which were audited annually by the SEC or other regulators, and the compliance work was mounting. I often worked until 2:00 a.m. to complete all the tasks of compliance, continuing education, and money management required in the industry. I also lead a team that managed the West Georgia

College Foundation investments and wrote the *Georgia Trend* column. To complicate my life, I worked under the supervision of an acting vice president who had an agenda that did not fit my plan for my academic division. I was within a year of fulfilling the requirements for an early retirement, so I began planning to leave the academic community, which I did in June 1996. I set up an office downtown in Carrollton and devoted my time fully to the practice of investment management, feeling that I was settled completely in God's plan for my life.

As I prepared to go full-time with the business, I received another surprise blessing. A friend offered me an office in his company building, which I gratefully accepted. This was not a cubbyhole in a remote part of the building. It was a plush space located just off the lobby with hardwood floors, high ceilings, eighteen-inch crown molding, window shudders, and rich furniture. He also routed my telephone numbers through his company switchboard and allowed me use of his world-class conference room on the top floor of the building. When God bestows a blessing, it is not going to be a "bunch of junk," and when He uses someone to provide for another, He blesses the provider as well. That plan is a principle of the kingdom that works in interpersonal relations as well as business.

God blessed us exceedingly after we opened an office, and the assets under management grew quickly. On the other hand, the compliance requirements and expenses became onerous; therefore, we de-registered the mutual fund in 1998 and the broker/dealer firm in 2000, concentrating on managing client portfolios. We have withstood two very difficult bear markets in this new century, and our performance has been quite good, particularly in the 2007-2009 recession and market crash.

Throughout the years in the business, we have tithed on the profits of the business and continued our personal tithes and pledge offerings. The *sine qua non* of our business and personal efforts is to "render to God the first fruits of the harvest."

Summary and Conclusions

This is a case history of a lifetime of stewardship. The emphasis is on, as researchers say, the longitudinal view of stewardship and the building of spiritual capital that is the repository of compounded blessings from a lifetime of investing in the kingdom of God. Stewardship is a means of worship and obedience and a condition for a multitude of blessings, the paramount of which is financial support in every walk of life. Also, stewardship is a basis for petitioning the Almighty for direction and provision in all circumstances and situations throughout a lifetime as well as a claim to eternal blessings in the New Jerusalem.

I have tried to show that God's faithfulness is not based on our goodness or any other character trait that we might think can earn His favor. His favor is an act of grace whereby He established promises, conditions, and blessings. However, we have to claim His favor by acting on His promises. He is looking for us to exercise our faith in His Word and His promised provisions in order for His favor to be upon us. He has established stewardship as a condition that merits His favor, the most readily discernable of which is financial blessing. God's pathway of favor is that we are good stewards, seek His plan for our lives, take steps of faith in new ventures, and confess with our mouths that God will meet our needs and vision.

These personal adventures attempted to entertain and illustrate salient points, but these life experiences reflect my vulnerability, faults, and uncertainty. Thank God we do not have to be perfect to receive the blessings that He has in His storehouse for us that can be claimed through stewardship.

A life of stewardship is not free from pain, disappointments, or uncertainty. Nevertheless, stewardship builds our confidence and our boldness to venture into the uncertainty in which God has planted a vision and to persevere in times when our dedication is challenged in fulfilling that vision.

The last point that I have attempted to make is that we can pass on to our children certain characteristics and traits that have their origins in stewardship. Parents who are good stewards evidence certain characteristics that can be learned by a child in a close knit household. Why is this? It is because stewardship, starting with sacrificial giving, is the ultimate sacrifice before God that we have available today. Sacrificial giving is the modern-day equivalent of Abraham's offering Isaac on Mount Mariah, under the direction and the watchful eye of Almighty God.

Stewardship over a lifetime establishes God as first in our lives, tests our trust in the Almighty, and sets us up for earthly and eternal blessings, just as accrued to Abraham and his posterity. I doubt that Israel would have been the chosen nation if Abraham had not been faithful to the sacrifice that he was directed to make.

Americans can learn from the Old Testament regarding the importance of tithes and offerings to the Almighty in preserving our strength as a nation. In 2 Chronicles 7:14, God spoke to King Solomon and related His formula for national strength, and that plan is applicable to the U.S. He said, and I paraphrase, if My people will acknowledge me, turn away from their selfishness and hedonism, and confess their other sins, I will heal and prosper their nation. God simply addressed His people, and in today's language that would be all believers. He did not at this point even address non-believers. Then the next step is for His believers to be faithful stewards of that which He has entrusted to them, which means bringing before Him their tithes and offerings.

Stewardship is pivotal in God's plan for the nations because tithing is evidence of where the collective hearts of His people are, demonstrating that God has first priority in their lives. The cumulative effect of this united act of obedience is that His people will reap bountiful results.

America will continue to face grave problems unless God's people are obedient to His commands and are faithful stewards. If the majority of the body of Christ in the United States would worship God with tithes and offerings and live out our Christianity, then our prayers for redemption of our country would be heard, faithfully answered, and result in a dramatic rehabilitation of America.

CHAPTER FIVE

Profiles in Entrepreneurship

The best way to build wealth is to start and manage a successful business. Starting a business can be a daunting task, and many new companies fail in the first two years. Undercapitalization is the main problem with business failures. Often entrepreneurs are forced to close their fledgling businesses when funds run out during the early stages of operation and before the public supports the new enterprise. Also, many failures occur after several years in business and during economic recessions when the company has insufficient capital to continue operations when sales and revenue turn down significantly. The recession of 2007-2009 is a haunting reminder of the impact of the economy on businesses.

Another reason entrepreneurs fail is their lack of personal preparation and diligence. Starting and running a business is hard work and very demanding of one's time and energy. Prospective entrepreneurs need the appropriate training, experience, steadfast work ethic, and patience to give their businesses the best chance of prospering. Studying successful entrepreneurs, particularly in your business sector, is the single most efficient and effective method of preparing yourself and planning and developing your business.

I have been privileged to observe, over a forty-year period, several friends who have started and developed very successful businesses. These friends are extraordinary people now, and indeed they evidenced certain skills and powerful characteristics growing up, as I learned piecemeal over the years of our acquaintances. However, they were not born and ready to fly, but they had to learn their businesses and take risks; their stumbles are as engaging as their triumphs.

I am presenting five of those friends and their development processes in the following profiles. In a series of structured interviews with these successful entrepreneurs, I focused on two features of their achievement. I wanted to present the founding and developing process of their businesses, and I also wanted to learn and to present to you the family lives of these people and report on those who contributed to their character, skills development, and other features of their maturation process. I found that some of these had to overcome impediments that lesser people would have seen as insurmountable. They all had mentors or supporters, and each had people who were pivotal in their lives.

The second feature actually is the most important in my ranking of insights into these entrepreneurs: their relationship to God and how God directed their lives. They all have powerful Christian testimonies. In fact, during the interviews, it seemed that the Holy Spirit guided our discussion, and each time we met in the one-to-one interviews, it was a moving encounter as these stalwarts talked about their salvation experience and their feeling that God called them into business and blessed them remarkably.

I hope that you will enjoy these stories, be inspired as you consider starting a business, identify the skills and characteristics of successful entrepreneurs, and learn how to rely on God for vision and wisdom in business. Now, I would like for you to get to know Ray Fulford, Bob Stone, Renee Keener, Aubrey Silvey, and Tommy Green.

Ray Fulford — RA-LIN & Associates, Inc.

From wearing patched pants and flour-sack shirts
*to Sunday school to donating a church building in Hondura*s

Ray Fulford oversees a four-company group of construction related businesses with just over $200 million in annual sales and a 500-person workforce. RA-LIN is an industrial/commercial building contractor, rated consistently in the top 25 producers in Georgia by the *Atlanta Business Chronicle.* The other corporations engage in commercial development and property management, retail building supply, and site-preparation. Mr. Fulford eschewed the traditional holding company organizational table and adopted an uncommon management structure that has worked very well for him and his businesses.

Mr. Fulford serves as chairman of the board of each corporation and has a president of each company who serves as chief operating officer. He serves as chief executive officer and chief financial officer and thereby advises on business development and operation strategies for each company. He meets monthly with each president and management team and helps set policies and accountability criteria, but otherwise he reviews the financial and progress reports on each project, leaving the operations to trusted associates.

I asked Mr. Fulford about lack of diversification in his businesses. He focuses on businesses that he knows best and can manage astutely during all phases of a business cycle. He would be at a disadvantage, given his organizational structure, trying to oversee a business that he had to rely on someone else to guide through the worst of times. Furthermore, he said that each business after the founding of RA-LIN was an opportunity addition that was a natural fit with the construction company. He saw a great opportunity for the new startup or acquired business to be a stand alone operation, support RA-LIN, and add significant value to the group. He started or built all the businesses with family members, except the site development company in which he was offered an opportunity to become a partner in the well-known and established business.

James Raymond Fulford was born to J. C. and Emma Jane Fulford in Johnson County, Georgia, in October 1942, the second of four sons. He was born at home on a farm in southeast Georgia, owned by a family member, on which his parents worked as share-croppers. The family moved from farm to farm five times by the time Ray was five years old as his father sought to provide better for his family. Eventually, J.C. Fulford secured a job in a gin mill and feed store in Wrightsville, county seat of Johnson County, and moved the family into town before Ray started school. Later J.C. bought an abandoned two-bedroom house with the help of his boss, moved it on a lot in Wrightsville, and upgraded the house over the years, to include their first bathroom, large porch, den and laundry room.

Ray said that his parents were good people who worked hard to provide for the family, and he learned his work ethic and values from both parents. While Ray was growing up, his father drove a truck, worked in different plants, and ran a service station. His mother worked in the cotton fields and in sewing plants. She took the boys to the fields with her early in the mornings to pick cotton when the dew was still on the boles in order to add moisture-weight to the pounds for which they were paid. The boys had to contribute to the family income and to help pay for school clothes and supplies by working on farms picking cotton and harvesting tobacco, vegetables, and pecans. Also, Ray delivered newspapers early in the morning before school and on Saturdays.

Although the family finances were grim in the early days, Ray still developed a good sense of humor and did not turn his depravation internally and make room for pity. He enjoyed life, and his father played a big roll in ameliorating the stressful conditions of a meager family income and clothes that would have caused some children to be bashful in the company of their peers. The Fulford family did not have a car for a few years, and Mrs. Lovett, the church organist, drove the family to church in her big Buick. Ray felt as good as anybody riding in that big automobile, although he wore patched pants and a flour-sack shirt. Church members made him feel good about himself, and he gained confidence then that has fortified him all of his life.

Ray Fulford was a spirited young boy who played boyish pranks and competed for the affections of one or more of his girl classmates. One of his favorite stories of childhood was about a grammar school girlfriend. He and a friend both had a crush on Betty Ann, and Ray took his turn to ask her to go with him to the movies on Saturday afternoon. She agreed, and they set a time to meet in front of the theater.

When he left home on his bicycle, he had only twenty-five cents to cover the twenty-four cent admission for two, which would leave no money for popcorn and a Coca-Cola. So he parked his bicycle behind the theater and took a hidden position behind shrubbery that bordered the theater. He waited until Betty Ann's father dropped her off in front of the theater, and then she, as if programmed by our young suitor, pranced to the box office, bought a ticket, and walked through the big swinging doors into the darkness of the theater.

Hallelujah, he thought; *now for my part of the plan*. So, he bought a ticket, a bag of popcorn, and a Coke and marched into the theater to find his true love. He found her and exclaimed, "You beat me here. At least I can buy you a drink and some popcorn." His heart was racing during his feigned enthusiasm. The bluff worked, and she saved him by saying, "No, I'm fine. I have money if I want something." Ray was relieved, and he wiped his sweaty palm and cradled her hand in his hand as they watched the movie.

Ray Fulford committed to Christianity, joined the Baptist church, and was baptized when he was twelve years old. He credits his father with rising early and accompanying the boys to Sunday school and church. His father was also fun-loving, easy to talk to, and played baseball with the boys in the fields near their home. "Daddy loved all of us so much. He was proud of his boys." J.C. Fulford took great pride in Ray's school and work accomplishments later. Ray remarked recently during our drive through a massive construction site as he gave me a tour during one of our interviews, "Daddy would have really liked this."

Mrs. Emma Jane Fulford was serious-minded and driven to achieve and provide for her family. She went in early and stayed late at a sewing plant to make production early in the week, thus increasing her paycheck for added piece-goods production. Her participation in production bonuses helped form Ray's business plan to offer project directors and later other employees an opportunity to share in any added company profits.

Ray's mother, although not given to an abundant display of affection, was very proud of him, particularly his college achievements at Southern Technical Institute. She showed her love and pride with weekly letters to him at Southern Tech. Her letters were brief but timely, and the love and support showed through each week. She always enclosed a few dollars, which helped him make it through the week.

Ray recalled fondly the fact that his mother liked to fish, and she took the boys fishing to a small lake at Camp Reed. "Taking us meant to walk down the railroad track about three miles one way. With our cane poles over our shoulders and a can of worms, we set out. If we caught any fish no matter the size, mother would keep them and cook them that night." Ray's father also enjoyed taking his sons to the Blue Hole, a large, sandy pool in the river nearby in Wrightsville, although his mother, who was very protective of her boys, regularly cautioned them not to "go near the water until you learn to swim," Ray recalled with a chuckle. Ray remembers fondly his Huckleberry Finn adventures: "I have never forgotten the good times, like going fishing at Camp Reed."

Mr. Fulford exuded deep respect for his parents and subtle pride in his humble beginnings during my interview. He implied that the experiences of his youth helped shape his philosophy of life and his concise theology. His stated beliefs are uncomplicated but yet profound: "God chooses people to do different things in life. He helps us out so we can help Him. He never gives up on us, and He never lets us out of His calling" (Romans

11:29; 12:6). He indicated that God put people, even young friends, in his path to help guide him into his calling.

Ray cited two teachers for their guidance, one of whom was Miss Wingard, his high school mathematics teacher. Miss Wingard had unique methods of challenging Ray to push himself to be a better student, although he was not an honor graduate from high school or college. Ray made a 78 on an Algebra examination during his senior year, and when Miss Wingard returned his test paper, she slapped it face down on his desk saying, "Boy, you just skinned your ignorance." Ray told me he never let that teacher down again.

One of his classmates also saw some potential in him, and he credits her with being another person who helped turn him in the right direction in life. In his senior year, he refused to take the SAT because he vowed that he was not going to college. He admitted that he did not have much ambition, and the best he could see for himself was eventually being a shift foreman at one of the local plants. But Diane had other ideas for him, and she insisted that he take the SAT with her when she took a make-up test. She registered him to take the SAT in Sylvania with her and showed up early at his house on the day of the examination. Reluctantly, he made the trip to Sylvania with her, took the SAT, and scored well enough to get into college at Southern Tech.

Bill Carraway, a local project engineer with the Georgia Highway Department, was the major influence in Ray's enrolling at Southern Tech. Carraway was a young adult himself who had never been to college but who evidently was very intelligent and ambitious. He also had ambition for Ray because he was not satisfied to see him settle for working in a local plant. He told Ray to go to college and study to be a civil engineer, and he outlined the student co-op plan with the state highway department.

Ray had not heard of Southern Tech and did not aspire to be an engineer. However, he agreed to try the plan, and he worked summer and winter quarters and attended classes in the fall and spring quarters. He graduated on time with a high grade point average but not high enough to graduate with honors, although it placed him among the top graduates in his class. Ray credits these key people and many others who wanted to see him succeed for their positive influence on him.

Mr. Fulford joined Richards & Associates (R & A), a utility construction company in Carrollton, Georgia, in 1965, with the assignment of starting a building construction department. When he arrived in Carrollton, he had just enough money to pay his rent at the rundown Carroll Hotel and buy a few meals. When the normal payday arrived on Friday, he learned that he would be paid monthly with the other salaried managers. So, he had little recourse but to call on his girlfriend that he had left in Atlanta with little encouragement of their having much of future together.

However, Linda Mills had other plans. She was attracted to this engaging but impoverished and reluctant young suitor and loaned him $25. Later he had to borrow another $50, and he pledged as "collateral" a commitment to spend more time with her. They were married in October 1966, and to this day, Linda claims that Ray still owes her the interest on his two notes.

When his boss, mentor and lifeblood of R & A, died prematurely in 1969, Mr. Fulford was forlorn. He had lost a brilliant associate and someone who backed his development efforts and otherwise was a strong and enterprising leader. After a series of fill-ins and failed company heads at R & A, Ray decided to start his own construction company in 1970. At first, he joined Kilgore Construction Company as a partner, but W.O. Kilgore wanted to retire and sell Ray the business. Instead, Ray decided to launch RA-LIN in April 1972. He operated the company in the first several years out of a trailer with a project manager and a trusted secretary/bookkeeper with whom he worked at Kilgore Construction Company. His first job was a $13,000 fire code upgrade project for a local manufacturing plant, and from there, he built RA-LIN into a regional industrial/commercial construction firm. RA-LIN grew dramatically in the early years as the company was awarded bid after bid in a highly competitive metro Atlanta area and then later throughout the state and some southeastern states.

The projects grew in numbers and size including school facilities, hospital wings and other medical facilities, shopping centers, office buildings, multi-family living complexes, warehouses, and distributions centers. During the period of expansion at RA-LIN, Mr. Fulford started two new businesses and bought into another. He formed the real estate development company in 1978 to manage speculative ventures constructed by RA-LIN, added the builders supply business in 1981, and bought into the site development business in 1993 to complete the construction group.

Mr. Fulford said that success came early, but he had to make some tough decisions to expand RA-LIN to take on larger and more complex projects region-wide and to deal with the recessions of 1974, 1991-92, and recently in 2008-09. The recession of 1991-92 was the low point in business for RA-LIN, because the industry was in chaos and subcontractors and suppliers were defaulting. He had to press legal action to deal with some of the issues. He considered closing the business, but his future son-in-law agreed to take on the role of regenerating and managing the business, and gradually the economy improved. RA-LIN stood in a good position to capture additional market share and basically reconfigure itself for greater expansion.

Building a business over time, which "was not modeled after any business that I ever saw," has been the high point of Mr. Fulford's business life. Throughout the development of the business, he has prayed for God's guidance and has received divine direction, even to the extent of not getting jobs that later turned out to be disasters-in-waiting. He said when you seek divine guidance, "God is going to let you fly your life, but you are not put on autopilot. He keeps a hand on your shoulder all the time, and He will guide you if you let Him. Then you need to give God credit and give back [*into the kingdom*]." Likewise, he said that in business, as in any human relations, practicing fairness and forgiveness and saying "thank you" is important. Furthermore, he is compelled to apologize when he has slighted someone in any way. He acknowledged that some people are not going to like you, but inasmuch as he is aware of any grievance, he will try to deal with the issue, and apologize or forgive, whichever is warranted.

I asked him what skills or characteristics constitute an entrepreneur. He said that first you have to be prepared to sacrifice. That dedication sometimes means you have to work two jobs, such as he and his wife did in owning and managing a trailer park when he was starting out in business. Next, learn to take calculated risks. You have to venture out, but use common sense and don't risk more than you can stand to lose. Mr. Fulford explained, "You can't be afraid to fail. You are defeated before you begin if you have that attitude. If you get knocked down, just bounce back quickly." When you bounce back enough and weather enough downturns, you develop confidence that you can succeed. You have to have confidence in yourself. Finally, he advises to seek the counsel of older and experienced people. "That is the reason that I sought out people like Fred Hutchins (late and revered local banker) for counsel and friendship."

I asked Mr. Fulford his thoughts on how to use leverage in business.

He acknowledged that in the early days of RA-LIN, he had to borrow money, but he does not favor "borrowing money to pay yourself." He did not draw a paycheck some weeks, but his employees never missed a payday. "Do not borrow money unless it is absolutely necessary. Grow your business out of retained earnings. Take matters a step at a time."

Ray Fulford has been driven to give back to others all of his life. When the Fulford daughters, Kristi and Andrea, and our daughter were young, we lived across the street from the Fulfords. We observed that this family "adopted" a distressed family and showered them with food and gifts at Christmas. Years later and after his success in business, Ray and his family established the Fulford Family Foundation with the mission of helping people to help themselves.

The foundation is also committed to Christian mission outreach programs. Recently, the foundation built a pastor's home for a native minister in Honduras. Previously, the pastor had to ride a bicycle for miles to arrive at the church; now he is available constantly for ministry at the church.

Ray Fulford is a hard-driving and enterprising businessman who has a heart turned toward God. He believes, as I do, that God has established a system that enables people to build wealth to put back into the kingdom. He said, "God Almighty decided that I can help you and you can help me." He went on to say that human beings are not ever going to be perfect, but we can grow and in our frailties still serve the Master. He acknowledges his human shortcomings, has learned how to forgive and seek forgiveness, and truly seeks to live at peace with all men (Rom. 12:18).

Mr. Fulford did not allow the deprivations of the early years to defeat him, but he learned to believe in himself, even before his ambition caught up to his confidence. He has implemented a brilliant business strategy and has acknowledged God's guidance in each enterprise and in his life in general. He has been a good steward of his financial blessings, and his fortunes moved him from wearing patched pants and flour-sack shirts to Sunday school to donating the money to build a church building in impoverished Honduras. He has grown in wisdom and service and is a venerable advisor. Aspiring entrepreneurs should consider his counsel.

Bob Stone — Systems & Methods, Inc.

*Going the extra mile for service and giving back
to the community and society in general*

Systems & Methods, Inc. (SMI) is an information technology firm that provides outsourcing services to state government departments that administer welfare benefits programs. Currently SMI processes child support payments under contract with eight states and the District of Columbia. The company generates $40 million in sales annually and employs 330 staff members in three major categories: information technology, welfare programs, and administrative services. Bob Stone is founder and Chairman of the Board of Directors, and three of his sons, along with a few other officers and managers, oversee the daily operations.

Bob Stone's watchword throughout his adult life has been to go the extra mile for service and to give back to the community and society in general. The company adopted the slogan, "Going the Extra Mile" from the beginning. This mantra has been practiced and taught by Bob and Tish Stone to six children and sixteen grandchildren. As the children and now the grandchildren have become old enough, they are connected to the company. The evolution of SMI is an engaging story and an exacting demonstration of a family business that is dedicated to serving an element of society that is often overlooked.

It is also a story of the rewards of putting God first and serving other people. As Bob Stone has insisted over the years to family members and staff, "God is going to provide the opportunities; we just have to stick to our values and otherwise be ready when the opportunities come." Although the mantle has been passed to the second generation of leadership, the story of Systems & Methods for the first thirty-five years since 1971 has been that of the founding, managing, and mentoring by Bob Stone.

Robert Joseph Stone was born in June 1940, in Atlanta, but he grew up and attended the public schools in Hapeville, a small town tucked in between the big city and the yet-to-grow Atlanta airport, known locally at that time as Candler Field. He was a good student and an enterprising youth who rose early each day to service his newspaper route and later sold Coca-Colas at his front yard stand during the summer.

Mr. Stone had a good role model in entrepreneurship in his uncle, J.W. Bulloch, who started and managed his own State Farm insurance agency.

J.W. Bulloch "grubbed out a living selling State Farm insurance," after working for years at hourly employment. Bob observed further that J.W. "rode around all day in a suit and tie and set his own schedule," to which young Bob asked, "Uncle J.W., when do you work?" His job appeared to be in stark contrast to his father's shift work as a mechanic at Delta Airlines. Bulloch also "dabbled in real estate," which also appealed to Bob, particularly when the uncle made a big sale.

Bob's parents administered the obligatory parental drilling in moral values, Christian principles, and the blue-collar work ethic, which was practiced and taught religiously by depression-era parents. Also, his father-in-law, Max Holt, had a great influence on Bob as his Sunday school teacher and mentor in the Christian faith.

Bob Stone's parents were not unlike many depression-era adults: sixth grade education, hard working, always seeking a better way of life for their children, unrelenting about getting more education, and expecting Bob to earn his own way.

Bob's father, Hinton "Rock" Stone, was a master mechanic, first honing his skills on Packard automobiles. He worked through the ranks at Delta Airlines as a mechanic, hanger supervisor, and Jet Base Superintendent, a vice president level position.

"We were a solid middle class family by the time that I graduated from high school, but our lives revolved around shifts at Delta," says Bob. "Rock" Stone also repaired automobiles in his backyard shop, and because of the income from that second job, the family was able to take vacations each summer.

Mrs. Stone was a pillar of community service organizations, school PTA, and band boosters, commitments Bob and his wife made years later in Carrollton. Bob's mother lectured to him and younger brother, Tom, that education leads to success. She demanded a great deal from the boys' schoolwork. Rock had been married before, but his first wife had died a year after giving birth to a son named Hinton. Hinton was born deaf and required special attention, but his stepmother was faithful to the motherly role.

Bob's parents contributed immeasurably to Bob's work ethic with directives such as, "You must learn to earn your own way," moral values, Christian faith, and community service. His father was a devote Christian, but it was his mother who made sure that the boys went to church and

Sunday school and said their prayers. His father made it clear that money did not come easy, and Bob had to earn his spending money as well as money to buy his first automobile.

The love of Mr. Stone's life and wife of fifty years, Lititia "Tish" Holt, appeared dramatically on the scene when Bob was fifteen years old, and she was almost two years younger. They met at a party given by his cousin, Linda Bullock, in the basement of the Bullock home in Hapeville. The first time Tish laid eyes on him, she fell in his arms—but quite by accident. Bob had arrived early at the party dressed in his new pink shirt, black pants, and white belt, in the best Elvis Presley fashion. Tish took her turn down the stairs to the basement, tripped, and went airborne toward the basement floor. In gallant fashion, our young gentleman stepped up and caught her in his arms.

Good news so far, but Tish buried her lipstick on Bob's shoulder and left him with a glossy-red badge of courage. He thought, *She is the silliest girl I have ever seen, and my mother will not like this.* But he was smitten because "she was a beautiful little thing." They had a good time together at the party, found they had a lot in common, and soon became sweethearts for the duration.

Tish moved with her family to Chicago where her father was transferred. Bob knew that it would take a lot of work to keep the romance going. But with Delta Airlines passes from his father and uncle, who also worked for Delta, Bob was able to visit the Holts each month until they moved back to Hapeville. The couple married soon after Tish graduated from Hapeville High School, but earlier Bob had a heaven-sent sign that she was the one for him, which he recounted during our interview. "As we were leaving Sunday school assembly going to our classes, I saw a faint halo form above Tish's head, and I knew that was a sign for me to marry her."

The couple married when Bob was a junior at Georgia Institute of Technology (Georgia Tech), where he majored in Industrial Management. Georgia Tech did not offer computer courses until his senior year, but in the meantime, he took all his electives in mathematics, thus further preparing him for the coming computer age. He learned the early computer language, FORTRAN, and Lockheed Aircraft hired him upon graduation as a computer programmer to help manage one of the first mainframe computers built in the southeast. He worked for Lockheed three years and completed his Master's degree at Georgia Tech while attending evening classes.

He moved on to Southern Railway, which was in the process of developing the first real-time tracking system for rail cars. However, Mr. Stone was assigned to payroll systems, so he soon tired of that and decided to pursue a Ph.D. at Georgia State University while teaching in the newly created quantitative methods program. He taught quantitative methods at GSU and completed all of the coursework for the doctorate by 1969. By that time, he and Tish had five children, and Bob thought it was time to find a permanent teaching job and finish his dissertation while earning a better living for his family.

In the fall of 1969, Bob Stone and family moved to Carrollton, where he began teaching as an assistant professor of business at West Georgia College. To supplement his income, he consulted with business and industry and governmental agencies in the area and taught continuing education courses to area professionals and business people. His expertise in computer programming became widely known, and one of his students asked him to assist a local CPA firm where the student worked part-time. Bob told the student, "I don't care about that work anymore; I'm teaching." However, he later consented and struck a deal, and months later, the partners of the firm offered the computer to Mr. Stone for his use as long as he gave the firm's work first priority. He reluctantly accepted the deal, formed a corporation, and brought in four partners to join him in a computer services business, while he still taught at the college. Systems and Methods Incorporated began operations in 1971, and its first job was a consulting job with a medical practice that paid $500 for the project, enough to pay for incorporation.

The company operated out of the living room of the Stone house for over a year, and the jobs and projects increased to the point that Mr. Stone and partners felt that the cash flow warranted the lease/purchase of an IBM System III computer. However, the computer cost $12,000 a month, but the company revenue was only $8,000 a month. The partners operated with the deficit for six months, hoping that the revenue would pick up, and they could pay down the $25,000 debt that had accumulated. However, the prospects dimmed even further, and the partners discussed splitting the debt and closing the company.

Mr. Stone had a different plan because he couldn't afford personally to pay $5,000 on company debt. Therefore, he offered the partners a deal: "Why don't I buy each of you out for a dollar and assume your part of the company debt?" Mr. Stone reasoned, "If the bank would let me assume the entire loan, I wanted to make SMI work. I felt like there was something coming." He had "thought" a prayer for guidance when he went into the meeting.

I asked Mr. Stone what made him think "something was coming," because conditions must have looked bleak at that time. He related his theology very succinctly: "God always gives us guidance and He provides opportunities. We need to be prepared to take advantage of whatever He sends. It does not matter what road you have taken. The Good Lord is going to give you opportunities. I feel strongly about that." Evidently, what Bob Stone felt was divine guidance that his company was ready to breakout, and breakout it did almost immediately after he agreed to assume the partners' debt and run the company himself. The break came as a result of a *pro bono* job to help a state government agency whose clients were on the bottom rung of the socioeconomic ladder: the Georgia Department of Family and Children's Services.

Mr. Stone was teaching a continuing education course in supervisory management in which the manager of the local DFACS Office was enrolled. She later learned about Mr. Stone's computer skills and discussed with him the problem that she had with processing the volume of paperwork in the issuance of food stamps. Mr. Stone agreed to analyze the problem, and in one weekend, he wrote a computer program to calculate the food stamp benefit due to each recipient. He said, "She brought the data to me on Friday, and on Monday, I handed her one thousand ATP (Authorization to Purchase) cards."

The manager was ecstatic about the help with her workload. She offered to pay, but Mr. Stone refused the money, telling her that was his contribution to the work, helping the less fortunate, that she was doing. The manager spread the word, and other managers came to him with the same request. He replicated the program for sixteen other DFACS offices without charge for a while, and then the state-level managers got involved and awarded SMI a contract for the sixteen counties.

Later the contract was expanded to sixty-four counties; within a year, all 159 counties in Georgia were under contract for ATP-form processing, and the company immediately made a profit. SMI paid off the note on the IBM computer, cancelled the lease agreement, rented computer time from local industries, and became debt free. The company computer fees dropped from $4,000 a month to $600.

Mr. Stone acknowledged that the DFACS work allowed the company to narrow its focus and perfect and expand its services. He observed that the food stamp distribution in the state was very inefficient, and his new hire, Dick Pickering, who had been one of the top managers in the Georgia food stamp program, persuaded him to take on the distribution process in the state. SMI entered the distribution agreement with one county and within a short time, the company contracted with the entire 159 counties for a direct mail distribution system pioneered by SMI. The company built a huge vault to safeguard the food stamps, which eventually totaled about $200 million in value. SMI competed for distribution contracts with other states and eventually provided services to twenty-six states located throughout the US.

By this time, Mr. Stone had bought all shares of minority owners outside his family, and he was managing the business as he had envisioned it years before, as a governmental outsourcing provider. He had tithed the earnings generated by the business from the beginning of the company and brooked no compromise with the moral code that was an extension of his values instilled from his parents and early influences. For example, when he was planning to expand the business within state government, he interviewed a lobbyist to work on certain issues with state legislators and agency heads. The lobbyist asked if SMI would provide cash to use in doing the deal. Bob Stone said, "No way. If that is what it takes to make the deal, count SMI out." The lobbyist was not hired.

In 1996, the federal government mandated that welfare transactions must be made by electronic transfer within five years and that the transactions could be made only by banks. Of course, this policy shift obliterated SMI's basis for operation. Mr. Stone related that this move could have potentially "destroyed a thirty million dollar business." He said that was one of two low points in the development of the business.

The other was a crisis of vision with one partner in the early days of the company. In 1971, one partner wanted the company to be a computer services bureau for local businesses, and Mr. Stone envisioned a business with a broader reach as a technology solutions company to focus on governmental agencies. However, the crisis in the mid-1990s had the effect of legislating the growing company out of business. "If what Al Gore wanted would have been put into place, we would have been out of business," Mr. Stone concluded. He agonized over this governmental policy change for over two years. Once again, Mr. Stone found that when God allows one door to be shut, He provides another opportunity; and SMI was prepared. This time preparation came in the form of the next generation of the Stone family assuming leadership.

Joe Stone, the oldest of three sons and an officer in the company, predicted on good evidence that the future benefits policy would shift away from family-oriented welfare to child welfare. Governmental changes were underway that eventually allowed private contractors to bid on services to child support agencies. SMI began preparing for this new venture, and the company issued its last food stamps in 2001. By that time, the company implemented new systems, such as the application of check imaging technology, and otherwise reduced the cumbersome process of issuing benefits. Furthermore, SMI made the distributions to recipients more efficient and more equitable. Currently, the company processes child support payments for eight states and the District of Columbia, and plans to contract with new states in the near future. The operation is being managed by the next generation of the Stone family with Joe serving as Chief Executive Officer; Bill is Chief Financial Officer; and Bart is Chief Information Technology Officer. Mr. Stone acknowledged that the transition to the next generation of leadership of SMI is the high point in his business career. Inherent in his acknowledgment is the fact that the company has reinvented itself twice in its thirty-eight-year history, and the facility to adapt to change has been literally bred into the new leadership.

Tish Stone was a steady advisor and worker in forming the enterprise, while being wife and mother of six active children. She served as Secretary/Treasurer and later Chief Financial Officer of the corporation until the second-generation transition. She has been active in community service locally and statewide for decades. She served as state president of the Georgia Federation of Women's Clubs and as national board member of the General Federation of Women's Clubs. She is a member of the board of trustees of Tallulah Falls School, owned and operated by the Georgia Federation of Women's Clubs.

In reviewing his career as an assistant professor of business and an entrepreneur, Mr. Stone said that business students or aspiring entrepreneurs need course work and practical experience in their chosen fields, like the Business Internship Program that he started at West Georgia College. "Most of all, you need to have a desire or a drive to be successful and realize that you will have failures, but you must persevere. It helps to find a niche business and fill that need by being the best in that business." Client service is the key to success in business: "You have got to serve the client, although you may have to educate the client sometimes. Nevertheless, the client is always right." He said when your business grows, "find the right people to help you and emphasize the importance of regular training and upgrading their skills." His business strategy is to control leverage and "only borrow to grow, not to pay yourself."

Bob Stone is a very intelligent, successful but humble man, and it is difficult to get him to credit himself. He deflects adulation and credits others in his company and in other businesses. He readily acknowledges the influences of his parents, uncle, and father-in-law, in addition is his wife, Tish. But he is smart, visionary, tough in negotiating, but fair in settling matters. He is a good steward of the increase of his labors and quick to credit the "Good Lord" with guidance and direction in his life and his company. He contemplated divinity studies soon after graduating from Georgia Tech, but felt lead that he could do more good by being a good steward in business.

Mission accomplished, Bob Stone!

Renee Keener — American Document Securities, Inc.

Whatever you do, work at it with all your heart,
as working for the Lord, not for man (Col. 3:23).

Identify theft and corporate espionage are the fastest growing nonviolent crimes in the United States, according to the Federal Trade Commission. Contrary to popular opinion, according to the National Association of Information Destruction (NAID) only about 25 percent of information theft occurs by electronic means, and nearly three-fourths of these crimes occur as a result of a paper trail. Rummaging through disposed trash, "dumpster diving," is still the most common method of stealing information, NAID concludes.

An entire new industry, documents destruction, has appeared on the industrial scene in the last two decades, and federal and state privacy acts have contributed to an allied industry, documents storage, since 1996. There are a few large, public corporations that engage in documents destruction and storage on a national or regional level, but the industry is dominated by small- to mid-sized companies, like American Document Securities, according to the NAID.

Renee Keener is the founder, chief executive officer, and chairman of a very successful NAID certified business. Ms. Keener was named Entrepreneur of the Year in 2006 by the Carroll County Chamber of Commerce, which also named her 2007 recipient of its Horizon Award, which recognizes outstanding women in business.

Renee Keener was born at Floyd Medical Center in Rome, Georgia, on June 17, 1961, to Truman and Jean Keener, residents of nearby Rockmart. Truman Keener was an engineer at the Goodyear plant in Rockmart, where he was a member of the team that developed the Goodyear blimp, which gained popularity in the early days of televised college and professional football games. He taught Renee the basics of money management and in later years was a strong supporter of Ms. Keener's entrepreneurial ventures, although he liked the safety of working for a big corporation himself.

Renee said that her father taught the "biblical side of me," but both parents taught her personal discipline, moral values, and the Christian faith. Jean Keener taught her daughter household and gardening skills and appreciations, but above all, she demanded that her daughter show respect to all people and humility in all her achievements in high school.

Renee was a good student in high school, beta club honoree, officer in the Future Business Leaders of America, and a notable tennis player. Her mother was a member of a large family, and young Miss Keener had many influences among uncles and aunts. She learned to seek advice from them, a characteristic that helped years later when she ventured into the business world.

Very early in life, Ms. Keener demonstrated independence and an entrepreneurial affinity, although somewhat ill-advised. At the age of seven years old, she raided her mother's kitchen pantry and sold the family cache of bread loaves to neighbors for a quarter. Another indication of her independence is Ms. Keener accepting a proposal of marriage from her husband of seventeen years while she was still in high school. As a young married couple, she and her husband were on their own, and with work and household duties, she did not have the time or money to go to college. Her husband, Phillip, did complete two years of college in engineering, and the young couple moved to Carrollton when Renee and Phillip began work at Dixie Converting.

They bought a small farm a few years later, and Renee started a horse-boarding facility that she owned and managed for ten years. She said that she was "not ever afraid of physical work," which has been evident in her entrepreneurial ventures and as you will understand later in her story.

When Renee was twenty-nine years old, she discussed with her husband an idea of starting a converting business to reduce large rolls of paper to smaller, more useful sizes. Phillip's father, who was a bi-vocational minister, had worked for a paper converting company; he advised against starting a converting business at the time. Nevertheless, Renee was undaunted in her plan because she reasoned that they eventually could be financially independent in their own business.

Soon after reaching a decision to pursue the idea, Renee and Phillip terminated their employment at Dixie Converting, and Phillip took a job operating a slitting machine at Sony Music in Carrollton. This machine cut the roles of tape to cassette size, an operation that added to his knowledge of the converting industry. Renee took the lead in researching and setting up the business, and in July 1990, they began operation as MontCo, Inc., a contract converting company.

The MontCo business plan was to reduce large label stock rolls to smaller sizes on which labels and other paper products could be printed, such as pharmaceutical prescription labels. They invested their life savings and all they could borrow in equipment and a building lease and set about to attract customers. "We had to hock everything, and if it [the company] failed, we would walk away with only the shirts on our backs," Renee recalled.

This was a time when interest rates in the US soared to 19 percent, business revenues slowed considerably, and the country sank into a deep recession. However, Renee never actually felt that they would fail because she had a quiet peace that God had "picked them to go into business" and that "He would see them through the deep waters." In God's perfect time at a trade show in Chicago, they made contact with a 3M Company representative, and soon afterward MontCo signed a contract with the massive business conglomerate out of Minneapolis.

MontCo steadily grew in operations and sales for the next five years, but the marriage failed and the couple divorced in 1994. However, they have retained the business relationship, because they have an abiding respect and admiration for each other and work well together in the business. Renee assumed her maiden name, and she entered into new ownership agreements with MontCo whereby she stills owns 49 percent of the company.

Understandably, she had a difficult time during the divorce process, particularly with forgiving herself, but she consulted other Christians, including a devoted friend and also her pastor. She and her prayer partners prayed for God to lift the burden, and God heard and answered their prayers. She was taking a shower one morning before going to work and praying her prayer for release. She felt the power of the Holy Spirit, and "it was like God said He was washing away my guilt and setting me on a new path." She knew "God had His hand on my shoulder," and she felt a new relationship with the Lord and a new confidence in the path in which she was being directed.

In 1996, the 3M Company approached MontCo with a business proposal for an expanded business contract. The company needed a converting facility in the Dallas-Fort Worth region, which would reduce time and transportation costs and further meet the conglomerate's needs. Ms. Keener researched the expansion idea and found that other businesses with installations in the Dallas area also could profit from MontCo's expansion to Texas. She spent about nine months looking for the right location and plant, and God led her to Mayor George Marti in Cleburne, Texas.

Mr. Marti agreed to build a first-stage 20,000 square foot building, designed to MontCo's specifications, and lease the facility to the company at a very reasonable price. Business revenues doubled over the next two years as a result of the new plant, and sales approached $5 million annually in the Carrollton and Texas plants combined. However, in 1999, the business felt the impact of the approaching economic recession in the US and Canada, and many customers over the next twelve months declared bankruptcy, several closing their businesses permanently.

MontCo suffered the greatest impact of this abrupt economic reversal in the Carrollton plant, but the Texas plant thrived, thanks to a large contract with Greenbay Packaging that God provided in answer to Ms. Keener's prayers. She prayed for God to intervene and send MontCo new business and help them otherwise to make it through the recession.

Within a matter of days, a representative of Greenbay Packaging contacted MontCo in Texas and set up a meeting for seven executives of the company to fly to Cleburne to meet with the MontCo executive team. The two companies reached an agreement, and business began to flow again to the Texas plant. No such big contract was in store for the Carrollton plant, and Ms. Keener knew that "It was a new chapter that God was going to redirect us into. Pruning helps you grow." She quoted the Scripture: "Count it all joy in times of trials because it produces perseverance" (paraphrase of James 1:2-3).

MontCo's last contract in Carrollton was executed in 1999, and Ms. Keener knew that in six months the company would cease to do business. At the end of the contract period, she heard from a machinery broker in Indiana, Nicholas Svetich, who is a Christian and was an unaware-angel to deliver a message of direction. Nicholas suggested that she consider starting a document shredding business.

She was unaware of such an industry, let alone how to start a business and compete in the new venue. But she realized that she needed to diversify her business, so she accepted the recommendation and spent a full year researching and planning the new venture, all the while maintaining her 49 percent interest in MontCo. From the beginning of the new direction, she felt confident: "For some reason, I knew it was going to work."

The actual day of the formation of American Document Securities, Inc. (ADS) was indeed a monumental day: September 11, 2001. About 9:00 a.m., she met with her CPA, company accountant, and a few other people. During the meeting, the group heard the news that the twin towers in New York City had been bombed by terrorists. She knew immediately that the word *American* or *America* had to be in her company name. She wanted to honor her country, the victims and their families, and the valiant public servants who risked their lives to save countless lives, maintain order, and fortify defense in New York City.

In order to operate a document destruction business, she needed a large truck equipped with a shredding machine and a generator. The nearest truck outfitter was Allegheny Paper Shredders located in Pittsburgh, Pennsylvania. She ordered the truck and soon bought a one-way airline ticket to Pittsburgh. Later when she arrived to pick up the deuce-and-a half loaded with shredding equipment, she shocked and amazed the Allegheny owner when she mounted the truck cab in preparation for driving back to Carrollton. Not only did she drive the six hundred miles to Carrollton, but she also drove the ten-wheeler to customer locations and operated the generator and shredder during the startup phase of ADS. A few years later, Allegheny featured Ms. Keener in their corporate newsletter that was distributed to a wide customer base and other industry contacts.

This in-house publicity launched her on another career, consulting with entrepreneurs who want to enter this new industry. Immediately after the article appeared, she was inundated with telephone calls that kept her from getting any work done for days. This experience prompted her to develop two courses of instruction for students to take in a classroom and in the ADS plant. In addition, she provides on-site consultation to clients after they complete the classroom instruction.

In 2003, Ms. Keener further developed her company by offering a documents storage service to small businesses and professional offices. Physicians, attorneys, and financial institutions are particularly good prospective customers. These professionals are required by federal and some state regulations to retain documents for unusually long time periods and to certify document privacy and confidentiality. ADS provides certifications that meet legal standards in case a customer is the subject of litigation both on privacy issues and document destruction.

The company uses the system termed "closed-loop" in destroying documents whereby documents of many customers are mixed and shredded together, making it virtually impossible for a thief or industry spy to reassemble a single document. The shredded material is bailed and sold directly to paper mills for baby diapers and paper towels.

Ms. Keener and her former husband continue as business partners. She owns 49 percent of MontCo and 60 percent of ADS, and Phillip owns the remaining percentages of both companies. He manages MontCo in Texas, and she manages ADS in Carrollton.

Ms. Keener's Christian faith is the foundation of her philosophy of life and business plan. She was taught tithing as a child; practiced tithing as an adult, taking "ten percent off the top;" and otherwise has been a good steward of her time, talents, and money. She is considerate of her employees even at her own expense. For example, she and Phillip reduced their salaries in tough times to avoid reducing employee salaries.

Renee believes that God selected her to be an entrepreneur, ordered her family and early experiences to develop her independence and determination, had His hand on her shoulder when times were tough, and blessed her bountifully. "It was like God painted the way for my future." Furthermore, her planning and decisions are based on prayer and research. "The deciding factor for me is when the good Lord says O.K. because then I don't look back." She indicated that with the assurance from the Lord, she knows that whatever she pursues under God's blessing will be successful and/or it will teach her something that will be pivotal down the road. I asked her how she has the assurance from the Lord: "Everything falls into place. Circumstances start happening [in our favor]; it is like a river [of support] starts flowing."

Ms. Keener does not have any children, but she is devoted to her older sister's children. "If my niece were to come to me about going into business, I would say that you have to get it right with God." If you do that, she concludes, you will have assurance, confidence, independence, and constant guidance. "I believe deeply in the Holy Spirit. He walks with me every day."

Unabashedly grateful to God, Ms. Kenner is publicly thankful. Even in the darkest times of her life, she could look around and see how blessed she was. In all things, "Count your blessings. Look at others who are worse off than you," she advises. She also recommends young people to become prepared by getting as much education as possible.

A higher education is helpful, Ms. Kenner believes, but advises those who cannot afford to attend college not to be discouraged from going into business if they are otherwise prepared. Perhaps, God even chose the non-college route for Renee in order to demonstrate how a young woman can be an entrepreneur without the benefits of a college degree. She does admit that above-average intelligence is important but concludes that a lot of very intelligent people do not have a college degree.

I did not specifically ask Ms. Keener for a list of cardinal rules that guide her, but in reviewing my notes from the two interviews, seven principles of management stood out. These are direct quotes from Ms. Keener, but I added the italics for clarification.

• Do not try to build wealth as your primary goal. Find a good product or service and "work at it with all your heart, as working for the Lord, not for men" (Col. 3:23 *from her business card and company website*).

• Surround yourself with knowledgeable and trusted people in your business and in your circle of friends and advisors. (*Two people profiled in this chapter were her early advisors, and one has always been a customer.*)

• Use common sense that flows from godly wisdom, your experiences, and wise counsel. Your judgment will be as good as anyone's will, so trust your own judgment.

• Do your due diligence. Spend much time in research and preparation. Continue to study and learn about your business and human relations.

• Never give up. Do not allow failure to deter you because early failures are probably only a test or a training ground. Failure is the avenue to success. (*It took her eight months of refusals before she landed a big contract with a regional hospital.*)

• Keep it simple. This is the key to life and business. Doing much of the work yourself will simplify your operations. (*The simpler your business model the easier it is to sell to customers and banks, teach to employees, and correct when problems occur. You may need to start your business as a proprietorship.*)

• Pay as you go and stay on top of your receivables. (*Do as much of the work yourself until you can really afford employees, expand your business out of profits and retained earnings, and pay your bills on time.*)

I met Renee Keener about two years before our interview when she was president of one of our Rotary clubs in Carrollton, and I read a couple of newspaper articles about American Document Securities. I knew she was a Christian and from all indications had developed a good business. I wanted to present a female entrepreneur in this chapter who loves the Lord and applies biblical principles in business. However, I really did not know her when I contacted her. At the end of a drop-in visit and our two-hour interview a week later, however, I left her office thinking that I had known her for years. Her enthusiasm and gracious manner, the way she thoughtfully and precisely answered a myriad of questions, and the unabashed acknowledgment of her faith, inspired me. I pray that her story will get into the hands of others who need motivation and general direction. No doubt, Ms. Keener will serve as a good role model for other young women who want to start a business.

Renee told me that she had prayed earlier in the day for guidance in the interview, particularly that God would give her the right words that would be helpful to others. If what I witnessed in two hours is any indication, her prayer was answered

Aubrey Silvey— Aubrey Silvey Enterprises, Inc.

On truth, honesty, integrity and being a man of his word.

Aubrey Silvey Enterprises is a vertically integrated company serving the electrical utility industry in the design, engineering, manufacturing, construction, and testing of electrical power substations. A substation's function is to reduce the high power voltage transmitted to a service area by utility companies and to transmit the usable low voltage over smaller lines to residential and business consumers. The company is organized into five divisions, which support each other or contract separately for services to other construction firms, utility companies, governmental agencies, and related corporations.

The EPC Division is somewhat unique in that it provides a single-source approach with integrated services in engineering, procurement, and construction for all electrical substation related projects. Also, the Wind Division and the Testing Services Group evidence the company's support of alternative energy sources and environmental protection issues. The company also owns five subsidiaries that provide related or supportive manufacturing, installation, and information technology services.

Aubrey Silvey Enterprises (ASE) employs almost four hundred technical and service personnel in five locations with an annual payroll of $19 million and generates $150 million annually in revenue. The company is qualified to conduct business in the forty-eight contiguous states and has actually done business in thirty-five states, Mexico, Canada, and several of the US territories.

ASE is now an employee owned (ESOP) company that is traditionally organized with a separate chairman, president/CEO, CFO, and numerous vice presidents/division managers. The Board of Directors oversees the policy role of the leadership team, and an employee advisory group also contributes to policy-related company planning and employee benefits and other well-being issues of the ASE family.

Aubrey Silvey is the founder, chairman, and general benefactor of ASE. Although he has relinquished the operations to a longtime associate, his influence and presence are very much felt at the corporate headquarters located in this rural, northeastern quadrant of Carroll County. The headquarters building and the serene work setting are typical old South, with headquarters offices and plants controlling about ten acres in the midst of the 450 acre Silvey estate just off a county road near Bremen, Georgia.

The Silvey estate is marked by open pastures, gently rolling foot-hills, and five lakes, some spring-fed and all pristine. Mr. Silvey wants people to know that the company is successful but that it conducts its business based on Christian principles and values. He feels that the serenity of the pristine lakes, pine and hardwood forests, and open fields convey something special about a company that operates in a highly competitive and hard nose industry. Most importantly, he feels that the serenity contributes to the high moral of the AES family of employees.

Mr. Silvey is seventy-two years old but evidences few of the lines and other markings of three-score and twelve. Although he is in the early stage of Parkinson's disease, he is still very much steady of feet and hands, and his recall and insightfulness show no signs of his announced condition. I interviewed him and his delightful wife of almost fifty years, Judy, around the dining room table where he started ASE in 1971.

After the discussion time at the table, he drove me around the property in his Gator ATV, and we viewed the future memorial site for him and Judy, already in place and built out of Georgia marble. Later we looked in on his state-of-the art woodworking shop where he had masterfully built collectors' pieces like the buffet in his dining room. When I drove away from the Silvey home, I drove very slowly through the estate/campus to soak up the last emotional fleck of this idyllic setting.

Thomas Aubrey Silvey was born October 20, 1937, in the village of Whitesburg, Georgia, located in the lower southeastern quadrant of Carroll County, to Tom and Ethel Silvey. Tom Silvey was a sharecropper farmer and the elected Mayor of Whitesburg. After the birth of four daughters, he and Ethel longed for a son. When Aubrey was born, the town celebrated along with the Silvey family. In fact, Tom Silvey got a ride down the main street of Whitesburg by the jubilant locals in a well-adorned wheelbarrow! Not long after Aubrey was born, Tom Silvey applied under a federal program for and was granted a seventy-acre tract of land in northeast Carroll County. This meant the Silvey family had a low-interest loan on a grayland farm in the foothills of northwest Georgia, where red clay is typical. Aubrey called it a two-horse farm compared to nearby farms that were small tracts and worked only by one mule. Tom Silvey's ambition to improve his provisions for his family and vision to seek ownership of land and equipment was not lost on young Aubrey. Also, Aubrey took note of his father's surprise visitations in the fields to check on his progress when he was plowing or doing other farm work.

Aubrey learned at a young age a valuable management principle: assign a job with appropriate authority to make decisions but check on the progress of the job regularly. Aubrey grew, matured, and acquired the family values of hard work, minding your own business, honesty, and integrity during the 1950s. "My parents were good people, and Dad worked hard to have a good name." They also taught him about the Christian faith, and Aubrey accepted Christ as Savior and Lord and was baptized in a cold creek at the age of twelve years old. He said further, "Dad was generous with his offerings, but usually we only had money when we sold a crop."

Aubrey graduated from Bremen High School in 1955 where he was influenced by his history teacher and the School System Superintendent, H. R. Jones, but the Carroll County Agricultural Extension Agent persuaded Aubrey to attend Berry College in Rome, Georgia. Berry was founded by the legendary Martha Berry to serve the mountain children of northwest Georgia.

The story is that Miss Berry sought a grant from Henry Ford to underwrite her fledging school, but Mr. Ford only gave her a dime coin. Undaunted by Mr. Ford's apparent putdown, Miss Berry bought a sack of peanuts, planted the peanuts, and months later harvested a large crop of peanuts. She sold the peanut crop and wrote to Mr. Ford about the profit she had turned on his ten cent contribution.

Henry Ford's plan of testing had worked, and he later contributed millions of dollars to Berry College during Miss Berry's life and after her death. Miss Berry's enterprising spirit was taught to the young students at Berry where a student could actually work his or her way through college. Aubrey flourished in that environment for a year before he changed his educational mission. Nevertheless, before young Silvey left Berry, he met the love of his life.

Aubrey was required to work two days each week by the college and was assigned to work with the paint crew on the campus. One day in 1956, he "looked out the window and saw a pretty young girl walking home from school." He soon identified her as Berry Purchasing Agent Herbert Muschamp's daughter, Judy, who was still in high school. Aubrey found out that she attended Berry basketball games with her father, so Aubrey started attending games himself and with the help of a friend, got a blind date with Judy. However, the date did not work out because Aubrey was "flustered and tongue-tied" and could not carry on a conversation with her. Judy recalled that he acted as if he "just jumped off a turnip truck. He had no car, no money, and little personality. Also, he did not call again for two weeks, but I found out that he did not have any money to date until payday."

At the end of his first year at Berry, Aubrey worked a summer job at

Southwire Company in Carrollton in the machine shop. "It was a hot and dirty job. One day I saw several men in ties and an air conditioned office in the plant, and I asked what they did; the shop foreman told me the men were engineers. I decided then that I wanted to be an engineer." He did not return to Berry but enrolled at Southern Technical Institute in the civil engineering program as a co-op student, working and studying in alternating quarters.

He wrote to Judy and saw her as much as he could, and he received some help from Judy's mother who remarked, "Don't upset that young man; he can make you a good living," which turned out to be a prophetic statement of no small measure.

Aubrey completed his degree program, married Judy the day after his graduation, joined the Marine Corps Reserves, and left for basic training within a few days of his wedding. Judy had a year of courses remaining before she could graduate, so she successfully petitioned the Board of Trustees to allow her to complete her degree as the first married student at Berry College.

The couple moved in 1961 to Carrollton where Aubrey worked ten years with Richards & Associates (R&A), an engineering and construction company affiliated with Southwire. Judy worked as home economist in Carroll County for the University of Georgia Extension Service. They adopted a son, David, in 1966 and daughter, Julie, in 1968, and built a house on the seventy-acre Silvey farm near Bremen.

"One of the first things that we did was pay off the final installments on that property," Aubrey recalled, and immediately, Aubrey and Judy began adding land to the family tract. Life was good: Aubrey was making a good salary as head of the substation engineering and construction department at R & A; they had a nice house and pristine acreage; and the family had settled in as members of the First Baptist Church in Carrollton. However, in 1968, Frank Rose, the visionary vice president of Richards & Associates, died of a massive heart attack, and the company was never the same. Aubrey surmised that he was not going to be appointed to head the company, so he made plans to start his own business. "I felt like I could do a better job of taking care of customers. Also, I had ten years of training in substation construction, and I was not going to let that go to waste." Therefore, in January 1971, he incorporated the business name because Silvey Enterprises was not available and came up with $24,000 of capital to start the company. The capitalization included the family auto, a 1970 Buick 225 valued at $5,000. He recalled, "Everything went into raising capital, and if we had failed, we would not even have our shoes."

Mr. Silvey drew up a list of potential customers, contacted everybody on the list, and submitted bids for announced projects. However, he did not get a contract for a job until after six months of operating as Aubrey Silvey Enterprises. Finally, South Carolina Electric and Gas Company in South Augusta awarded ASE its first contract, and Mr. Silvey contacted a close friend, J. T. Becker, who lived in Atlanta, to help him with the project.

ASE did not own the necessary tools or other equipment, so Mr. Silvey started the company's first job with rented or borrowed tools and equipment. In order to complete the contract, he enlisted the help of friends as a crew, some of whom took a few weeks of vacation from their regular jobs. While work was in progress, Mr. Silvey contacted other potential customers, and projects came more frequently as he submitted numerous bids. The first job for South Carolina Electric and Gas made a small profit, and in the first year, the company realized $187,000 in gross sales.

Mr. Silvey had taken a 50 percent reduction in salary from his previous employment at R & A, but the effect of that set-back was minimized by the prospects for business growth. In 1972, ASE received new opportunities to bid projects, and the results were so successful that the company was hard-pressed to cover all the jobs with one crew. However, Mr. Silvey had a plan for development that also turned out to be the basis for an ultimate business succession plan with the hiring of Tommy Muse Sr. in the substation assembly department. In 1973, Mr. Silvey formed a second construction crew and named Mr. Muse as superintendent.

Aubrey Silvey Enterprises grew its substation construction business dramatically over the next ten years. By 1982, the company worked five fully equipped construction crews, operated in twelve southeastern states, and generated over $3.7 million in sales. Although by 1982 the company was successful by every measure, two major changes were set in motion that would have a lasting effect on Mr. Silvey personally and his company in general. First, SEFCOR, a Griffin, Georgia, company that had been the sole source supplier of electrical connectors to ASE, approached Mr. Silvey about his company's buying all of SEFCOR. He visited SEFCOR, was impressed with their operation, saw a good opportunity for a compatible subsidiary, and bought the company within six weeks of the initial plant visit.

SEFCOR continues to operate as a wholly owned subsidiary and sells electrical connectors to all major utilities in the US, Canada, Mexico, and several other foreign countries. This acquisition set in motion a corporate policy of being open to acquisitions and new division startups. Also, the organizational framework was established with divisions/groups operating within AES and five subsidiaries functioning independently. With the acquisition of SEFCOR and the emerging expansion policy, Mr. Silvey realized that he "needed more training in managing a growing business."

Mr. Silvey applied for and was accepted into the Harvard University Business School's Owner/President Management (OPM) program in 1982. He had already established a capable and experienced team of officers, managers, superintendents, and support staff and had delegated authority commensurate with each employee's responsibilities. His selection, training, and management methods worked to his advantage while he was in Cambridge for the numerous in-class sessions of the three-year OPM program.

He told all the staff to solve their own problems and not to call him in Cambridge unless they could not handle the job. He reported, "Nobody called me." This was in stark contrast to other students who were repeatedly returning calls to their offices. Mr. and Mrs. Silvey both observed that the Harvard training was a pivotal experience in the growth and development of the company. He said that after the Harvard experience, "I had the confidence that whatever we did was just as good as or better than that of the competition."

After Mr. Silvey completed the Harvard OPM program in 1985, ASE started Associated Substation Engineering, Inc., EPC Division, Power Equipment Services Division, and Testing Services Group before 1990. In 1996, when ASE could not get satisfactory service for its computers, the company started Silvey Information Services, Inc., to deal with its own information technology and to offer its services to other companies.

The climb to the top of its industry was not without obstacles and job shortfalls for ASE. In fact, in the early 1980s, the company lost $1 million in the construction of a steel mill in Kentucky when the project estimators made several inaccurate assumptions. He said also that in the mid-1980s that he could not get jobs because of the cost of borrowing and a deep recession. Fortunately, the company could rely mainly on its retained earnings until the economy improved. However, at one point, ASE needed an extension on a one million dollar note held by an Atlanta bank, but the bank denied the extension. "That hurt," Mrs. Silvey said. However, they turned to Textron Corp in Atlanta who bailed them out and carried them through the crisis.

I asked Mr. Silvey how he dealt with the risks of estimating projects and with the inevitable reversals in business. He said that he and his wife asked for divine guidance daily and spent a lot of time talking to the Lord. "I give credit to the Lord for his leadership and guidance, and without His guidance, we would have never done it [founded and developed ASE]. God is still Number One."

Soon after starting ASE, the Silvey family felt they owed God His part of the profits that accrued to them from the business. Mr. Silvey told the story about when he began tithing and how much tithing meant to him and his family. In 1965, when he taught a Sunday school lesson on tithing, he told his class, "From this day forward, I will tithe."

I asked Mr. Silvey if there was an incident, situation, event, or relationship that the resolution or break could have resulted only from divine intervention. He immediately told me about a $26 million job in Anaheim, California, that ASE was awarded in the bid process for a gas insulated substation against international competition.

"The job was in a high population area on expensive real estate. We found the job, bid on it, and built it," he said. "ASE was awarded a lot of jobs as second bidder because the low bidder could not qualify for the job."

He concluded that these jobs particularly stand out as ASE being favored by the Almighty. He further acknowledged that probably many jobs that ASE did not get would have been disasters, but the company was spared because of divine protection. He has been very thankful for these blessings.

We continued our discussion regarding spiritual matters, and I asked him if he would verbalize his theology. He said that God provided man with a helpmate, and "one of the most important things a man can do is to find the right helpmate." He added also that he has a good helpmate and that she has been by his side through everything, including serving as corporate secretary, office manager, and member of the board of directors of all Silvey companies. He said further that a faith in God is essential in order to get through life and to pursue one's vocation, and we should not forget to "expect His promises to be fulfilled."

Mr. Silvey is a strong advocate of education and lifelong learning. He said that the Harvard OPM was an "eye opener" for him, and he dedicated himself to providing similar opportunities to his staff. He talked about how important it is for a person in business to continue learning by reading and taking courses. He cited the numerous educational programs that ASE officers and staff have attended.

I asked Mr. Silvey his thoughts on two final points: using leverage in growing a business and developing a business plan. He said that he had to borrow money to grow AES but that he relied on retained earnings for as long as the built-up profits lasted. His most impressive financial coup was obtaining a Development Loan guaranteed by the federal government in order to buy SEFCOR in 1982. Regarding business planning, he has developed business plans over the years, particularly after his training at the Harvard OPM program in 1982-85. However, he acknowledges that business plans are general guides, are often outdated well before their time, and are useless when circumstances change significantly. On a personal note, he certainly did not plan to build wealth, although he did plan to add acreage to his estate when land became available. "My sole purpose was to provide for my family, by whatever means, and I've been pleased that I've been able to do that."

I have known Aubrey and Judy Silvey and their children, David and Julie, for over forty years, and they are the same gentle, humble people that they were starting out in business. He has been a steely-tough businessman but has maintained a high standard of values for himself and his associates. One of Mr. Silvey's strengths has been his ability to identify and nurture excellent leadership in ASE, and the company continues to grow under the executive leadership of Tommy Muse Sr. As stewards and philanthropists, Mr. and Mrs. Silvey have been generous with their church and Berry College, and Mr. Silvey served twenty-four years on the Board of Visitors and two years on the Board of Trustees of Berry College.

Mr. Silvey has been also recognized for his achievements in business, such as being named Georgia Small Business Person of the Year in 1994. Despite these accolades and appointments, he has not changed one iota. He is the same unpretentious man of the late 1960s. He has always maintained his mantra of truth, honesty, integrity, and "being a man of his word." Surely the proverb about the Lord blessing the ways of an upright man applies to Aubrey Silvey.

Tommy Green — Greenway Medical Technologies, Inc.

Making health care better for the benefit of all

Thomas Wolfe's 1940 novel, *You Can't Go Home Again,*[1] started a catch phrase that warned young people about returning to their hometowns to seek their fortunes. Likewise, when the citizens of Nazareth did not receive Jesus, He said that a prophet is without honor in his own country. However, Tommy Green never considered the specter of failure when he returned to Carrollton in 1965 after graduating with a business degree from the University of Georgia. Furthermore, Mr. Green, as the heir apparent of a group of retail stores, did not succumb to the pattern found by academic studies that second and third generation business owners frequently do not succeed in the family business.

Tommy Green's life over the next forty-five years spent in his hometown form an intriguing and inspiring story, which includes starting and developing a successful high-technology business and more importantly relates his spiritual growth. His story serves a unique role in this group of entrepreneurial profiles, because it sends a message to those who, with a similar inheritance, may want to say "soul take thine ease" and open themselves to atrophy from complacency.

Greenway Medical Technologies (Greenway) is an information technology business that develops, markets, installs, and supports practice management and electronic health record software for physician practices and clinics. Over 1,100 physician offices located in all states but one use the software that runs on PC's and handheld devices, and manages administrative and clinical data for these practices. The administrative component includes patient scheduling, insurance, and other financial tracking; and the clinical component records patient diagnosis and treatment information.

Annual sales in 2009 were $48.8 million, and the company employs just over 300 software engineers, sales staff, and management personnel. The startup of Greenway evolved over forty-three years, beginning with the family business of NAPA auto parts stores and later the startup of a check-imaging technology business, both of which were sold for large profits. This powerful story of entrepreneurship and Christian faith begins and ends with Tommy Green.

Wyche Thomas Green Jr. was born in May, 1944, to W. T. "Buddy" and Louise Green in Carrollton, Georgia. He is the only son and second child, and he and his two sisters were born four years apart. Buddy and

Louise Green grew up and later married during the Great Depression, and they purposed that their children would have the benefit of a college education. Buddy persuaded Louise that they should have their children four years apart, so they would not have more than one child in college at the same time, thus being able to afford the best education available for their children.

Buddy Green grew up in LaGrange, Georgia, where his father owned a Nash automobile dealership that did not make it through the Depression. Buddy Green could not go to college; but he was smart, industrious, and observant. He parlayed his job at a service station into a career choice. He frequently ran errands to the NAPA store to pick up parts for the service station mechanic, and he realized that he could make a good living selling auto parts. The Depression elevated auto parts stores to strong business positions because owners had to repair their cars and trucks, since they were unable to afford new vehicles.

Buddy Green acquired a NAPA franchise in 1936 and was awarded the Carrollton territory. He also persuaded his father to open a store, and grandfather Green was awarded a territory in south Alabama. Over the years, Buddy Green and his father added to their stores, and by the time Tommy was ready to enter the business, he was heir apparent to a NAPA chain of eight stores, which he also added to during his tenure as chief executive officer of the group. Therefore, father and grandfather bestowed on Tommy a viable business group and invaluable education in entrepreneurship. Likewise, his parents encouraged him and provided the resources for him to attend the university of his choice to learn, mature, enjoy himself, and find a good wife.

Tommy was a good student in high school and the all-American boy. He played football in a town of rabid football fans that elevate their Friday-night heroes to near mythical status. However, he was not big enough or fast enough to attract college football recruiters, and he had other plans for his time in college. He enjoyed himself in high school, but his Christian education and faith-building were not neglected. His parents were pillars in the First Methodist Church, and Tommy accepted Christ as Savior and Lord in a revival at FMC when he was in the sixth grade.

Tommy was a normal high school student but was serious about preparing for the University of Georgia, which he entered in 1962. He pursued a degree in business administration at the university, joined a fraternity, and by his own admission enjoyed himself as "Joe College," drifting away over time from his Christian consecration.

Along the way, he had a blind date with Betty Jenkins, a dark-haired and brown-eyed beauty from Augusta, and it was "lights-out" for Joe College from then on. Not only did the college romance survive, the couple married in 1966 after they both graduated. Before they married, Tommy served on active duty with the Air Force Reserve.

The couple moved to Carrollton in 1966, and Tommy began his career in the family NAPA store chain. However, in 1968, he was called up with his Air Force Reserve unit during the USS Pueblo crisis off the coast of North Korea. The Reserve unit, permanently stationed at Dobbins Air Force Base in Marietta, Georgia, served almost twenty months of call-up duty at Dobbins.

Tommy was the Non-commissioned Officer in charge of the immunization detachment for his unit, and he was able to take the weekend shift for thirty-two consecutive hours and also work on Mondays; then he could be off duty for the remainder of each week. Therefore, he was able to return to Carrollton and work in the NAPA office at least four days each week. This brutal regimen continued for twenty months until the Air Force Reserve unit was discharged from active duty.

The Green family NAPA business grew, in large measure due to Tommy's dedicated service and acquisition policy, and at one point, the chain owned twelve stores located in Georgia and Alabama. Tommy and Betty had a good life, popular in society and community service, and Tommy followed his father on the Board of Directors of West Georgia National Bank. The couple started a family after five years of marriage, and over nine years birthed three children, Tee (W. T. III), Beth, and Andrew.

By 1972, a major spiritual change was underway in the Green household. The changes began when Betty felt the need for spiritual growth in her life, and she began attending a Bible study. She studied the Bible, read expository books at home, and later began teaching a Bible study session. Tommy "saw the difference in Betty and noticed that she was easier to get along with, because she loved me with a deeper capacity."

Betty urged Tommy to get involved with Bible study in some way, but he was not moved until Betty backed off from her steady coaxing. As Tommy related the story, she was praying one day and felt that God was telling her, "Live your life and leave Tommy to Me." In 1974, after observing Betty's great passion for Jesus Christ for two years, Tommy concluded "what Betty is into can't be all bad," although he still chided her about praying for specific blessings. However, God taught him a lesson about prayer, but in a loving and fatherly way that yielded a powerful blessing.

Tommy and Betty had wanted for years to buy twenty-seven acres of land adjoining their property, but the owners had been adamant about not selling. Betty asked Tommy to pray with her about the matter, and Tommy agreed, although skeptical about God having time to answer about a specific desire. They knelt in prayer that night, and Betty prayed for God to "work it out where we can buy the property." As Betty prayed, Tommy received a dollar figure that came into his mind.

The next morning, the property owner called Tommy. After six months of no contact about the property, he indicated he might be willing to sell, while admitting he did not know why he changed his mind. Tommy met with the owner, who offered to sell at a "subdivision development price." When Tommy balked at the price, the owner offered the exact amount that God gave Tommy the night before. The deal was done, and God used the transaction to teach Tommy that He answers prayers about our desires as well as our needs.

Soon after the property blessing, Tommy began attending a men's Bible study and the meetings of the Full Gospel Businessmen's Fellowship International in Carrollton where he soon became a leader in the group. He met business leaders in Carrollton and in Atlanta who were successful and had powerful testimonies of God's grace and blessings. He said these were "men's men who liked to hunt, fish, and play golf but were spiritual. I did not see that growing up."

Driving back from Atlanta one night after a Full Gospel meeting, he said he had a "Damascus Road" experience. "I was praying and told God if You are really as real as these men say You are, present yourself to me and I will spend the rest of my life with You. I started crying and cried all the way back to Carrollton. We started attending a spirit-filled church with a very humble, anointed preacher who preached the Word of God like I had never heard."

Tommy said that his life has never been the same, and he has tried to serve God and proclaim his faith in Jesus Christ consistently since that experience. For years, in the late 1970s and 1980s, he traveled the country giving his testimony to businessmen in churches and meetings of the FGBFI.

Tommy Green's personal life in the mid-1980s was blessed and rewarding, but he began to question the direction of the auto parts business. He observed that NAPA's three-step distribution system was squeezing profit margins as compared to the new NAPA competitors' two-step distribution. During Mr. Green's tenure at the head of the group of stores, sales grew from $1 million annually to $7.5 million, but the industry was becoming saturated with competition. Tommy decided to sell the business, and his ailing father endorsed the plan. Therefore, in 1986, Tommy began selling eight of the NAPA stores to each of the store managers, a process that took six years. During the selling process, Tommy began looking for another enterprise project to pursue.

Mr. Green had served on the Board of Directors of West Georgia National Bank four years by the time that he sold the NAPA stores, and he had observed that the banking industry, particularly the small banks, was burdened with physically canceling and returning checks to its customers. This laborious process was an ideal target for his search for a troubled industry that had an extensive problem that could be solved with technology. These were the days when Microsoft introduced its Windows NT operating system, and Mr. Green and the small group of advisors and associates that he assembled took a big gamble that Windows eventually would become the operating system of choice for the banking industry. Also, he identified check-imaging as the format necessary to solve the check handling burden for these smaller banks. Check-imaging was not a revolutionary idea, but the application to the Windows NT operating system was. Larger banks used mainframe technology, which was very expensive and complicated to operate, to take pictures of checks and sort them by these images.

Mr. Green could see this check-imaging system in smaller banks greatly reducing bank expenses and effecting maximum efficiency of bank personnel. He envisioned a vast market for this software on a PC platform. Therefore, Mr. Green contributed $1 million to the capitalization, raised another $3 million from investors, and incorporated Greenway in May 1994. Software engineers and technicians were hired, and the technical staff began writing the software in May 1994.

Greenway began marketing its check-imaging software in August

1995, and the product was a major success. Within four years, almost 300 banks in five countries bought and used the software, and Greenway offered separate maintenance contracts and services to its customers. Greenway's major competitor was BISYS Group, and Greenway captured a significant portion of BISYS' market share and attracted some of the leading technology engineers and sales force in the industry. Consequently, BISYS offered to buy Greenway, and after meeting with the shareholders, Mr. Green and the shareholders sold the corporation to BISYS for $47.5 million in November 1998. Mr. Green, his son Tee, who agreed to serve as a regional vice president of sales, and most of the technical staff remained with BISYS; however, after five months, Mr. Green resigned to follow another entrepreneurial venture. Tee followed his father in the new venture after eighteen months with BISYS.

Mr. Green sold many shares of Greenway stock to several medical doctors, and five of these he dubbed as "techno docs" because they "could see what was going on in physicians' practices regarding the use of electronic health records." Even before the sale of Greenway, these physicians were making the case to Mr. Green to develop software that would meet the needs of physicians in private practice. He and his associates investigated the field and found the EHR field was crowded already, and they had no interest in pursuing EHR development. However, two of the physicians, Dr. Thomas Fitzgerald and Dr. James Ingram, persisted and called a meeting of thirty physicians who were interested in the project. They met with Mr. Green and his associates, and he listened to their complaints about the software already on the market.

The physicians said that the software systems on the market were difficult to integrate into their practices and slowed their work flow. Mr. Green saw great opportunities to improve health care, particularly in the diagnosis and health care research. Therefore, he formed a team to consider the issue, including several technical staff; his son Tee, who was experienced in patient diagnosis and health care research issues; and his son-in-law John, whose specialty was customer support.

The Greenway Medical team saw an opportunity to build a more efficient and productive computer technology based system using PC technology. After studying the problem, the team came up with several ideas to begin testing.

The sale of Greenway check-imaging business occurred in November

1998, and by that time, Mr. Green had settled on his next entrepreneurial venture, which was later named Greenway Medical Technologies and incorporated in 1998. Fortunately, BISYS did not contest the name Greenway, since the new company would not be in direct competition with BISYS. Mr. Green raised $84 million in capital dedicated to develop state-of-the-art electronic health records and practice management software.

Contributing to the risks of a software project is the fact that the technology has to be developed and sold before a dime of revenue can be expected. Therefore, the complete package had to be in the hands of physicians and practice management staff before Greenway could begin billing. Fortunately, Greenway Medical began selling the software in 2002, and sales have grown steadily over the last seven years.

During fiscal 2009, the company sales grew 38 percent over fiscal year 2008 and now provides electronic solutions for 1,100 medical practices and is used by 27,000 individual health care professionals. Most physicians in a practice use a wireless tablet to input data for patient records, and these data points are coded to produce a variety of patient information that can be used to enhance patient diagnosis and care, practice efficiency and effectiveness, and medical research.

Mr. Green is particularly excited about the medical research uses and potential of the software. The software can sort patients' records to catalog drug compatibility and reactions, symptom assessment, and a myriad of other diagnosis and patient care evaluations. Likewise, the software administrative and financial suite enhances the efficiency of the practice immeasurably. The electronic health records suite virtually turns the small medical and clinical practice into a laboratory for solutions in-house to vexing diagnosis and other health care problems and safety issues.

Mr. Green said by getting away from the paper patient records, health care is penetrating a new frontier. "It is complicated, but this technology is going to make health care better, and I am glad to say that Greenway is making a difference for the benefit of all."

I asked Mr. Green to what does he attribute his long-term success, and his simple reply was the leading of the Holy Spirit. "I would not think of driving to work without spending my travel time asking for leadership. I know that when I pray, the Creator of the universe hears and answers. If we are really successful, it is to God's glory."

I asked Mr. Green to identify his personal characteristics and talents that might form a checklist for aspiring entrepreneurs to use in evaluating themselves. "Some people think that I am a smart technology inventor. But I am just a guy that had the vision, organized the business, and recruited the people." He said that you need to have good people, organize your business, and thank God when He gives you an idea of where to start.

I have known Tommy Green for over forty years, and my characterization of him, in a single word, is courageous. I believe his courage really became evident when Betty and he sought a deeper relationship with the Lord. His zeal for the Lord and his testimony drew mixed reactions locally in the beginning, but he sowed spiritual seeds that helped awaken many pedestrian Christians during a period of spiritual renewal in our town. His spirit-filled theology challenged the established practices and customs of mainline church members, like me, when he taught about spiritual gifts and knowledge that were not taught in our churches. Some practices conflicted with our more formal and structured customs in worship.

He was right. More is available beyond salvation to empower Christians for service and in fulfillment of worship, and Tommy Green's courage is exhibit one. As one of his associates in the Full Gospel Businessmen's Fellowship stated, "Tommy came forth with an enthusiasm for Jesus and an excitement [for what he had found in the Lord], and he wanted everybody to know the fullness of the Lord's message."

He has been courageous in starting companies, raising enormous capital, venturing into a field that he had no training or prior experience, and being accountable to powerful investors. However, he had a belief in himself, and more importantly, a faith in God to lead him and protect his business. He has made and will make significant contributions, through Greenway Medical Technologies, in health care in the future that will be responsible for saving lives and otherwise improving patient care. Tommy Green, over the years, has been renewed with a spiritual vigor, blessed with a vision, and empowered with courage. He has the vision to know the truth and the courage to accomplish it.

Conclusion

Entrepreneurship is a powerful force in the US economy, and starting and managing a successful business can be the best way to build wealth. But starting and building a new business is risky, and indeed the operational definition of an entrepreneur is one who "assumes the risk of a business venture." [2] How does one succeed then in a new business? What are the life experiences, skills, and characteristics that prevail among successful entrepreneurs? Is there anything special about entrepreneurs in God's kingdom on earth?

I believe that God calls and trains successful entrepreneurs. He knows our latent skills because He blessed us with these talents. He then shapes our life experiences in our families, schools, and otherwise, to enable us to become aware of our talents and to be drawn to work that is compatible with those skills.

David High in his book, *Kings & Priests*, [3] says that priests minister in the name of God, and 'kings' give tithes and offerings in abundance into the earthly kingdom to spread the Word of God and care for the poor. (Of course, 'kings' is used in the generic sense.) He says that the call of 'kings' is as sacred as that of priests and that neither should interlope in the other's charge. One of the entrepreneurs profiled in this chapter, Bob Stone, ironically, had to make a choice between divinity school and business, and all of those profiled acknowledged in some way that God had lead them into starting their own businesses.

Pastor Steve Davis observed that "sometimes we church leaders have given the affluent only one option: feel guilty. However, we need to run from two extremes. One is materialism, and the other is asceticism. They are, ironically, a lot alike. Materialism you will recognize as the religion of the golden calf, where we fall down and worship money and possessions. Asceticism is a brand of faith where we obsess on possessions by demonizing them. And when we do, we are rejecting the good gifts of our Lord." [4]

What are the characteristics that successful entrepreneurs evidence as they build their businesses? I read biographies and academic studies about and directly observed entrepreneurs for many years, including of course the friends profiled here. Four main character groupings seem to prevail in each new creator of an enterprise. You may find this short checklist helpful in determining if you are called to entrepreneurship:

Visionary—They are very intelligent, have a keen awareness of their role in business, can analyze their future prospects, and can formulate a way to get things done. Ray Fulford and Aubrey Silvey left a failing Richards & Associates and started their own construction firms. Bob Stone left college teaching to devote all of his time to his new business. Entrepreneurs do not normally make detailed business plans, except for a loan application when demanded or a stock-offering prospectus, but they carry in their minds continuously where they are leading their enterprises.

Driven—They are highly motivated, indeed driven to succeed. When impediments occur, using their vision and determination, they find a way to succeed. The entrepreneurs profiled here gain an inner strength and direction from the Almighty, and they understand that God is not going to allow their enterprises to fail. Hardships growing up often harden their "metal" of determination. They are willing to take risks to achieve their objectives.

Irrepressible—Successful entrepreneurs are resilient, which is meant to refer to their emotions and personalities. They are enthusiastic, optimistic, and personable; and they can communicate their ideas and sell their products or services. They never think that they will not succeed, or if they do, it is just about a unit that has to be excised. Renee Keener had to close one of her units, but she soon found a more viable business. Tommy Green became concerned about the NAPA stores, sold them, and invested in a more viable business.

Indefatigable—Entrepreneurs are diligent, and they work long hours and do much of the work themselves in the startup stage. They have a high energy level, and this physical quality and other characteristics combine to form good leadership.

Entrepreneurs grow their businesses by investing their earnings in the business, and they further grow their wealth by investing in a company retirement plan and other investments. Fortunately, all of us can likewise grow our wealth by investing, and in the next chapter, we turn to the investment principles and practices that will produce a good return on investment over a lifetime of investing.

BOOK TWO:

WALL STREET METHODS

People don't need extraordinary insight or intelligence [to invest and build wealth]. What they need most is the character to adopt simple rules and stick with them.

—*Benjamin Graham, the late legendary investor, Columbia University lecturer in finance, and mentor to Warren Buffet*

CHAPTER SIX

Vision and Wealth

A vision of wealth and building wealth are inextricably connected, much like conceptualizing a fine home before you even talk to an architect or contractor. People who have even modest fortunes did not arrive at financial independence by aimlessly amassing wealth. Of course, there are always the unusual exceptions, such as someone who wins the lottery and the Beverly Hillbillies.

Wealthy people start their wealth-building by seeing the end before the means. They do not scurry around willy-nilly trying different projects without some concept of where they are going with each venture. They know where they want to be financially at some time in the future, and they make plans to achieve their goals, even if their goals are modest in the beginning.

Having a vision does not mean the absence of dead ends, even with the best of planning. For example, you may be faced at some point with a deep recession and bear market that is much worse than expected, such as in 2007-2009. How will you manage your portfolio under these conditions? Answer: have a sell strategy, such as using technical indicators that I describe in chapter 9. Adjustments will have to be made at every phase of your plan, but you will be adjusting your plan, not adjusting your goal.

Your first step is to define the meaning of wealth to you because everybody will have a different view of the financial condition that will be sufficient. As noted previously, vast disparities in perception and expectations are in evidence among people in the US and in other countries.

Bob and Tish Stone, whom you met in chapter 5, made a three-week trip to China in November 2007, and they returned home on Thanksgiving Eve. Their observance of Thanksgiving was like none other that they had ever experienced because of their fervent thanksgiving for the blessing of being born in the United States. They told about the poverty and unsanitary conditions in which most of the people of China live. However, they said the people were very courteous and friendly, except perhaps the motorists on the streets of the major cities. The hotel service personnel and shopkeepers were good ambassadors for China. They said that the trip was very worthwhile to learn firsthand about that vast country and to compare the striking differences between the US and China.

As a special feature of their excursion, the Stones spent the night in the home of a farmer and his family. This farm family lives in a very modest cottage, but it has a guest room upstairs where the Stones slept. However, most of the farm families live in tiny huts and work the government allocated one-sixth acre "farm." Tish said that the people were very hard working and frugal, but even then, they were malnourished and had very limited health care opportunities. She said that Americans who receive welfare would be considered middle class in China, and American retirees living on social security and with Medicare health insurance would be considered wealthy.

No doubt, the perception of wealth is relative, not only in contrasting a third world civilization to that of the United States, but there are vast disparities among the people of this blessed United States. As I indicated in chapter 1, the sharecropper farmer and the farm day-laborer view wealth much differently than a land-owner farmer and a small-town banker. We all have to define what wealth is to us or stated in more action-oriented terms, we have to set goals or a series of goals as we work toward the financial conditions that will satisfy each of us.

How much do you need to accumulate by various stages in your life in order to have sufficient financial resources at your time of retirement? People are living longer than even a decade ago, and a retiree could live twenty-five to thirty years after the customary retirement age of 65. Furthermore, many people are determined to retire early, and some workers are even forced to retire before normal retirement years. Therefore, your wealth-building goals should include provisions for a long life and plans for early retirement.

These plans should include a system for adding to your wealth during your retirement years in order to maintain your standard of living, cover the effects of inflation, and provide for any extraordinary expenses. I urge you to set goals that include increasing your wealth into your advanced senior years. This suggestion represents modern thinking by financial consultants because of the significant increase in the life expectancy of men and women during the last twenty years.

When I started in the investment consulting business in the mid 1980s, we used a simple formula to allocate money among stocks, bond, and cash for seniors. We subtracted the age of the client from 100, and the result was the percentage of a client's portfolio that we allocated to common stocks. The remainder usually was devoted to bonds and money market funds. Therefore, a seventy-year-old retiree would have had only 30 percent allocated to stocks.

These days, I might allocate 50 percent of that portfolio to stocks, although the stocks are usually dividend paying and are securities of the finest blue chip companies in the US. Also, the seniors need their portfolios actively managed, and in that regard, I buy undervalued stocks and sell them as they get overvalued or under-perform. I plan to grow that senior's portfolio for the rest of his life, and you should devote a portion of your portfolio to growth for as long as you can do the homework that I am going to show you.

I recommend that you consult a fee-based, certified financial planner to review your life insurance and long-term health care program. You might also want to get his or her ideas about your investments also, but you should be in charge of your investment goals and portfolio management. Financial planners who charge for their time and do not sell products usually develop a portfolio of mutual funds for their clients. I use individual stocks to build a portfolio for a client, and you should consider doing likewise.

As you set your investment goals, you undoubtedly will arrive at your definition of wealth. Your definition of wealth and your net worth goal should be private matters between you, your spouse, and God. These goals that you set grow out of the vision that you feel God gives you, and your vision might differ from the recommendations from your financial planner. Your financial planner will produce for you a financial plan, based on your salary and a modest return on your monthly investment. In addition, he or she will make recommendations for life insurance and long-term care insurance, but your vision likely will exceed the modest goals in your financial plan.

As you determine your investment goals, on one hand you will look at what is reasonable to expect based on your income, current age, and modest investment return as reported in your financial plan. On the other hand, you will begin to dream about what you would like to do in the kingdom and where you need to be financially to be able to achieve these spiritual and financial goals. The two goals will blend together in your mind and soul, and you will be able to produce a vision of the wealth that you will set about to realize. You should bring this proposition before the Lord in prayer to make sure that you have followed His leadership in setting these goals and the benchmarks to use in assessing your progress over the years.

Continue your stewardship plan and constantly seek to grow closer to God and to be more like Christ, as will be evidenced by your diligence, humility, and discretion. You will be amazed at how God will work in your life and how He will prosper you. In all probability, God will redirect your income earning capability, possibly by setting you up in a business or making it possible for additional education, such as a study for a professional certification or a degree or advanced degree. Whatever your age or financial condition in life, God has a plan to make you more like His only Son, Jesus Christ, and He has a plan to prosper you.

Defining Wealth

Simply stated, the age-old definition of personal wealth in the United States is a net worth of $1 million. Of course, net worth is defined as total assets minus total debt. Millionaires were in this country long before there was a United States. There is evidence of large fortunes even in the English colonies among planters, shippers, and manufacturers. But after the Civil War, the number of millionaires increased dramatically, with large fortunes made in industrial sectors and banking. On Jekyll Island off the coast of my native Georgia, a winter sanctuary operated in the late 1800s and early 1900s called the Millionaires' Club. Legendary tycoons such as J.P. Morgan, Joseph Pulitzer, Marshall Field, William Rockefeller, and Cornelius Vanderbilt were a few of the barons of industry and banking who spent the winter months on this barrier island, no doubt planning their next enterprises.

Of course, these tycoons were worth more than a million dollars, but in the minds of those on Main Street, everybody then and now who is worth $1 million is assigned to the wealthy category. Although that amount today was equivalent to about $50,000 in Cornelius Vanderbilt's day, millionaire is still the venerable title much sought after by most Americans. Net worth of $1 million is a reasonable goal and an exalted measure of wealth, particularly for someone who has not yet accumulated a six-figure net worth.

As you set your goals, I recommend that you refine the net worth definition and subtract depreciating assets from you calculations. Motor vehicles of land, water, and air and household furniture should be deducted, but art and other valuable collectibles should be included. The value of depreciating assets is hard to appraise, and my experience has been that people far overestimate the worth of these items on the secondhand market. If you insist on listing these, use a wholesale price and not an asking price.

Stanley and Danko in their book, *The Millionaire Next Door,* devote a few pages to defining wealth. They do not include "material possessions," including the main residence, in their calculations of net worth. They define wealth in terms of a net-worth range of $1 million to $10 million, "because this level of wealth can be attained in one generation. It can be attained by many Americans." However, the authors exclude trust fund principle and the income collected from trust funds or other instruments of inheritance from their calculations of net worth. [1]

Stanley and Danko also have a unique way to determine a relative measure of wealth based on age and income. They say to "multiple your age times your realized pretax household income from all sources except inheritances. Divide (that amount) by ten. This less any inherited wealth is what your net worth should be," to be considered wealthy at any age. [2] I like including your spouse's income in this calculation and reporting as a family, but I question the exclusion of income from inherited assets, since this would be a reliable portion of your annual income to be spent or saved as you determine.

Also, I question not referencing the cost of living in these calculations, particularly if your primary residence is left out of the calculations. I recommend that you consider the cost of real estate where you live in your goal-setting process. Does your salary cover any premium that you have to pay for a residence in your region of the country, or do you and your spouse have to maintain two residences if your jobs place you in different locations?

The authors do make a good point that your ability to accumulate wealth from salary and smart investing are the most important factors in determining what should be your net worth now. If you have a shortfall between your current net worth now and where you should be according to this formula, the difference should be your near-term to intermediate-term goal. [3]

Let us work through an example of Stanley and Danko's formula for defining wealth as net worth at any time in your life. A forty-five-year-old person with a family income of $90,000 a year would project a net worth of $405,000 (45 X 90,000 = 4,050,000/10). [4] As you see, the equity in your primary residence is not included in this calculation, which makes good sense to me. You have to have a place to live, and it is not likely that you would convert the home into cash to live on, unless you are in advanced years and were to move to assisted living.

However, you could make the case that your payments on your home are reducing your ability to accumulated savings from your salary; therefore, the residence is an investment and should be included in the calculation. I cannot argue with that reasoning, so make your calculations as you wish. I am only giving you ideas about relevant calculations as you think through your net worth goals.

One more point that Stanley and Danko make repeatedly about what defines the person or people setting goals for their wealth building is that wealth accumulators are very frugal, and they do not buy "showy" items that are normally associated with high net worth individuals.[5] Basically, the formula is simple in my way of thinking: people who build wealth must save from their joint incomes and put that money to work in appreciating assets like real estate, common stocks, and/or a private business.

A great deal of wealthy people have practiced extraordinary frugality in their wealth building. James E. Stowers Jr. and his wife, Virginia, of Kansas City are two such people. Jim Stowers is the founder of 20th Century mutual funds, renamed American Century in 2000. The Stowers story is chronicled in his book, *Yes, You Can Achieve Financial Independence* (2000). Stowers tells of what he and Virginia did to save money to invest and to build a business. My favorite of those is his using a razor blade in his shaver much longer than normal in order to save $22.50 a month to contribute to their investment pool. Frugality and setting investment goals were the Stowers' secrets for building wealth.[6] Incidentally, the Stowers are also very generous people now and have been throughout their lives. In this decade, they have donated over $1 billion, mainly to the Stowers Institute for Medical Research in Kansas City.

My definition of wealth is relative to your individual household, the cost of living in your location, and the lifestyle of your household. Wealth is the value of your liquid assets that can sustain your standard of living and old-age needs if you were to retire or otherwise discontinue your salary today. The liquid assets should include also valuable investment property that can be easily converted into cash. This definition is not perfect, but it does contain the basic elements for a comfortable and financially secure life.

Does this definition address your most fundamental financial goal? This interpretation allows for personal decisions now and in the future regarding living standards, which includes where you live and your cost of living. If you live in some counties in California or major metropolitan areas, for example, you will have to cover higher property taxes and upkeep of your expensive primary residence. As another example, if you desire a new car every two years, your net worth goal must allow for this.

Just to show you a real example of my definition of wealth, my parents would have been wealthy according to my definition of wealth. Here is their background. Mother died in 2004 within three weeks of her ninety-third birthday, and Dad died in 2005 at age ninety-six. They lived until death in their own home, with twenty-four-hour care the last two years of Dad's life, and prior to that, regular daytime in-home care.

Their home was a very modest three bedroom, two bath ranch style house that they bought and paid cash for at retirement in 1974. In the last thirty years, they drove a Buick or Oldsmobile sedan, which they bought new every six years. During their retirement years, they went out to eat in very modest restaurants a couple of evenings a week and for Sunday lunch. Obviously, they did not need a large cash flow each month, but they were comfortable and did not sacrifice for anything they wanted.

My parents were very disciplined and steady folks. They started tithing at church early in their married life, which began in 1932 in the midst of the Great Depression and soon after the stock market crash in 1929. My father worked in a textile mill for a while and operated a barber shop to get through the Depression. About the time I was born, he began selling life insurance and moved up quickly with American National Life. Mother did not work outside the home. In 1948, after serving as a lay minister for a few years, he accepted the call into full-time ministry and served as a pastor until his retirement in 1974.

In all his years in ministry, he never made more than $14,000 a year, and even then that salary was not earned until the 1970s. Granted, they lived in church-owned houses for just over twenty years. Of course, in 2008 money, his top salary would have been less than $50,000 a year. Their keys to building wealth were being steadfast stewards, everlastingly grateful to God, frugal, and disciplined in their planning and savings.

My father was twice-removed Scot-Irish, and he and mother were the most frugal people I have ever known. They were ample evidence that Scots have a frugality gene imbedded in their Celtic physiology. But they dressed in style, entertained guests often in their home, and always drove a nice car. When I was living at home as a teenager, I never felt that my father's income was lower middle class. They paid for my college education without borrowing a dime, but with some scholarship help in my senior year. Here is the key to their wealth accumulation: they saved some money each month, "socking" their cash away in certificates of deposit at different banks to qualify each CD for FDIC insurance.

Their choice for accumulating wealth was too conservative for me, but this no-risk practice was typical of people who lived through the financial calamities of 1929-39. Nevertheless, I was amazed to discover the amount of money they accumulated and the interest they received when my wife and I had to take over writing their checks about three years before dad died. Their strategy had been to add money each month to savings, reinvest the interest each quarter before they retired, and let compounding build their wealth. Their standard of living before and in retirement was simple, but they were comfortable. They never changed their lifestyle in retirement, except they went out to eat more often.

If they had retired to the west coast of Florida, they would not have fit my definition of wealthy. They would have paid more for a house than their home sale in Georgia would have brought, and their property taxes and living expenses no doubt would have eroded their comfortable monthly cash flow. They planned for what they wanted in retirement and home health care in old age, and with God's blessings, they realized their vision of retirement comfort and remaining in their home for their entire lives.

In this commentary, I simply have intended to give you ideas and a few challenges for your consideration as you write your vision for the future and your financial goals. Also, let me add, you are probably more affluent now than you think, particularly if you have been frugal over the years, own your own home that requires minimal upkeep, and are investing 10-15 percent each pay period in a company 401(k) plan or investing the allowed limit in family IRAs.

Here is what you should do when you finish reading this book and taking further steps that I recommend. Write your definition of what is wealth for you. Next, determine your specific financial goals, write each goal in detail, and have both spouses sign each goal. Then write a plan for how you are going to achieve each goal. Lastly, send me a note every five years detailing your progress toward your wealth-building goals.

Setting Goals

When you are determining your financial goals, you certainly need to start by being realistic about what you can accumulate and then work through the next phase of your planning based on your vision. You must follow the dream (vision) that God has given you, and my experience is that His vision will not allow you to be too conservative. Certainly, you do not want to plan to just "sock" money away in certificate of deposits as my parents did, no disrespect intended to them.

You need to take advantage of the growth of corporate America and buy shares of common stocks in good companies that have excellent growth prospects for the future. Study past stock market trends and understand the historical returns of stocks in the last 100 years. Study the economy and understand about interest rates, money supply, and a few other basics of economics. That is just a little shameless promotion for chapters 7-10 in which I instruct you in all you really need to know about building wealth.

Another reason for not being fearfully conservative is that you are in this enterprise with your heavenly Father because you have prayed and asked for a vision or plan from God for what He wants for you in ministry and finances. Therefore, refresh that part of your goal setting and write down what you feel like God is saying to you. You certainly may not have an actual vision like the one Jacob did in the Old Testament, and you might not hear an audible voice from God as Moses did. However, you eventually will have an inspiration that will come to you in the form of a thought, or you will hear a story that will spark a dream or hope in your spirit.

Ron Blue in his book, *Master Your Money,* outlined the goal-setting steps two decades ago that are still pertinent, and I quote:
• Spend time with God.

- Record your impressions [about what He seems to be saying to you].
- Make your goals measurable.
- Take action at the appropriate time[7]

Ron Blue set the course very poignantly:

You do not test God by dreaming up goals; that is why the process of setting the goal is so important. When you spend time with Him, you receive assurance and conviction that this is what He would have you do. Therefore, resources are of no concern. They are God's responsibility. You do not set the goal and then go to Him asking for the resources. You let Him speak to you and develop the goal, and then you trust Him for the resources. [8]

This quote nails the reason that I unabashedly claim that Christians may seek to build wealth. If Christians satisfy the biblical priorities, God will supply the resources in abundance to bring to fruition the vision that He gives us to accomplish His mission and to bless us. Delilah, the nationally syndicated radio host, says, "God gives us big dreams so we can grow into them."

You may need to establish several goals for your selected time periods or target dates. This series of goals and the commentary that you use to define your goals and measurable benchmarks evolve into your investment plan. For example, you might define wealth as $1 million of liquid assets. Then you should prepare a net worth statement of your liquid assets held by you and your spouse. You might have a net worth statement of liquid assets that looks like this when you are forty years old and your spouse is age thirty-eight.

$1,500	checking account
4,500	bank money market account earning interest
45,000	your IRA/401(k) plan
24,000	spouse's IRA/401(k) plan
8,000	(200) shares of a local bank stock
20,000	investment portfolio
$103,000	total liquid assets

You then decide that your long-term goal is to increase your investment portfolio to $1 million before you retire. Next, establish benchmarks or sub-goals for every period of five years to use as measurable goals against which you can assess your progress. Another goal that you might establish is to be a good steward of the profits that you make on your investment portfolio. Therefore, you state that you will tithe to your local church and other ministries on the capital gains that you realize from the sale of stocks during the lifetime of the portfolio. Also, you pledge another 5 percent for offerings to charities from your realized capital gains and dividends over the lifetime of your investment portfolio. You might choose neglected and abused children as your ministry.

Make a list of the prospective charities and programs that you will support, which might include a children's home, CASA, and an orphanage in a war zone. These entries form the essential elements in your investment plan, which is probably not going to be more than two type-written, double-spaced pages. However, you might want to include some unique elements for your family.

In my situation, I included a few items about my business with regard to client total assets under management and a statement regarding the fee structure that I adopted for ministers, teachers, elderly citizens, public servants, and clients with at least five years as a client. I also pledged to help clients with small investment accounts. If you own a business or have control of policy-making in your profession, I encourage you to include goals and pledges for churches and charities in your investment planning. The most important element in all this is to write your investment goals and set quantifiable benchmarks for selected time periods.

Quantifying Goals

Translating the vision that God has given you into quantifiable goals, which you can use to measure your progress over the years, will require some research. Many people freeze when someone mentions research, but the Internet has made information available to the individual investor that a decade ago only the professional money manager and financial planner could buy. Now numerous websites allow you to test various investment strategies. Go to Google and conduct a search for *investment calculators* and check out the plethora of offerings available, most of which are free. Look for a financial calculator that allows you to test various strategies. You will need an (1) Investment Goals Calculator, (2) Investment Distribution Calculator, and (3) Asset Allocation Model.

Your investment goals calculator should allow you to establish a hypothetical goal and to produce projections of future valuations of your portfolio based on various rates of return that are compounded, years required for accumulation of assets, periodic contributions required to meet your goal, and any initial investment that you might have. Your withdrawal calculations will need to establish the number of years and the amount of monthly withdrawals that you can make from the accumulated assets in your portfolio. Also, you will need to project your total payout over your lifetime factoring in future capital gains in your investments throughout the life of your portfolio.

The final application in quantifying your goals is to set targets for the percentages of money to invest in a diversified portfolio of stocks, bonds, and cash. Incidentally, cash is any stable-value asset, such as 30-day Treasury Bills or money market accounts that maintain a steady $1.00 a share value. This asset breakout of your investments is called *asset allocation*, and it is a method of spreading risk over at least three different asset classes, each reacting differently to economic and market conditions from the others in the portfolio.

The interactions among assets in a portfolio can be measured, and it has been established that you have diversification when the components, in most cases stocks, bonds, and cash, correlate negatively or do not correlate highly with each other. For example, when stocks are going down in a poor economy, bonds will likely increase in price, and cash will retain a stable value. I will describe more about asset allocation in chapter 7, but for now, I need to introduce the concept because it is strategic in your setting quantifiable goals for your portfolio performance during various time spans.

I have searched the Internet for websites that are free and are easy to use, and I recommend www.dinkytown.net calculators. This is the most uncluttered and easy-to-use site that I reviewed. There are hundreds of sites sponsored by mutual funds, banks, and others who have something to sell, but each site is so cluttered that it is a nuisance to navigate, not to mention that you can get bombarded with spam mail from these vendors who capture your URL. Simply log on to the site that I have recommended and then click on Investments under Categories in the left panel. This will open a page of fourteen calculators, including the three essential modes that I mentioned above: investment goals, investment distribution, and asset allocation.

Investment Goals Calculations: The first step is to review the several rates or return and accumulation periods that you want to use in determining an investment goal for your portfolio. This Investment Goals Calculator will allow you to review as many rates of return and accumulation periods as you wish. Listed below are projected ending values for rates of return of 8, 10, and 12 percent and 20 and 25 years of asset accumulation based on an initial investment of $20,000 and $1,500 a quarter.

Table 6-1. Investment Value Projection

Rate of Return	Years of Accumulation	Projected Value
8%	20	$375,896
10	20	490,831
12	20	644,235
8	25	588,553
10	25	828,465
12	25	1,175,155

These accumulation periods and projected values are based on contributions of $1,500 each quarter, but you will be able to improve your return over time by simply contributing $500 a month. Of course, if you invest more money, the years of accumulation can be reduced significantly because of the effect of compounding contributions.

Investment Distributions Calculator: The second step in quantifying your investment goal is to run a few screens of the investment distributions calculator, which will provide you with the amount that you will be able to draw monthly, quarterly, or annually from the amount that you select as your investment goal. Remember to estimate a percentage of return during the withdrawal years to allow you to increase your withdrawal to keep up with inflation. I developed several withdrawal schedules and used an average annual return of 6 percent and an average inflation rate of 3 percent.

Listed as follows are the monthly withdrawal amounts for the several goals presented in Table 6-1, and I have included a column devoted to the beginning amount you could withdraw, if you elect to increase your withdrawal each year by the 3 percent average inflation.

Table 6-2. Withdrawal Projections
With and Without Adjustment for Inflation

Yrs of Distrib.	Starting Value	W/D Not Adj.	W/D Adjusted
20	$ 375,896	$ 2,646	$ 2,084
20	490,831	3,455	2,721
20	644,235	4,535	3,572
25	588,553	3,717	2,783
25	828,465	5,232	3,918
25	1,175,155	7,422	5,557

Studying the distribution tables should move you a step closer to quantifying your investment goal(s). Of course, these starting values may not meet your needs in 20 to 25 years because the purchasing power of the starting value will be greatly reduced over the years due to inflation. Therefore, you might need to adjust your goal upward, which of course will require you to contribute more to your investment portfolio, realize a higher rate of return, or extend the contribution period.

Listed below is a table of the adjusted projected values necessary to approximate the purchasing power of 2008 dollar amounts. I have used a 3 percent inflation factor for 20 and 25 years to project future values required to approximate the current value. (Search Internet for Compound Value Interest Factor [CVIF]. Multiply factor for each year and inflation per cent by Investment Goals.)

Table 6-3. Investment Goals Adjusted for 3% Inflation

Accumulation Years	Investment Goals	Adjusted Goal for 3% Inflation/Year
20	$ 375,896	$ 678,868
20	490,831	886,441
20	644,235	1,163,488
25	588,553	1,232,430
25	828,465	1,734,806
25	1,175,155	2,460,775

I need to show you one additional item of information, and that is the effect that a significant lump-sum investment can have on your portfolio

over time. Remember the assumption that I made in setting up these examples is that you had $20,000 invested at the time that you established
your investment goals. In other words, the calculations that I gave you in
each of the above tables included the effect of a $20,000 lump sum invest-
ment. The lump sum might be a rainy day savings account, a rollover IRA,
an inheritance, or countless other possibilities. Also, the hypothetical ages
that I have used are forty and forty-five years, and the projected withdrawal
ages are sixty, sixty-five, and seventy years old. That $20,000 invested now
in a diversified portfolio of stocks, bonds, and interest-bearing cash, such as
a money market fund, can have a significant effect on your reaching your
investment goals. The following table shows the effect of the lump-sum investment and specifies the amount you would need to invest annually to
reach the adjusted-for-inflation goal.

Table 6-4. Effect of Lump Sum Investment on Annual Contribution

Adjusted Goal	Years of Accumulation	Rate of Return	Original $20,000 Grows over Years	Your Annual Contribution
$678,868	20	8%	$ 93,220	$ 12,798
886,441	20	10	134,540	13,128
1,163,488	20	12	192,920	13,470
1,232,430	25	8	136,960	14,985
1,734,806	25	10	216,680	15,437
2,460,775	25	12	340,000	15,906

These calculations assume that you make lump sum contributions at
the end of the year, but I recommend that you contribute at least quarterly.
Quarterly contributions take advantage of the fluctuations in stock prices
to lower your average share purchase price over time and add to the compounding effect of your contributions. You can determine the amount that
you need to contribute each year by dividing your goal for future accumulation by the compound-value interest factor for a one-dollar annuity
(CVIFA). Remember to subtract the compounded value of your original
$20,000 for each of the years of accumulation and rates of return to calcu-
late a revised investment goal for each periodic contribution.

Now go to the CVIFA table. (Remember to subtract the compounded
effect of your original $20,000 investment from your adjusted goal to get

your revised investment goal.) You can locate these tables by searching the Internet for CVIFA. When you find these tables, locate your rate of return goal across the top and then locate the number of years of accumulation under the year column on the left side. Where the year of accumulation intersects with the rate of return that you have chosen, you will find the factor that you need to divide into your projected investment goal. The result of this long division is your annual contribution goal.

An alternative method of estimating the amount that you will need to invest in order to reach your goal over the specified number of years is the Savings Calculator offered by MSN Money. Go to www.msn.com and click on Money. Click on Personal Finance on the Menu, then Savings & Debt, and finally, Savings Calculator. You will see the screens to input your criteria for years of accumulation and rate of return to achieve your goal. This program calculates a return based on quarterly compounding, which is typical of bank interest rates; therefore, these investment amounts will be less than the annual compounding effect that is typical of an investment portfolio.

Your annual contributions based on the listed rates of return assume that you will invest in a diversified portfolio of stocks, bonds, and cash and make no withdrawals over the accumulation period. I want to show you how much more of annual investment you will have to make if you choose to put your money only in certificates of deposit in order to achieve your inflation-adjusted goal. I have used the annual contributions required in a 5 percent certificate of deposit, which is the high end of the CD range in most economic cycles. Occasionally, you might get a higher CD if a bank has a special promotion, but you cannot count on a higher rate for the duration of your accumulation period. For the CD calculations below, I used the CVIF tables to calculate the growth of the original $20,000 at 5 percent annually and used the CVIFA to calculate the annual contribution and 5 percent interest for each time period.

Table 6-5. Comparison of Required Contributions to Diversified Portfolio and CD to Reach Inflation Adjusted Goal

Inflation Adjust Goal	Accumulate Pd. in Yrs.	Div. Port. Return	Div. Portfolio Annual Cont.	5% CD Annual Cont.
$ 678,868	20	8%	$ 12,798	$ 18,926
886,441	20	10	13,128	25,204
1,163,488	20	12	13,470	33,582
1,232,430	25	8	14,985	24,404
1,734,806	25	10	15,437	34,930
2,460,775	25	12	15,906	50,142

Obviously, you will have to contribute significantly more to your CD than your diversified stock portfolio in order to reach your investment goal, which is a high price to pay for a modest reduction in risk. (See table 6-6 that follows.)

As you begin making contributions into your portfolio, you might have a struggle to invest $3,000-$4,000 each quarter, but over time as your salary or salaries increase, due to inflation and to your learning the tricks of saving money, you will find that your investment program will become easier. Of course, another way to make contributions is to designate a percentage of your income to invest, and the amount will grow over the years as your income increases. Other plans for making contributions include making a change in the invested amount every five years.

I recommend that you use the CVIF and CVIFA tables for a precise calculation for investment purposes. Again, I remind you that the tables in this chapter are just examples. Certainly, you might set lower goals or higher goals, but use the calculators to identify the numbers that will work for you. I remind you also that you are engaged in an enterprise that is fortified by biblical promises, and the One who makes these promises is looking for you to have faith in His promises and to lay the groundwork for Him to bless your effort.

This stretching yourself in setting your investment goals might ultimately lead to a significant change in your life spiritually and vocationally. God might lead you into a different work or otherwise change how you make your money. Nonetheless, the point is that this method of financial planning that I am recommending is not your ordinary fee-based planning methodology, not to minimize the professional planner's assistance, but you will have to persevere to establish your faith in financial matters that is outside the norm in professional planning. Do not be timid in these matters, but be bold and watch the hand of the Almighty move greatly on your behalf.

Investment Plan

After you have determined your goals and quantified them, you must develop an investment plan. This plan probably will be one type-written page or less, but it will address your goal and the various inputs for achieving your goal. If you are investing for retirement, you would need to address your various tax-sheltered investments and Social Security. Most people have a 401(k) plan or a form of an IRA; therefore, you should state in writing how you are going to invest each portion of your retirement program. If your goal is simply to realize $1 million by an age that you have determined, then your written plan will be something like this:

> *My wife and I seek to realize an inflation-adjusted amount of $1 million in our combined investment portfolios in addition to any retirement accounts that we own. We will invest in a diversified portfolio of stocks, bonds, and cash equivalents such as money market accounts and three- to six-month Treasury Bills. We will begin with a mix of these securities in the proportions recommended by an asset allocation program that sets the percentage mix. We will manage the investment portfolios using growth stocks of financially sound US companies and foreign stocks, US Treasury Notes and Bonds, corporate bonds of US companies, and high-grade cash equivalents.*

You might have other items that fit your investing style that you will learn from chapters 7-8. I will suspend further observations of the items that you might select to include in your investment plan, except to comment on your asset allocation percentages.

In your diversified portfolio, you probably will have stocks of large-cap, medium-cap, and small-cap companies. According to academic studies, different size companies in the mix spread the risk and enhance the growth potential. Of course, the word *cap* is the abbreviation for capitalization, and this figure is the result of multiplying the per share price of the company's stock by the shares outstanding, which is the number of shares held by investors.

Various stock research services rank the size of companies differently, but large-cap companies have huge numbers of shares to sell to the public, and the multiplied amount is usually $10 billion or more. Mid-cap companies usually have capitalizations between $1 billion and $10 billion. Small-cap companies usually have total shareholder capitalization of less than $1 billion. The reason for having each of these three-size companies in your portfolio is to take advantage of the unique contributions of small, medium, and large cap companies in a portfolio during various stages of the economic cycle.

Each type of company has its own cycle when it will outperform the other two types of stocks. Also, each size company has its own patterns of volatility: small-cap is usually the more volatile, demonstrating greater fluctuations in price than the other two. But over the years, small-cap stocks have outperformed large-cap stocks. Mid-cap is a good compromise between growth and stability in price fluctuations. The role of large-cap stocks is steady growth, dividend payments for total return, and reduced volatility.

Foreign stocks add to diversification because many times the economies of Europe, the Pacific Rim, and underdeveloped nations grow at different times from the economy of the US. Stated differently, when the US economy is in a recession, Europe and other counties might be still growing, and vice versa. This disconnect among economies has been the case in years past, but the investment world and the international economies have become more connected.

A higher correlation exists between domestic and foreign stocks at this time, and the trend is for greater correlation. Nevertheless, for now, let us continue with our plan by including foreign stocks as a component to add diversification to your portfolio. See chapters 7-8 for a further explanation of corporate capitalization and the role of each size stock in your portfolio.

Historically, stocks have outperformed corporate and government bonds, and bonds have outperformed US Treasury Bills (T-Bills) of twelve-months duration or less. Small-cap stocks have outperformed large-cap stocks, but with greater volatility. Listed below is a table that compares the average annual returns and relative volatility of the several types of securities, as published in *Stocks, Bonds, Bills and Inflation 2006 Yearbook,* compiled by the venerable Chicago investment research firm, Ibbotson Associates. The S & P 500 Index is the proxy for the large-cap (large-company) stocks, and a small company index is used as the proxy for the small-cap stocks. Therefore, average annual returns are based on a very large grouping of stocks in each asset class.

Unfortunately, you would not want to invest in some companies in these indexes. Selective stock-picking can improve your return, and hopefully, you will be able to select stocks that will give you a greater return as you perfect your application of the methods and strategies that I am going to show you in chapters 7-8. Nonetheless, let's look at the historical average returns, volatility (standard deviation) of each security, and the relationship between average annual return of a security class and its relative volatility.

Table 6-6. Asset Class Historical Returns and Ratios

Security	Avg. Annual Return	Standard Deviation	Relative Volatility	Ratio AAR/RV
Large Company Stocks	10.4%	20.2%	6.5	1.60
Small Company Stocks	12.6	32.9	10.6	1.19
Long-term Corporate Bonds	5.9	8.5	2.7	2.19
Long-term Government Bonds	5.5	9.2	3.0	1.83
Intermediate Government Bonds	5.3	5.7	1.8	2.94
US Treasury Bills	3.7	3.1	1.0	3.70
Inflation	3.0	4.3		

Source for Average Annual Return and Standard Deviation: *Stocks, Bonds, Bills and Inflation, 2006 Yearbook,* Ibbotson Associates, Chicago. Used by permission.[9] Relative Volatility and Ratio AAR/RV are the author's calculations.

Note: Standard Deviation (SD), a measure of risk, calculates the spread of readings of the index or other distribution from its arithmetic mean. The higher the standard deviation, the greater the risk. Relative Volatility compares securities' SD to the riskless T-Bill.

As you can see, small-cap stocks have an average return greater than any security, but they have a considerably greater relative volatility rating.

Based on a simple ratio of average annual return to relative volatility (AAR/RV), small-cap stocks have the lowest ratio of return to risk, and US Treasury Bills have the best return, historically, in relation to its volatility but barely cover the average inflation. In fact, sometimes Treasury Bills produce a negative return when measured against inflation, such as in 2008-09, when money market rates dropped almost to zero yield.

Table 6.6 shows that you will have to take on disproportionate risk in order to have a chance of reducing the time it will take to realize your investment goals. However, by mixing the percentage of investments in each security class, you can lower the risk and realize an optimum rate of return. Run your criteria in the Asset Allocator to see the model's recommendation for mixing security classes to seek the highest return with the lowest risk. Here is a chart of the Asset Allocation Model for thirty, forty, fifty, and sixty-five-year-old investors, including additions that the Asset Allocator made for mid-cap and foreign stocks.

Table 6-7. Asset Allocation Model by Selected Ages

Security Allocation Class	Allocation 30 Yr. Old	Allocation 40 Yr. Old	Allocation 50 Yr. Old	65 Yr. Old
Large-cap Stocks	32%	27%	25%	20%
Mid-cap Stocks	19	16	13	9
Small-cap Stocks	14	11	9	5
Foreign Stocks	14	14	12	9
Bonds	8	12	15	21
Cash Equivalents	13	20	26	36

One objective of the asset allocation model is to help preserve your portfolio value in bad times, which is based on the age-old principle: do not lose money in any year. If you keep from losing money in any year, you can afford to realize a smaller return from year to year. This model reduces the volatility of your portfolio according to your age and in relationship to the broader market, as measured by the S & P 500 Index. The principle is that over rolling five-year market cycles, you will make up for the weaker gains in up-markets in relationship to the S & P as your portfolio outperforms the S & P during down-markets. However, you may need to adjust your allocation at different times during a market cycle in order to improve your return, and I will explain these strategies in chapters 7-8. For now, this asset allocation model according to your age is a good place to start.

Conclusion

In order to build wealth, you will have to organize your effort and conduct research as you establish and implement a strategy to realize your vision over the remainder of your life. If you have prepared yourself spiritually and have sought God's guidance in financial matters, He has given you a vision of what He has in store for you. As often as not, you may have to carry your vision in your heart and mind for many months between receiving the vision about your future and the revelation of the next steps. However, do not despair; God is faithful, and He will deliver (see Habakkuk 2:3). Some days you might be preoccupied with the vision, and you will catch yourself mumbling a prayer or having a discussion with God about "whence and whither" from here, Lord. You will find that these are cherished moments because you will feel very close to God, and you can imagine His enjoying the fellowship with you on these matters. Just picture Him as getting as much out of this as you are.

One reason that God put us on earth, established the institution of work, and gives us these dreams that require work and consequently discussions with Him is for His enjoyment. He loves a business/financial partnership, and you could not have a better associate. But you will get more out of the relationship if you can see God as enjoying working with you and see yourself as fulfilling your purpose in life as you fellowship with your Business Partner.

As you seek God's direction to fulfill the vision, He will reveal the next steps, in His own time and according to His perfect order. Your job will be over time to give form to the vision by defining what wealth is to you and writing goals to make specific your long-term plan. Quantify your goals that will be sufficient to bring this vision to reality. Write everything in your secret notebook and let these goals begin to incubate in your mind, heart, and spirit; and then begin to implement your plans as God gives you direction and opportunity. In the next three chapters, I will provide instruction in how to approach the investment portion of your vision and show you how to invest using time-honored methods.

CHAPTER SEVEN

Wall Street Words and Wisdom

Every enterprise has its own terminology, measurements, and customs, and the investment group certainly is no exception. In fact, investors should know the language, measurements, and customs of investing completely before committing any money to the stock market. This is in contrast with learning piecemeal about other enterprises. For example, with my physician, computer technician, and mechanic, I can give them a glassy stare when they describe my illness, computer malfunction, or automobile breakdown; and they will go ahead and make the necessary repairs to my body, laptop, or SUV. But with my investments, I have to make more decisions than in most enterprises in which I function, and I had better make the right choices or I suffer irrecoverable losses.

The more I learn about the terms, measurements, and customs of my body, my computers, and my vehicles, the more I can participate in the discussion and even some decision making regarding necessary repairs and maintenance. After years of dumb questions and some reading, my tolerant physicians and mechanics at least have taught me the difference between cardiac defibrillators and catalytic converters. But if you are going to invest in stocks, do not plan to learn as you go. No doubt, you will be a more gifted investor with experience, but you need to identify and master the fundamentals of investing before you commit any money to stocks.

Some investors still rely exclusively on a broker or money manager to select stocks and otherwise manage their investments, and many investors rely on mutual funds. Even in these cases, investors should be knowledgeable of the language, measurements, and customs of Wall Street, a study which will help them tolerate the anxiety that is inevitable in the volatility of today's stock market. Most investors will not persevere in their investment program if they do not understand the basics of economics and investing.

To complicate matters, more and more investors are being forced to manage their investment programs because of the shift in the nature of corporate retirement programs. The 401(k) and the 403(b) programs require that the participating employees select the investments for their retirement program. While most retirement programs use mutual funds, these mutual funds are invested in stocks and bonds. The basics of one's retirement planning should focus on an understanding of the components (stocks) of the mutual funds in which they are invested.

If you can possibly do so, I recommend that you invest your entire investment program in common stocks and a few bonds and money market funds to satisfy your asset allocation plan. I much prefer to see you manage a well-diversified stock portfolio than to see you in several mutual funds. All investment recommendations from here on relate to common stocks.

Fortunately, in order to function in the investment world, you do not have to know everything about investing. You just need to know the terms, measurements, and customs that support your investment style and your investment strategies. My approach in the next three chapters is to focus only on what you really need to know in order to build wealth in your stock portfolio. You can contrast my approach to the experts and near-experts that traffic their wares on CNBC and the other financial programs. You can ignore everything that you hear on CNBC's *Fast Money* and a few other programs. I am not criticizing *Fast Money* or any other financial program, but I do not think that you need to know anything other than what I am going to teach you in order to build wealth in stock investing. Too much is presented in the media for you to learn, and it is confusing to try to absorb all you see and hear; therefore, minimize your frustration by focusing only on what you need to know in order to be a successful investor.

CNBC and other financial programs are good for news, ideas, and amusement but not good for learning how to invest. The same is true for *Money* magazine and other financial periodicals. All of these visual and written media focus on a multitude of opinions, methods, and strategies with little consistency in the messages among the experts. The same is true for trying to learn to play golf from *Golf* magazine. Every money manager and golf pro offers opinions, methods, and strategies from different backgrounds, styles, and techniques; and listening to or reading about different approaches is confusing as you perfect your own personal style and methods.

Let me illustrate my point. Because I am tall, I have learned that I should take golf lessons only from one golf pro that is over six feet tall. The average-height to short-in-stature pro does not fully understand the problems that tall golfers have with swaying and not properly pivoting away from the ball. Tall golf pros will spend a lot of time working with me to deal with the physique aspects of the game. Furthermore, and most important, one golf pro will teach a complete golfing system that links (excuse the pun) every aspect of the game and is consistent from day to day.

In the early days when I took up golf at the age of twenty-two, I did not want to spend the money on golf lessons. Instead, I searched for the best book on golf that I could find, and I settled on Ben Hogan's *Five Lessons: The Modern Fundamentals of Golf.* I bought the book because it was very thin and had large print. Of course, I recognized Ben Hogan as one of the all-time greats of the game, but the conciseness of it was the main reason that I bought the book. I felt like I could remember more of his lessons because he covered only what I needed to know to start playing and perfect my game.

You need a consistent investment style that links every aspect of your investment program, and it needs to be concise and focused. You do not need a complex scheme to be able to build wealth by investing in common stocks. Ben Graham, the legendary Columbia University professor and mentor to Warren Buffet and many other celebrated investors said, "People don't need extraordinary insight or intelligence [to build wealth]. What they need most is the character to adopt simple rules and stick with them." In keeping with that wise advice, I am going to show you all the vocabulary, measurements, and customs that you need to learn to be a successful investor and build wealth.

Wall Street Words

Here are the terms and concepts that you need to know in order to function effectively in the investment world. First, let me define how I use Wall Street. **Wall Street** is the term that represents the entire US investment community of professionals who are located from the namesake street in lower Manhattan in New York City to Manhattan, Kansas, and points beyond and in between. Brokers and securities dealers, investment advisers, investment researchers, and investment bankers are the main enterprises in the Wall Street community. The remaining terms you need to know are as follows:

- **Equity** is an accounting term that means the sum of money paid in by investors during the issuance of stock and the retained profits by corporations. Equity is also another term for stock.

- **Stock** is a unit of ownership of a corporation. New issues of stock are sold by corporations through investment bankers (broker/dealer firms) to raise money to enable the company to expand or otherwise develop its enterprise.

- **Debt** is simply the money borrowed by the corporation. Usually, this is in the issuance of bonds of different maturities to investors who wish to own dividend paying securities. These bonds are rated on investment quality by one of the rating services such as Standard and Poor's or Moody's. The sum of debt and equity form the capitalization of the corporation, which the company uses to generate revenue and make a profit.

- **Capital** is a corporation's debt, equity, and retained earnings.

- **Capitalization** (abbreviated **Cap**) includes common and preferred stock, corporate bonds, and retained earnings.

- **Capitalism** is an economic system that uses private (non-government) money to make money in business. In contrast with capitalism, socialism is defined by the central government owning all property and allowing only minimal personal assets.

- **Capital market** is where buyers and sellers of stock strike a deal. With original issues of stock, capital market applies to the process whereby investment banks raise money on behalf of corporations from the private sector (you and me) to finance private enterprise.

- **Investment banks** are large broker/dealer firms that underwrite new issuance of stock and then sell to the public.

- The **Securities and Exchange Commission (SEC)** operates to protect investors, maintain fair, orderly, and efficient markets, and to facilitate capital formation.

- **Private sector** or **private enterprise** means any non-government enterprise; however, corporations that register with the SEC to sell large issues of common stock to more than 100 private citizens is said to go "public." Corporations that sell shares to less than 100 individuals do not have to register with the SEC and remain private corporations, but their stock is not traded on the exchanges.

This private/public designation can be confusing, so let me attempt to clarify the matter. Corporations registered with and governed by the SEC are publicly traded companies, but they remain in the private sector. These companies are represented by stocks traded on the New York Stock Exchange and the automated system administered by the National Association of Securities Dealers (NASDAQ). We will focus on these publicly traded corporations as we develop a strategy for building wealth.

The Securities and Exchange Commission enforces corporate compliance with laws, rules, and regulations that have been established by Congress for the protection of investors. The SEC enforces corporate accounting standards and reporting regulations, which are the basis of investment analysis. Sometimes corporations are subject to SEC enforcement procedures ranging from simple restatement of earnings or accounting procedures adjustments to more serious penalties such as fines and sanctions.

In these cases, the company's stock price usually trades lower on the public announcement that the SEC is investigating the company because investors worry about added costs of doing business and a myriad of uncertainties that can result in future setbacks to the company.

• **Bull markets** and **bear markets** typically follow the economic cycles marked by protracted up and down moves, respectively, in the price of stocks as measured by the several market indexes, such as the Dow Jones Industrial Average (DJIA). For example, investors typically sell stocks when the economy looks like a recession is impending.

The most plausible explanation of how bull market and bear markets were introduced into our investment lexicon is from the early days of stock trading in eighteenth century London. The British brokers at the end of a trading day posted the trades on a BULLetin board outside of the trading establishment for all traders and interested parties to see. Brokers called their postings bulls. If the board was full of bulls, that was a bull day, but if the board was "bare," that was a bad day for traders.[1] I do not know how the animal symbols were added. Nevertheless, bull and bear markets of the twenty-first century have communicated the best and worst of conditions, although the bears had control mainly for the last ten years. The term *bullish* expresses optimism about the future for stocks, and *bearish*, pessimism.

• **Market sector** is one of ten groupings of industries that represent corporations that are in competition with each other. The Global Industry

Classification Standard lists twenty-four industry groups classified under one of ten sectors. (Search the Internet for GICS to see the complete sector and industry listings.)

• **Market rotation** is an investment strategy whereby investors sell some industries and buy others depending on their perception of the next big move in the economy and bull and bear markets. For example, when higher interest rates are anticipated, investors might sell bank, utility, and other stocks that are interest-rate sensitive. In these times, investors might then buy **blue chip** consumer staple stocks, which hold up well during recessions. **Blue chip** stocks are the most financially stable and well-managed corporations that normally sell a diversified group of products or services. For example, these companies make up the thirty stocks in the DJIA.

• **Growth, value, and momentum investing** are the three basic styles of investing. **Growth** investing is picking stocks whose earnings are growing substantially from year to year. Typically, these companies grow sales by developing and marketing new products or services, buying competing companies, and broadening their marketing target groups. Technology stocks and small and mid-cap companies are usually growth stocks. These companies might have higher price to earnings ratios than value stocks.

• **Value** stocks are usually bought for the value of their assets that can produce a combination of high dividends and slow and steady growth, although not nearly as high-growth as typical growth stocks. Value stocks typically have low price to earnings ratios and offer higher dividends than the Standard and Poor's 500 average. Banks and utilities are considered value stocks.

• **Momentum** investing says that a stock that is going up in price is likely to keep going up until acted on by some significant event, such as the appearance of a strong competitor. These stocks typically will have very high price to earnings ratios that will be disregarded by investors. Momentum stocks often are the province of traders who like to buy the dips and sell on any bad news, such as a penny shortfall below consensus earnings predictions. Technology stocks of the mid to late 1990s were the darlings of momentum players.

I have defined these three basic investment styles as if they were mutually exclusive, but actually, many investment **strategies** include features of each. For example, I like to buy growth stocks that are very much undervalued in relation to their historic price to earnings ratios. Some strategists call my style **growth at a reasonable price (GARP)**, which is a blend of growth and value. Frankly, I am not fond of these strategy labels, but I have included them in our discussion because you will see them many times as you conduct research in building your stock portfolio and even more so if you invest in mutual funds.

• **Asset allocation** is an investment strategy of apportioning investment money among several different asset classes such as stocks, bonds, and **cash equivalents**, which are ninety-day or less US Treasury bills. The objective is to spread the risk among assets that do not correlate highly with each other. For example, in a perfect negative correlation, if one asset class goes down in price, the others either go up or remain relatively stable. Asset allocation is one method of **diversification,** but to be adequately diversified, investors should select stocks that represent several industries in different market sectors. Large, medium, and small-cap stocks with different betas diversify further.

• **Beta** is a calculation of the volatility of a stock in comparison to the market in general as measured by a standard market index. A stock with 1.00 beta is in lock-step with the market, and a stock with a 1.50 beta is 50 percent more volatile than the market, and so on.

• **Earnings** are simply the profit of the company after all expenses and income taxes are paid. The common abbreviation for the smallest unit of earnings is **EPS,** earnings per share. **Revenue** represents the gross income to the company, and **sales** are the income from the distribution (selling) of goods and services only. Also, sales do not include dividends, interest, rents, and other revenue.

• **Cash flow** is sometimes used to analyze a company's net income instead of relying on EPS. Cash flow is the simplest form of reporting profits and is calculated from net profit (sales less expenses) plus depreciation. Cash flow is very much like the balance in your checkbook at the end of the month.

• **Earnings predictability** is a term reported by *Value Line* **(VL)** *Investment Survey,* the venerable stock research firm, which is a rating of VL's accuracy in predicting earnings. A 100 rating is a perfect prediction average, and a 50 is accuracy only one out of two times. **Financial strength** is a VL rating of the investment quality of a company based on the company's financial statements and other reports. VL rates from A++ (highest) to UR (unrated for poorest quality). I do not buy any stocks rated below B.

• **Intrinsic value or fair value** is a term used to address the value of a company based on its earnings or cash flow projections for years in the future and mathematically discounted back to the present value. I compare a stock's current price to its intrinsic value to make sure that I am not overpaying for the stock.

• **Cost basis** is an accounting term that simply means the total price you paid for all shares of a stock. It is best to keep the cost basis of each block of stock and the date of purchase in order to match your sales with the appropriate block of stock.

• **Tax loss selling** is done to reduce income tax liability during a given income tax year. As a strategy, if you have large profits that you have held at least one year, you might want to sell a loser to offset the gain if both are long-term holdings or both are short-term holdings.

The above defined terms form the vocabulary that you need to know to function successfully in selecting stocks, but there are still the measurements (ratios and calculations) and customs (economic and market maxims) that are essential to shaping your investment strategy and managing your money. I will address measurements first.

Wall Street Ratios and Calculations

The grandfather of all the measures of value of a stock is the **price-earnings ratio (PE),** whereby the earnings for the past four quarters, the projected four quarters, or a combination of the two are divided into the current price of the stock. Therefore, as the earnings go up, if the stock price trades in a close range, the PE will go down. If earnings continue to grow from quarter to quarter, a PE that goes down indicates improving valuation for the stock.

On the other hand, the PE of a rapidly growing company will go up because investors anticipate higher growth for many quarters in the future; therefore, they will buy the stock even as the PE escalates. Eventually, the PE (sometimes called the **multiple**) exceeds all reasonable expectations for earnings, and the number of buyers of the stock will decrease and sellers increase, and the stock will drop while the PE adjusts to a more normal level. This is what happened in the period 2000-2003, particularly with technology stocks. Keep an eye on the PE of the Standard & Poor's 500, which historically is around 15 but increases as a bull market roars ahead, and this average PE will give you a benchmark for determining an acceptable PE for the combined stocks in your portfolio. A **forward PE** simply means making the ratio calculation using the **projected earnings** of the next four quarters.

The **price/earnings to growth ratio (PEG)** is another calculation to use in assessing the valuation of a stock. Since the earnings growth of a company is so important in evaluating the investment worth of a company, the PEG has been popularized as a way to express this future value in relation to the current stock price. For example, if a stock is projected to grow 20 percent during the next four quarters, and it has a PE of 30, the PEG would be 1.5, but if the stock has a PE of 20, the PEG would be 1.0. The latter would be the better value, because you would pay less money per share for the growth of this stock. Investors who focus on PEGs like to buy stocks with PEGs below 1.00 and sell when PEGs rise to 2.00.

Relative value (RV) is simply a historical comparison of a stock's PE. Over the years, a stock will establish a PE range that will define the underpriced value and over-priced value of the stock. For example, a stock with a historical average PE of 20 and the current PE of 30 will have an RV of 150 percent. But if the current PE is 15, the RV will be 75 percent. I like to buy stocks that are priced at the low RV of 75 percent and sell at an RV of 150 percent.

Price to cash flow (P/CF) is normally lower than the PE, and many analysts like this number to evaluate a stock rather than the PE because the P/CF is less subject to company manipulation than are earnings. *Value Line* reports a cash flow multiple, and you can multiply this number by the current cash flow per share to determine if the current stock price is under, ahead, or in line with current cash flow. If the price is well ahead of the cash flow trend line, that is a good time to sell the stock because the price will correct back to in line eventually. If the price is below the trend line of the cash flow, that is a good time to buy because the price will increase eventually to normal along the cash flow line.

There are three financial ratios that I focus on when analyzing a company to determine its investment merit. **Debt to capitalization (D/C) or debt to equity (D/E)** are the most important ratios for determining financial strength in my analysis. **D/C** is the relationship between the company's long-term debt and the paid in capital by shareholders plus the long-term debt. **D/E** is the long-term debt divided by the shareholder equity.

(Shareholder equity includes the retained earnings held by the company.)

I use debt to capitalization because it is easy to determine from a page of *Value Line Investment Survey*. I look for a low debt to capitalization of 33 percent or less, which converts into about a 1:2 debt to equity ratio. The lower the debt per cent or higher the equity in the mix, the stronger financially the company will be in an economic downturn. If a company has little or no debt service, the company will be more likely to sustain itself during dire economic conditions as revenue and earnings fall than will a company with a heavy debt service.

Return on equity (ROE) is another powerful financial ratio, which is a calculation of the percent of annual net income compared to the total shareholder paid-in capital (equity). This is a good measure of the efficiency of the company and the effectiveness of the company management. I look for a minimum ROE of 15 percent with minimal year to year swings. I had rather see a consistent 15-20 percent annual ROE than a 10-30 percent figure.

I like to use ROE in combination with the company's **operating margin (OM),** which is the profit margin calculated on normal business activity. Operating margin does not include expenses for taxes, interest, and non-recurring activities such as buying or selling a subsidiary. The operating margins will vary for different industries, so you will have to do some work to find out the average **OM** for each industrial sector. On the other hand, a consistent ROE that exceeds 15 percent is a measurement of an efficient and effective company management.

There are several **technical** indicators that are useful in determining when to buy or sell a stock or in assessing the conditions of the entire stock market. Technical analysis is simply the measurements and calculations using price and volume fluctuations in contrast to **fundamental** analysis, which focuses on the business-related factors of a company, such as earnings and management, to assess the investment value of a company. Charts and **moving average (MA)** lines are the technical indicators that I use most often in the investment strategy that I will focus on in chapters 8 and 9.

A moving average is calculated by adding the most recent number to a sum of the numbers, and subtracting the oldest number and recalculating the average. I often use the 50-, 200-, and 400-day moving averages of the Standard and Poor's 500 Index as an indication of the trends of the stock market in general. Also, I use these same moving averages to calculate the trend of the price of an individual stock, and both the S & P and the individual stock moving averages can be presented in a chart with a moving average line showing the history of the particular MA.

The assumption in using these technical indicators is that collectively investors send a message about the market in general or an individual stock that is worth your consideration as you make buy/sell decisions during any given day of market trading. In effect, the MA is a continuous measurement of the combined knowledge and sentiment (emotions/confidence) of all investors in the stock market or in an individual stock. Even an investor who relies on fundamental analysis in stock selection and trading can enhance the performance of a portfolio by properly applying a few technical indicators in making buy/sell decisions.

McClellan Oscillator (MO) is a technical calculation based on the number of stocks advancing in price minus the number of stocks declining in price on the New York Stock Exchange and the NASDAQ. These daily calculations are represented in graphical form and a moving average of the daily calculations is plotted. The **MO** is used to assess whether stocks are **overbought,** in which the market has run up too far too fast, or **oversold,** in which the market has declined too far too fast in the recent past. The McClellan Oscillator is very helpful in deciding when to buy or sell a stock that is on your watch list. When the market is overbought, it is likely to have a sell-off for a brief period as stocks decline in price to adjust to new information about the economy or about corporate earnings revisions, for example, and this decline attracts new buyers.

When the market is oversold, it is likely to rally as new buyers come into the market and bid stock prices up. Therefore, if you want to unload a poor performing stock or raise cash to buy another stock, you might wait until the market rallies to an overbought position on the MO to sell. The reverse would be true for a stock that you are eager to buy but would like to buy at a lower price. I will detail this method further in chapters 8 and 9.

The best measurement for determining your asset allocation for stocks and fixed income is the **Comparison of the S & P 500 Earnings Yield to the Yield on the 10-Year US Treasury Note.** That may appear complicated but it is not, and I will show you the composition of the two indicators. The **earnings yield** is best defined as the earnings divided by the price of the stock or index then converted to a whole number (E/P X 100). The yield for the 10-year US Treasury is simply interest divided by the price of the Note multiplied by 100 (Interest/price X 100).

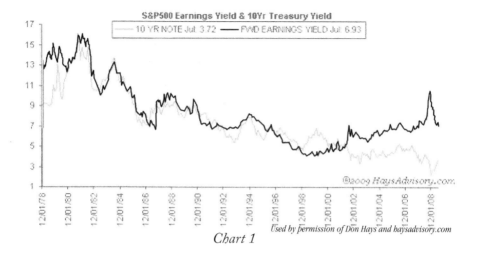

Chart 1

The two yields normally track each other (see Chart 1), but sometimes they separate as indicated for the years 2002-2008. Chart 1 demonstrates that stocks (black line) have better return prospects than fixed income (gray line). You can also compare the whole numbers as reported in the box of Chart 1. Earnings yield (stocks) is 6.93 compared to the yield on the 10-Year Treasury Note of 3.72; therefore, the prospects for stocks are much greater than fixed income. If interest rates (gray line) were to rise to above the earnings yield (black line), that relationship would be negative for stocks.

The forward earnings for the S & P 500 Index were $67.63 for July 2010 as projected by IBES (International Brokerage Estimating Service) (Chart 2). With that information, you can estimate the future value of the S & P 500 Index by dividing the current S & P 500 price (976.29) by the estimated earnings ($67.63), which will provide the current PE based on future estimated earnings. (976.29/67.63 = 14.44 PE). Now calculate the projected PE that will approximate the 3.72 percent yield on the UST Note (Chart 3) (1/3.72 X 100 = 26.88 PE). The PE will go up as the earnings yield goes down and vice versa.

Now multiply the estimated future PE (26.88) by the estimated forward earnings for the next twelve months ($67.63), and these figures calculate the estimated S & P 500 Index of 1,818 in twelve months from July 2009 (26.88 X 67.63 = 1,818). Of course, many conditions will affect stocks within that twelve-month period, which of course will affect the PE that the market is willing to pay for the earnings. So you can set a reasonable PE, such as 20, and multiply your selected PE by forward earnings ($67.63), and the results will be a reasonable expectation for the market return in twelve months.

The effect of these comparative calculations is that you gain more confidence in setting your asset allocation. In this case, the estimated PE of 20 times the forward earnings calculates to the S & P 500 Index of 1,353 by July 2010, which would be a 38.54 percent gain from the current 976.29.

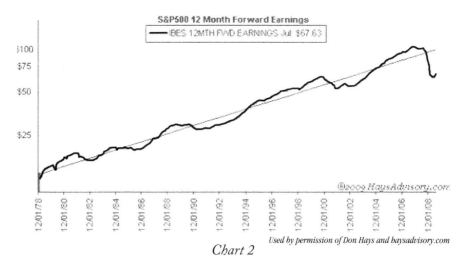

Used by permission of Don Hays and haysadvisory.com

Chart 2

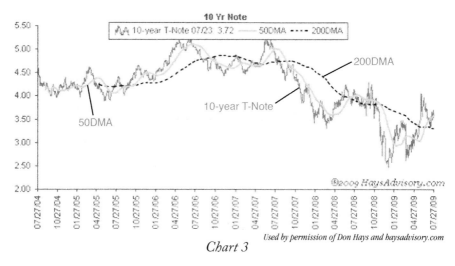

Used by permission of Don Hays and haysadvisory.com

Chart 3

You might be concerned about calculating these fundamental and technical indicators, but the good news is that you do not have to make any calculations. Publications and websites are available that calculate the technical and fundamental indicators that I have reviewed in this chapter. Go to www.zacks.com for the PEG. See www.bigcharts.com for the moving averages, and visit www.haysadvisory.com for the McClellan Oscillator and the Comparison of the S & P Earnings Yield and the 10-year UST Note yield. See *Value Line Investment Survey* for the price/earnings ratio, debt to capitalization ratio, return on equity, operating margin, and the price to cash flow line.

For calculating the RV, I recommend Toolkit 6 software. In addition, you can get projected earnings, earnings predictability, and financial strength from *Value Line*. You can find the intrinsic value from www.valuepro.net or www.diamond-hill.com (see the Financial Model page). *Value Line,* Toolkit 6 software, and www.haysadvisory.com will cost you some money, but zacks.com, valuepro.com, and diamond-hill.com are free. Additional research resources are included in chapters 8 and 9.

You can make several additional calculations that are very simple but can be very useful as you analyze a stock and compare with other stocks:

Earnings Yield (EY) calculated from the Current Price Earnings Ratio (P/E):
Current PE = 14.44
1/PE = EY X 100 (1/14.44 = .0693 X 100 = 6.93 percent)

Forward Earnings (Fwd EPS)(est.) calculated from Earnings Yield (EY):
Current EY = 6.93 percent
EY/100(Current Price or S & P 500 Index) = EPS
(6.93/100 = .0693 X 976.29 = 67.63)

Current Price Earnings Ratio (PE) from Earnings Yield (EY):
Current EY = 6.93 percent
1/EY= PE X 100 (1/6.93 = .1444 X 100 = 14.44 PE)

Fortunately, these calculations are available on several websites. Haysadvisory.com is the most comprehensive, but its annual subscription is $250. More on this subject later.

Customs and Practices

The US economy is fairly predictable because it is highly influenced by the monetary policy of the **Federal Reserve,** and consequently, the stock market is highly influenced by the Federal Reserve. For that reason, if you study and understand the Federal Reserve actions, you can stay ahead of the movements of the stock market in general or at least understand why stocks react significantly when the Federal Reserve raises or reduces interest rates and otherwise affects the money supply.

Since the US economy is estimated to be about $13.8 trillion a year, the swings from growth to recession and back to growth take many months to complete; however, the stock market anticipates these swings and moves well ahead of each move. Therefore, studying the Federal Reserve, the overall monetary policy of the US government, and the economy in general are well worth the effort for investors.

The **Federal Reserve (Fed)** is governed by a seven-member board appointed by the President, and the Board's **Open Market Committee (OMC),** also includes five Federal Reserve Bank presidents. The Fed OMC meets eight times a year to set monetary policy such as short-term interest rates: **Fed Funds** and the **Discount Rate.** Fed funds are cash reserves that member banks can loan overnight to each other, and the Fed sets the rates that banks in the Federal Reserve System can charge to each other. Discount Rate is the interest rate the Fed charges its member banks for loans. The changes in either of these rates up or down are strong indicators of the Fed's monetary policy for the future and the future rates, such as prime, that affect consumers, businesses, and investors.

Interest rate trends that are higher add to the cost of doing business by corporations and cost of living for consumers, all of which are negative for stock prices. When interest rates are lowered by the Fed, this act can reduce the cost of managing a business and a household, and as a result, lower interest rates are positive for stock prices.

The Federal Reserve OMC also influences the total money supply in the entire economy by selling and buying government securities to and from, respectively, its member banks. Selling securities in the banking system reduces the money supply to meet the borrowing demands of businesses and consumers; therefore, interest rates inch up until the demand for borrowing is significantly reduced. However, when interest rates inch up, investors start to buy certificates of deposit from local banks and interest-bearing instruments from securities brokers. Typically, the money to buy these low-risk, fixed income securities flows out of stocks and stock mutual funds. Money in checking and money market accounts usually rise also, in addition to funds added to certificates of deposit. This process raises the money supply, and it takes many months of Federal Reserve selling government securities to soak up the added money available to banks to buy government securities.

When the Fed wants to reverse its course of action and increase the money supply, the Federal Reserve starts buying government securities from the Federal Reserve Banks. This action provides more money for banks to lend, and usually, the Fed reduces short-term interest rates, which prompts major banks to lower their prime rate, and businesses and consumers ramp up their borrowing. Gradually, the economy heats up with all this renewed spending by business and consumers, and then the business cycle starts over.

Dr. Carole Scott, professor emeritus of economics at University of West Georgia, succinctly describes the Federal Reserves' impact on money supply, interest rates, and economic expansion. "The Fed reduces banks' reserves by selling them securities. This reduces their ability to lend. By adding to the supply of securities, the Fed lowers their prices. This and reducing how much banks can lend raises interests. Fed purchases have the reverse effect. The bond market is affected by interest rates. Investors move between stock and bond markets; so what happens in one of them affects the other." Of course, fluctuations in interest rates affect consumers and businesses. "If goods' prices rise more rapidly than do wages, real wages—the real cost of labor—decline. This lowers the unemployment rate and raises profits; so the economy expands. If the reverse takes place, the effect is the reverse. So the relationship between rising prices of goods and wages is very important."

Keeping alert to monetary policy of the Fed, such as the Fed funds rate and discount rate and the money supply reflected in local bank rates offered for CD's, can help investors make judgments about the future allocations to stock positions in their portfolios (see www. Federalreserve.gov/fomc).

When the Federal Reserve keeps interest rates high, over a period of time such as twenty-four months, the economy slows significantly. Unemployment goes up, consumer spending and confidence go down, and corporate earnings are reduced. If business slows for an extended period of time, deflation occurs and prices for products and services are reduced or level off.

In the 2000-2002 period, even modest attempts to increase prices were met with consumer resistance, and companies had to restore prices to a lower level. This economic condition is deflationary, and a protracted period of reduced or level prices would result in little or no salary increases for workers. Jobs usually are reduced and depressed economic conditions snowball. The economic deflation of 1929-34 was so bad that officially it was termed a depression, and history books now refer to the period as the Great Depression. Depressed prices occur in each economic slowdown and unemployment spikes.However, general economic depression is quite rare, although the recession of 2007-2009 was termed by a few observers as a depression. Nonetheless, recessions occur at the end of most business cycles, and these economic downturns seem to repeat every four to five years. These cyclical downturns are what investors need to be able to anticipate.

The **yield curve** is an excellent means of depicting Fed policy. When Fed policy is accommodating, the interest rate yield will slope up and to the right on a chart showing the relationship between interest rates and maturities, with higher rates on longer maturities. When short-term rates are higher than long-term rates, the yield curve is inverted. An **inverted yield curve** historically is a precursor to recession twelve months in the future.

Recession is a period of decline in the economy, and varying definitions by economists and federal bureaus quantify the percent and duration of these declines. The common definition of recession is a period of two or more quarters of zero or negative growth in the **Gross Domestic Product (GDP).** The GDP is the annualized output of goods and services in the economy as measured on standard indicators that are proxies for the overall economic activity in the US. Recessions occur in large measure as a result of the Federal Reserve raising interest rates over a period of time to slow down business activity in order to head off inflation. Turning the $13.8 trillion US economy without over-stimulating or under-stimulating the overall commerce of the nation is almost impossible.

Inflation is a function of supply and demand in the price of goods and services. As the economy grows, businesses and consumers buy additional goods and services until demand is greater than the supply or availability of such products or services. Typically, unemployment is reduced during a growing economy, and more wage-earners with increased salaries buy more

174

merchandise and services. Therefore, demand stimulates price growth. Inflation typically pushes bank interest rates higher because more money is in demand than is available to borrowers. Mild inflation is not entirely bad for the economy. Inflation growth of 3 percent or less is usually absorbed easily by the economy, and then interest rates will stay in check around 3 percent or slightly more on short-term Fed funds. Inflation and interest rates over 3 percent affect negatively the economy, stock prices, and fixed income securities. The effect is compounded when inflation and interest rates move up significantly from much lower percentages.

The negative effect on stocks is because of the anticipated added costs to business. The effect on fixed income securities is that investors will demand higher bond yields on new issues in the US Treasury auction to be compatible with Fed policy. Also, old bonds and preferred stocks will have to compete with new issues that will offer higher rates and in some cases higher quality securities. Therefore, existing bonds and preferred stocks suffer lower market prices to provide for increased yields.

Inflation is a major key to the health of the economy, and of course, the health of the economy is a major factor in the health of the stock market. Early signs of rising or falling inflation can be determined by the changes in the **Consumer Price Index (CPI)** and the **Producer Price Index (PPI),** which are keyed to changes in prices over a benchmark year. The **CPI** is a retail index measuring the cost of living, and the **PPI** measures the wholesale price of production.

Business cycle is the economic period marked by "feast to famine." During times of low rates of inflation and interest rates, business flourishes; but business turns down when inflation and interest rates escalate. This is a **cyclical** trend. By contrast, secular trends in business and the stock market are long-term trends that are established over numerous business cycles.

Summary and Conclusions

The vocabulary, measurements, and economic and Wall Street practices that I have outlined are all you need to understand in order to invest profitably in common stocks traded in the US. If you are new to investing, you will need to study and practice using these concepts until you are very comfortable with the contents of this chapter.

If you need further elaboration on some of these concepts, use your favorite web search engine and identify further resources for study, but do not take any side trips that introduce concepts beyond our focus. If you are an experienced investor, this chapter might simply be a review, but my doctrine of narrowing your focus and mastering the details might improve your return and settle your emotions during stock market crises.

I have attempted to be concise in this chapter to facilitate your understanding as we narrow our focus in succeeding chapters on the specifics of buying and selling stocks, and managing a portfolio that is diversified among at least three asset classes: stocks, bonds, and cash. Too many potential investors get discouraged reading or hearing in the media the myriad of economic and market related details that in the end many times are useless. Even experienced investors get caught up trying to understand and some even making decisions to buy and sell on information that may be flawed, irrelevant after a short-time, or just inconsequential for long-term investors. Remember, much of what you hear or read regarding common stocks is for short-term trading or for the best interest of the analyst. I get amused occasionally watching some of the TV investment debates or discussion that is irrelevant long-term. Some evidence suggests that TV producers are scrambling for a "timely" show that day that will attract and hold investors, and they project enthusiasm about issues that are really just the natural course of market swings. It is too bland to say, "This is no big deal, but here is what the market is doing today." Do not get caught up in this excitement (even the euphoria) and panic of merry-go-round TV stock and market analysts and the program personalities.

If you are going to listen to anyone, I recommend *The Kudlow Report* show on CNBC at 7:00 p.m. (ET), Monday through Friday. Lawrence Kudlow has a Ph.D. in economics, and takes a conservative view of market swings and government intervention in commerce. I also recommend Dave Ramsey's radio and television shows. Mr. Ramsey takes care of individual investors. However, at all times, follow your tightly-focused investment discipline such as I have outlined here. Chapter 7 is an attempt to get you ready to narrow the focus even further as we discuss the details of my recommended investment discipline that follows in the remaining chapters.

CHAPTER EIGHT

Selecting Stocks and Managing a Portfolio

Sir John Templeton, founder of the Templeton funds, said to buy stocks at the price that reflects the maximum pessimism about the company and the economy, and sell stocks at the price of maximum optimism. The short and sweet version is buy low and sell high. Of course, stock prices do not fall to the buy range unless there is something pessimistic about the company, the company's stock sector, or the market in general. Likewise, stocks do not rise in price unless there is generally investor optimism about the company, the company's stock sector, or the market in general.

Investor sentiment moves the market; sometimes the sentiment is rational, based on sound investment fundamentals, and sometimes the sentiment is irrational and just fed by emotion for a relatively short-term. However, for whatever reason, stock prices move in cycles from maximum pessimism to maximum optimism, and John Templeton's mantra should be a rule of investing: move in and out of stocks at the extremes of price swings. The challenge is to determine when the low point is in the sentiment about the stock and when is the high point that characterizes the extreme in investor optimism.

The secret to meeting the challenge is to develop a thorough system of selecting stocks and managing your portfolio. Your system should tell you when investors have sold off a good company and when they are too enthusiastic about the future of a stock that has had a sudden appreciation in price but has poor fundamentals.

I am going to show you in this chapter my system for selecting and selling stocks. The system begins with identifying research tools that will become the basis for your economic and market assessment, stock analysis, and portfolio management. The process begins with determining the most useful research tools that you can use or buy that will be either free or modestly priced.

Research Sources

In order to use the best research and to track your portfolio, you will need to spend a little money each year. I have selected resources that will allow you to invest like a professional by spending about $1,000 a year, but you can subscribe to most sources on a trial basis for a fraction of the annual fee. Also, included in my recommendations are several free websites that are just as good as similar expensive sources. The research tools can be grouped under one of three main headings: market strategy, stock analysis, and portfolio management.

Market strategy simply means an analysis of the economy and current investment conditions in addition to projections for the economy and the stock market. This is the top-down approach, which is the practice of looking at the overall economy and the trend of the stock market as reflected in the major indexes, like the Standard & Poor's 500 Index. I like to begin with the assessment of the overall market conditions because making money in stocks is very difficult if the trend of the overall market is down. So determine the market trend and that will help you determine the percentage of your portfolio to allocate to stocks, bonds, and cash.

The market strategist should offer you a bank of data covering a myriad of research and provide you with commentary to interpret the data. Use this information to decide where and how much of your money to place in the several asset classes, including the three most popular: stocks, bonds, and cash equivalents. The resource that I recommend helps interpret economic and market conditions such as money supply and Federal Reserve policy, investor sentiment (psychology, emotions), overbought/oversold market conditions, stock valuation vs. bond valuation, and future relative performance for each asset class to name a few research items. In addition, a market strategy resource should recommend the allocation percentages of your portfolio among the asset classes, usually concentrating on stocks, bonds, and cash.

My recommended strategist helps you determine when to be heavily invested in stocks and whether to invest in growth, value, or cyclical stocks; when to be mainly invested in income producing investments, such as bonds and/or preferred stocks; and when to heavily allocate to cash equivalents for income and capital preservation.

Good market strategy advice can help you take the emotion out of investing, trust time-proven instruments that appraise value in stocks and other asset classes, and keep you invested at times when you should not retreat to cash. My assumption is that stocks in the early stage of a bull market can produce the greatest percent of appreciation in a portfolio, and you want to be heavily invested in stocks at those times. On the other hand, when it is time to reduce exposure to stocks, you need to reduce your stock allocation, regardless of how ebullient the news about the economy and stocks is, in order to preserve your gains. Remember, investors at the end of a bull market throw money after overpriced stocks even when the market is topping, and these investors bid prices up beyond reasonable valuation of stocks. Hopefully, your market strategist will help you identify these conditions and preserve your profits. Of course, the usual caveat is in order because nobody gets it 100 percent correct each market swing; therefore, be prepared to ride out the tough times with your strategist.

The market strategist that I recommend is Hays Advisory of Nashville, Tennessee. Their website is www.haysadvisory.com, and it is loaded with charts and commentary. I like the Premium annual subscription for $250, which provides all the charts you will ever use, sector studies, twice-weekly commentary, and an asset allocation model, based on Hays' appraisal of Psychology, Monetary, and Valuation. Psychology is often referred to by some market researchers as market sentiment. Psychology uses several instruments, such as the various measures of option trading, to estimate how much fear or exuberance is in the market.

The Monetary gauge is a measurement of the availability of liquidity in the marketplace, most notable of which is the action of the Federal Reserve and its money supply policy. Of course, the notion here is that a tight rein on money by the Fed will lead ultimately to a slowdown in the economy and a downturn in stock prices. On the other hand, when the Fed is more accommodative in its monetary policy, such as low interest rates, the economy and stocks rebound eventually. Valuation basically measures whether it is better to be more heavily weighted in bonds, cash, or stocks.

Don Hays started Hays Advisory in 1999, and soon after that, began offering market advice on the company website. He now has a four-member team, composed of his two sons and a director of research and technician. The senior Hays was market strategist for two firms, J. C. Bradford & Company and Wheat First, for about thirty years before starting his own research and money management firm.

Hays and his associates provide twice-weekly commentary regarding current movement of the economy and stock and bond markets. The commentary is replete with charts and references to illustrate the writer's point. Sometimes senior Hays may go into more detail than you think that you will need, but if you stay with him, he will make his point and provide wise counsel in up and down markets.

Unfortunately, he missed the call of the horrific bear market of 2007-2009, like so many of us in the business. Therefore, he has installed another element in his three-prong approach (Psychology, Monetary, and Valuation) which will address the overall trend of the market. At this writing, the Market Trend Indicator is too new to evaluate, but Hays' research and back-testing indicate to me that the market-timing indicator should dramatically improve the usefulness of the Hays model. Hopefully, Hays can accurately tell you when to sell because preserving capital in bear markets is as important as capital appreciation in the bull markets.

The plethora of Hays' charts may overwhelm you on your first review of that section of the website, but the good news is that Hays has provided an extensive Glossary for each chart. The Glossary provides an excellent teaching tool for researching the economy as well as the stock and bond markets. For example, you can determine the best time to buy or sell a stock based on the likely short-term movement of the market by studying the NYSE McClellan Oscillator vs. the 21-day Oscillator. I reviewed the purpose and method of oscillators in chapter 6. When the oscillator rises above a certain level (100 on the Hays charts), that is a good time to sell stocks because stocks are likely to turn down in the near term. Of course, the opposite is true for buying a stock. Also, you can keep up with the fluctuations on major interest rates worldwide.

In 2008 the three-month LIBOR (London Interbank Offered Rate) spiked to over 5 percent during the credit crisis compared to the much lower three-month US Treasury rate. This spread indicated that domestic and international banks simply were not inclined to lend money to each other, thus the operational definition of a tight credit market. Soon after the stimulus packages and guarantee programs by US and foreign governments began to work into the banking system, the LIBOR fell precipitously. You should check many other charts periodically to get a good indication of what is affecting the economy and the stock market, and the trend changes that are likely to occur.

If you decide not to take my recommendation of the Hays website and to engage another market strategist, I warn you to check out your choice of strategist on what I call the Adulation and Arrogance Indicator (AAI). I have observed for years that when a professional money manager or researcher gains national attention by making an astute call on the market or a few stocks, if that person does not deflect the praise of the media or even worse boosts in writing or in public view about his or her achievements, that person is not a good candidate for your market strategist.

You may say that you want someone who has a stellar record of calling market turns and identifying ideal market sectors. Of course you do, but baggage accompanies pride and arrogance. I have observed this lack of character in several well-known people in the investment world, but I hesitate to call names; you can do your own research on this issue if you are interested. My point is that a spiritual issue regarding pride and arrogance is evident in all settings, and the biblical wisdom of *pride goes before a fall* should be of utmost counsel as you choose your investment strategist.

The market strategist should provide you with the global economic and investment picture, and this top-down approach sets the framework for where and when you should invest. Then when you have settled on an investment strategy, you should move from the general to the specific and analyze individual stocks in the market sectors and size of companies that appear most rewarding and safest for the projected time period.

FUNDAMENTAL ANALYSIS

The purpose of **stock analysis** is simply to identify the best stocks that comply with your investment strategy based on the fundamentals and/or technical indicators of the company. Fundamental analysis includes the numbers that are reported quarterly and annually by the company, such as earnings and cash flow growth, return on equity, profit margin, and the ratings reported periodically by research agencies that appraise financial strength.

As I noted earlier, I am focusing on investing in stocks in this book, and I use bonds and cash simply to add some dividends but mainly to help preserve capital. I recommend using US Treasury notes and bonds in addition to money market accounts that invest in government securities to fulfill your bond and cash allocations. However, stocks will be where you make or lose money, and stock analysis is the focus of my investment research. Of course, you can read and study the annual reports of the companies that you want to follow and do your own calculations. I recommend getting the annual and quarterly reports from the Securities and Exchange Commission website for periodic corporate fillings. Just go to your favorite search engine and look for 10-K and 10-Q reports for your selected companies.

By far the best resource for **stock analysis** is *Value Line Investment Survey*. Arnold Bernhard founded Value Line in 1931, soon after he started out on his own in managing client portfolios. He had been laid off from Moody's after the stock market crash in 1929, where he saw many people lose their life's savings. He developed the statistical system of picking stocks soon after the 1929 crash and began publishing the system in 1931. Currently, *Value Line* (VL) rates about 1700 stocks, reviewing every stock each quarter prorated over thirteen weekly reports. The basis of the system is rating stocks for "Timeliness," from 1-5 with 1 and 2 stocks being buy rated, 3 rated stocks for hold, and 4-5 stocks sell rated. These ratings are predictive of the stocks future performance over a six to twelve month period with 1-2 stocks expected to outperform all other stocks rated by *Value Line*.

The rating system provides a 1-5 number for the stock's Safety, which is based on *Value Line*'s financial rating of the stock from A++ to a lowly C- and the capitalization of the company with heavily indebted companies receiving the lowest ratings.

The Technical rating is the third of the *Value Line* ratings, ranging from 1-5 for predicted stock performance over the next three to six months. This rating is based on price action and earnings momentum.

The Value Line system could be used to manage one's portfolio by simply staying in 1 and 2 rated stocks, and Value Line boosts an enviable record over the long term. However, in 2008, the ratings were not good. Their Group I stocks representing the best companies in the US declined 52 percent. That one-year record notwithstanding, I am recommending *Value Line* because of the valuable data the research group provides.

In addition to the individual stock analysis, Value Line publishes each week a Selection and Opinion newsletter, which provides economic and stock market commentary, four model portfolios, and detailed information on the economy, interest rates, and stock market performance. Furthermore, a third publication, Index of Stocks, is included in the weekly package of information mailed to subscribers or available online at the www.valueline.com website.

The Index of Stocks updates all 1700 stocks regarding the three ratings: Timeliness, Safety, and Technical in addition to numerous projections and current financial data. This is the most comprehensive stock analysis resource that I know of for its universe of 1700 companies, and it is available for $599 a year with a slight discount for the electronic version. However, you can subscribe to a thirteen-week trail offer for $65, which is ample time to allow you to evaluate the product. I believe that you will find that VL is worth the money.

The ratings are excellent resources, but the reason that I recommend *Value Line* for stock analysis is because of the plethora of data provided on each stock for each quarter. [See Figures 1 & 2 on page 192 and 196 (Garmin and Emerson) provided by Value Line Publishing, Inc.] The system that I recommend for stock selection follows a discipline that can be accomplished only with comprehensive, dependable, and reliable data that are delivered to you in a manner to enhance your efficiency. Having all the data in one source conserves your time and improves your accuracy in making your calculations.

Value Line's only drawback is the mail delivery of the weekly package. *Value Line* promises delivery on Thursday of each week, but it hardly ever arrives on time at my office. The tardiness is not VL's fault, except for their choice of the third class mailing permit. The US Postal Service has leeway in determining delivery date under third class permits, so your copy may be late, depending on your regional postal center. Of course, the electronic delivery is always on time and is less expensive. However, you have to print the documents if you want a hard copy, which I do, and I like the mailed copy format for storage and quick review if I am traveling. Of course, the electronic format is available and recommended for the sake of punctuality.

I will go into more detail about *Value Line* in the Stock Selection section of this chapter. Also, I will refer to Morningstar Premium Membership later. I like this service for the individual investor, which is $299 for the Premium package, because it is inexpensive and has many good features, although it does not have the plethora of data on individual companies like the *Value Line Investment Survey*. Morningstar rates stocks from 1-5 stars, with 4-5 star stocks rated buys, 3 star stocks being holds, and 1-2 star stocks recommended sells. They base their recommendations on their calculations of fair value or intrinsic value, which is the present value calculation of future expected cash flows generated by the company. Morningstar also provides an analyst report on 2,000 stocks and provides a recommended "Buy At" price that is based on a "margin of safety." The margin of safety is a calculated discount from the fair value.

Morningstar analysts also assign grades for Financial Health, Growth, Profitability, Stewardship, Fair Value Uncertainty, and Moat. The Moat is a concept popularized by Warren Buffet. A Moat rating is likened to the pool of water surrounding a castle during medieval times for protection from warring avengers who would try to destroy the castle and its inhabitants. The Moat rating, such as Wide or Narrow, is a means of expressing the durability and magnitude of the competitive advantage of the company in competition with other companies in its sector.

The Moat rating is closely correlated with the company's stewardship of management and the analysts' ability to predict the Fair Value of the company. The other ratings for Financial Health, Growth, and Profitability reflect the ability of company management to produce consistent profits that enable the company to survive and prosper in economic downturns.

You can set up a portfolio or watch list in Morningstar that will give you constant updates on each stock as the data changes. Use the My View tab to create the portfolio and then Customize My Portfolio with the following entries:

- Company Name, Symbol, and Current Price
- Morningstar Rating, Economic Moat, Fair Value, and Price/Fair Value
- PEG Ratio (PE to Growth Ratio), Dividend Yield, Percent below 52-week high
- Relative Strength vs. S & P 500: 1 year, 3 months, 1 month
- Grades for: Growth, Profitability, and Financial Health
- Fair Value Uncertainty

Morningstar's Rating reflects the current price of the stock in relationship to its calculated intrinsic value. Morningstar uses the term Fair Value, which includes intrinsic value and their analysts' cognitive evaluation also. The intrinsic value of a stock is paramount in the buy/sell system that I will go into later. So, you should learn more about this measure and to use a software or website that provides these calculations for many stocks. Of course, a formula can be used to calculate these values, and those of you who are math and computer experts can set up a spreadsheet to do the calculations.

For the rest of us—and if you do not want to pay for Morningstar's Premium service—I recommend two free websites. I have reviewed Valuepro.net, which is relatively simple to use, and its intrinsic value calculations appear to be based on *Value Line* numbers for the several inputs in its calculation screen. After you enter the site, enter a stock symbol and click on Get Baseline Valuation. A screen will appear with the intrinsic value at the top left and a Recalculate button next to the intrinsic value. Also, that page has numerous data points that you may alter as you wish. Compare the earnings growth rate, profit margin, and revenue to *Value Line's* numbers. If you make changes, simply clicked on the Recalculate button to determine the new intrinsic value. You can check the other data points against *Value Line's* numbers to make sure that the current data are listed in Value Pro, but usually it is up-to-date.

The second free site is Diamond-Hill.com, which is provided by Diamond-Hill Capital Management. After logging in, click on About Us for the drop-down menu and select Investment Model. Read the Acceptance Page and click on Accept. That will bring up The Valuator. You can then enter a stock symbol and click on Calculate. At the bottom of the page under Calculated Values, you will see Derived Model Value. This is the intrinsic value of the stock, which of course is the present value of the projection of future earnings and cash flow. At the bottom of the Calculated Values section is the Estimated 5-Year Annual Total Return in percent.

You can also enter the current stock price during the day and click on Calculate to see the revised Estimated 5-Year Total Return. I like this feature because if a stock price declines during the day, that price might meet your target, whereas at the end of the day the price might run up to a price that is out of your buy range. The same is the case for selling a stock.

Another feature of this website that I like is the ability to compare another stock with your featured stock. Simply follow the steps above in the second column, which is easily identified. You can compare a stock in the same industry or several stocks to select the best projected return for the stocks in one industry. As you will see, you can use this feature in many ways.

Another tool that I recommend is IClubCentral's Toolkit 6 Stock Selection Guide. This is the system developed by the National Association

of Investment Clubs in the 1950s, now offered through the succeeding organization, National Association of Investors Corporation and sold
through IClubCentral. The Stock Selection Guide software produces a buy
price and sell price for a stock, based on historical data and projected revenue and earnings.

The SSG uses the past five years of prices, earnings, dividends, and
price/earnings ratios to calculate a plethora of data, but it simplifies the
data to give you a projected annual total return percentage (price appreciation and dividends) and a risk/reward ratio, which Toolkit 6 calls the up-
side/downside ratio. Please review Figure 3 on page 211 (Stock Selection
Guide), and review Toolkit 6 at www.iclub.com/products. Toolkit 6 was released in 2008 at a price of about $180. Download it or order the disk, and
study the manual and tutorials that are available. I will refer to Toolkit 6 in
your stock selection and portfolio management in chapter 9.

TECHNICAL ANALYSIS

My recommendations so far about analyzing a stock have focused on
the fundamentals of the company. However, another method of **stock
analysis** focuses on the mood of investors, and that is **technical analysis**,
which simply measures the price movement of a stock and of the total
market in general. I hasten to add that the technical analysis that fits my
investing strategy is not day-trading but technical analysis for long-term
investing, whereby the majority of your gains will qualify for long-term
capital gains for income tax purposes.

Why use technical analysis? The mass of investors will tell you a lot
about the stock, so you will need a method of measuring the investor sentiment about the stock or the stock market in general. What does investor
sentiment tell you? First, investor sentiment reflects the cumulative knowledge and expectations of all investors. For example, little known facts about
a company's products or services might be reflected in how some investors
trade the stock, whether they are buying or selling. Also, if there is any hint
of fraudulent dealings by company officers, somehow the market will pick
up on this.

Other investors who might not have the same understanding about the
company see the price movement, and they become curious and investigate
the cause of the price downturn or upturn. Then a massive sell-off or
break-out to the upside can occur. Next, investors can tell you the expectations for the overall economy and thus the future of stock prices. This ex-

pectation can be measured for one or more industry groups as well, which can give you an idea about which industries to avoid or allocate a dispro-portionate amount of your cash resources.

The main purpose of technical measures in my investment strategy is to get out of stocks that are in a hopeless downtrend. If you can cut your losses in a stock that is headed for a large loss and might not recover in a long time, you can significantly improve your investment return, not to mention insulate you from abysmal anxiety.

Seeing a stock lose most of its value or even become worthless is a bitter pill. I did this with WorldCom in the fraudulent debacle of the 2000-2002 bear market. Some analysts on Wall Street were still touting a buy for the stock as it headed to oblivion. I did not buy to the end, but I held to the end because the story on the stock was still reasonable from the analysts and the company. But there was extensive manipulation of the quarterly earnings for years; and of course, the stock looked good while the numbers were being manipulated. To finish the story, diversification kept us from holding a lot of shares of WCOM and thus minimized the loss. However, a loss in a small position can affect the performance of your port-folio, and I could have improved the performance of client portfolios and my own portfolio if I had sold WCOM when it broke below its 400-day moving average.

Another purpose of using technical analysis is to assist in the timing of your stock purchase. This is a secondary objective in my investment strategy because if you just buy stocks that have good fundamentals when they are beaten down, you can do quite well in stock investing. However, by using simple technical analysis, you can determine when a stock is begin-ning to show some price appreciation. This technique is not foolproof; in fact, nothing about technical analysis is foolproof, but the only downside that I can see is that you might have to trade sooner than you would without using technical indicators.

Stocks sometimes have fits and starts in their moving from the dirty-clothes hamper to the clean-clothes drawer. In other words, when a stock shows up well on a technical measure like a 200-day moving average, it might fall back below the 200-day MA line several times before it takes off; conversely, the price may pull back and not return to the moving av-erage line again for years. My strategy for using technical analysis on the buy side is to make sure that the technical indicators for the broad market, such as the S & P 500 Index, are showing strong upside momentum and then to look for the same in the stock that I wish to buy.

Monitoring the technical indicators for the broader market, such as the S & P 500 Index, provides good information for setting your expectations for the movement of the market in the intermediate future, such as the next six to twelve months. The technical indicators simply express graphically the mood of the mass of investors without one sector of the market, such as the financial sector in 2008-09, unduly influencing the expectations for the intermediate future of broader market.

Here are all the **technical indicators** that you need to be a successful investor. First, I remind you that the strategy that I am suggesting is for long-term investing and not day trading. Day traders use the technical indicators that I recommend, but they also use many other charts and patterns. The technical indicators that I use will move you into stocks or an individual stock when it is showing upward momentum and move you out when the momentum has changed significantly. Here is the list of three technical indicators and the way to use them. All three are moving averages (MA); please review the definition of moving averages in chapter 6:

- 50-day Moving Average
- 200-day Moving Average
- 20-month Moving Average

I will suggest several websites that have moving average components, but for now, here is how the moving averages work. The software or website calculates the moving average for the period that you indicate in the setup for an individual stock or the index, and the website produces a chart with a wiggly line that shows the plot of your choice of daily, monthly, or quarterly day-ending prices for the stock or index. The software may also show a straight line that connects the low points or the high points. Also, you can set up to plot an index, such as the S & P 500 Index, and the stock that you want to study, thus giving you a picture of how the stock has performed in comparison to the market in general over a period.

In its simplest form, here is how you should use the moving averages. The 50-day MA alerts you to an early price movement of the stock or index. The 200-day MA confirms the trend and triggers a buy or sell. When the stock price moves above its 50-day MA, put it on a short list to monitor daily, and when the stock price moves above its 200-day MA, buy it. If you want another confirmation, wait until the S & P 500 Index day-ending price goes above its 200-day MA.

You use the same method on the sell side. When the day-ending stock price goes below its 50-day MA, put it on a short list, and when the stock price goes below its 200-day MA, sell it. For added conformation, you might want to wait until the S & P 500 Index ending daily price goes below its 200-day MA. When you hold a stock for several months, you should have a profit as the stock price and the moving average move together.

There are **two free websites** that I recommend for plotting the simple **technical indicators** that I use in my investment strategy. Big Charts and Yahoo Finance will work as well for you as the most expensive professional services. Go to www.finance.yahoo.com and click on My Portfolio to create a watch list of stocks. This will bring up a blank screen in which you can type the symbols of all the stocks that you want to follow. Just skip a space between each symbol that you enter. You can also create a watch list for the industry groups and the broad market indexes that you want to follow.

Yahoo will help you identify the symbols for the industry groups and the indexes. The indexes that I follow are the Dow Jones Industrial Index, S & P 500, NASDAQ Composite, and the Russell 2000. The Russell 2000 gives you a measure of how the small cap stocks are performing. The Wilshire Total Market Index is also a helpful measure of most of the publicly traded stocks.

Go to My Portfolios in www.finance.yahoo.com to create a portfolio or watch list. Click on Track a Symbol Watch List, enter a name for your portfolio or watch list, and click on New View to select the technical indicators that you want to follow. Select a name and symbol and then follow this sequence in setting up your watch list with these technical indicators: 50-day MA and percent from 50-day MA; 200-day MA and percent from 200-day MA; and percent from 52-week low and percent from 52-week high. Just click on your choice and move it to the Add column.

You have all you need in www.finance.yahoo.com to track your watch list or portfolio using technical indicators. Here is how to use your moving averages: when your percent from 50-day MA turns to green, that is a signal to begin watching that stock for a possible buy. When the percent from 200-day MA turns green, that is a signal to buy the stock. The sequence is the same on the downside when the indicators turn red.

Sometimes these indicators might turn around and show a red or a green soon after you buy or sell. That is the time to check the major indexes that you think fit this stock. Usually, that will be the S & P 500 Index. If this index is trading below its 200-day MA, a conservative investor will not buy the stock in the first place. However, if you are aggressive and bought the stock after it moved above its 200-day MA, without a confirmation from the S & P 500 Index, you should make one more check before you sell the stock that has suddenly reversed. Check the 20-month MA in Big Charts or you may use a 400-day MA that approximates a 20-montha MA.

Go to www.bigcharts.com and click on Advanced Charts. On the left under Advanced Chart is a DRAW CHART panel; enter your stock symbol in the box. Scroll down and click on Time Frame and enter 2 years and click on Frequency and enter Daily. Scroll down and click on the Indicators box and click on Moving Averages. Click on SMA (simple MA). In the right box, enter 400 and go back to the top and click on DRAW CHART.

This will bring up the graph of the daily prices of your selected stock and line indicating the 400-day moving average over the last two years. You can see where your stock is trading now in relation to its 400-day MA. If the stock is trading below its 400-day MA, it is a candidate to sell. However, if its stock price is above its 400-day MA, you might want to hold it for a while, if you recently bought the stock and it has reversed its up-trend and fallen below its 200-day MA.

Once you set up My Portfolios in Yahoo, you will then be able to review your watch list and portfolios quickly every day to see if there are any transactions that you need to make. Likewise, you can save your setup in Big Charts and review as many stocks as you wish by changing the symbol in the DRAW CHART box.

After you have a setup to do economic and market research and fundamental and technical analysis, you will need a system for managing your watch list and portfolios.

Yahoo and *Value Line* both provide **portfolio management** resources, but each is in a secondary role to my recommended **portfolio management** resource. I recommend Quant IX's Portfolio Manager 5 management tool sold through Better Investing (BI). Portfolio Manager 5 sells for $169 or if you join Better Investing (BI), PM5 sells for $129. It can be downloaded from

Better Investing or you can buy the disk. Go to www.BetterInvesting.com for ordering details.

Portfolio Manager 5 provides the four main requirements of good portfolio management software. If you have a BI membership, the software provides access to S & P stock and Lipper mutual fund services that allow daily price updates; download of investment income for stocks, bonds, and mutual funds; cost basis accounting and reports; and automatic backup. All of these four elements are important to facilitate your portfolio management, income tax reporting, and security for your system.

If you have a taxable portfolio, you will see the benefit of PM5's tracking each incremental purchase of a stock while you are building a position in a security. For example, if you build a position in a stock with three incremental purchases, you need to keep each purchase separate because you may need to sell in increments, and you need exact cost information to report your sale on your income tax return. Likewise, tracking mutual fund reinvested dividends for a taxable portfolio can be a simple matter with an effective and efficient software product like Quant IX's Portfolio Manager 5.

Yahoo Finance can support your **portfolio management** by giving you buy/sell signals as discussed earlier. Also, *Value Line* provides daily portfolio updates that can help you manage your stocks. Set up your portfolio and your watch list on the web-based components of www.finance.yahoo.com and Value Line. On ValueLine.com, log in and go to the Home page, where you will see Subscriber Portfolio Online in the left panel. Click on Subcriber Portfolio Online and click on Portfolio to set up a New Portfolio by selecting New Transaction. As I described earlier, at finance.yahoo.com, you will work in My Portfolios to create and edit you portfolios and your watch list.

Watch List Selections

The next step is to identify a group of stocks to follow that match your investment criteria. You can screen for these stocks on various websites, but I recommend reviewing the *Value Line Investment Survey* for your selections for the watch list. If you pay for the paper subscription to *Value Line*, you can also have access to the *Value Line* website, where you can screen stocks in the VL database using a variety of criteria. Of course, you can do just as well reviewing the weekly issue of Ratings and Reports. I am going to show

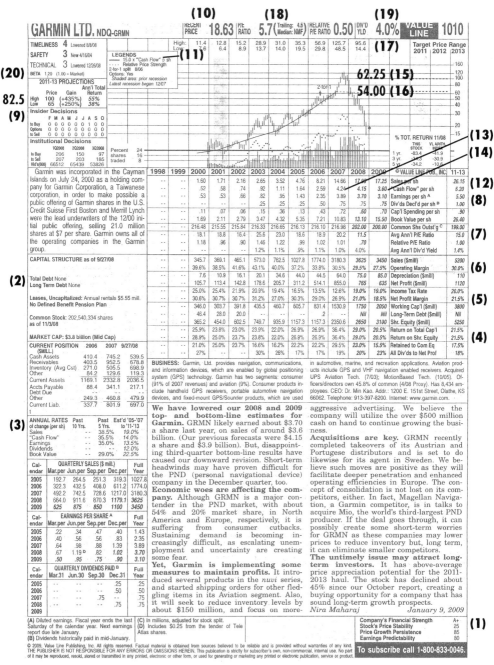

Used by permission of Value Line Publishing, Inc., New York, NY

Figure 1

192

you how to review a page of *Value Line* to evaluate a stock for possible inclusion in your watch list.

Let us assume that we are going to look for growth stocks, so we focus on stocks that historically have grown sales and earnings more than 14 percent a year. We can assume further that if sales and earnings grow 14 percent annually or more in the next five years, that the stock will appreciate at least 14 percent a year. At that rate compounded, the stock price will double in price in the next five years, which is a very rewarding goal.

After scrolling through the pages of a recent issue of *Value Line*, I selected Garmin Ltd. (GRMN) (Figure 1 on p. 192) as a stock to review. Garmin meets all my criteria for being included in my watch list. First, it is a financially sound company. *Value Line* gives it a Financial Strength rating (1) of A+ which is next to the top rating of A++. Also, I reviewed the Capital Structure, and the company has no Long-term Debt (2), which further evidences its financial strength and bodes well for the company in tough economic times such as the 2008-2009 recession.

Next, I looked at the Annual Rates (3) to get a picture of Garmin's past and projected growth rates. The estimated sales and earnings rates for the next five years exceeded my criterion of 14 percent, so all is well there. Next, I looked at the Return on Shareholder Equity (ROE) (4) to see how effectively management has used the paid in capital from shareholders. The ROE has been very high but is projected to be 20.5 percent in 2009, which is still greater than my criterion of 15 percent or greater and exceeds the Electrical Industry statistics reported by *Value Line* at the introduction to the Ratings and Reports for each industry.

The last quick review that I make is the operating and profit margins numbers (5 & 6), and I compare them to the other companies in the industry. Garmin's past and projected margins significantly exceed the industry averages. Based on this initial review, I concluded that Garmin is a leading stock in the Electrical Equipment Industry and that it has excellent growth potential for the next five years. I read the analyst's comments and considered the *Value Line* Ratings for Timeliness, Safety, and Technical; but at this stage, I did not make a judgment about buying the stock at this price (10). I am just looking for stocks that fit my objective of growth potential, financial strength, good management, and wide profit margins.

To further estimate the growth potential, I made a few calculations. Of course, *Value Line* makes their own stock price appreciation projections, as listed under the Timeliness box in the upper left corner of the page (9), but I wanted to check how realistic these numbers are. To that end, I multiplied the projected Average Annual P/E Ratio (7) by the estimated Earnings per share (8) and the result is 82.50 (9) [15.0 X 5.50 = 82.50]. I divided 82.5 by the current price which is 18.63 and get 4.43, which indicates that if earnings reach $5.50 annually and investors bid up the P E to 15, Garmin could more than triple [82.5/18.63-1] in price over the next five years.

As a further check on the five-year price appreciation potential, I use the cash flow to make a projection. I multiple the Cash Flow historic multiple (11) by the projected Cash Flow per share for the next five years (12) and the result is 93 [15 X 6.20 = 93]. Of course, 93 exceeds my P E and earnings per share projection, so I feel good about the projected price in five years of 82.5.

The last calculation that I make in this process is to estimate a current fair value. I use the Cash Flow multiple (11) and multiple it by the past year's Cash Flow per share (13) and the current year Cash Flow per share (14). In this case the 2008 calculation is 62.25 [15 X 4.15 = 62.25] and the 2009 calculation is 54 [15 X 3.60 = 54]. I post these at (15) and (16) for future reference.

Therefore, the current price is much less than its fair value based on the cash flow of the company. You can see in 2008 that Garmin's price was as high as 95.6 (17), so it is not out of line to expect the stock to appreciate to 82.5 at sometime within the next five years.

Additional numbers that I note is Garmin's current P E is 5.7 (18) compared to its historical average of 15.0 (7), and it is yielding a healthy dividend of 4.0 percent (19), which is a significant bonus for a growth stock. Needless to say, Garmin goes on the watch list.

As you review the *Value Line* stock report, you should focus on the little box in the lower right corner of the page (1). In addition to reporting on the Company's Financial Strength as mentioned earlier, the box (1) reports on Stock's Price Stability, Price Growth Persistence, and Earnings Predictability. Each one of the numbers assigned to these components tells how volatile or steady that the stock's price is likely to be.

I like to focus on the Earnings Predictability, which is the percent of accuracy that *Value Line* analysts have recorded historically in predicting the annual and quarterly earnings. I like to add stocks to my watch list that are easy for analyst to predict earnings such as with recorded percentages of

70 and above. Earnings drive the price of a stock, so if *Value Line* analysts can predict the earnings accurately each quarter, the stock is less likely to sell off because of negative earnings surprises.

The stock's **Price Stability** is a ranking of weekly price variance with 100 being most stable. **Price Growth Persistence** reports the stock's tendency to appreciate as compared to the average stock. Now look for Beta in the top left box (20). Beta is the measure of fluctuation of the stock's price compared to the price changes of the New York Stock Exchange Composite. For example, a beta of 1.00 would track exactly the NYSE Composite, whereas a beta of 1.50 would be 50 percent more volatile than the NYSE Composite, and a 0.50 beta would be 50 percent less volatile than the NYSE Composite.[1] Each of these components will help you decide if the stock measures up to your profile of stocks based on risk and volatility.

You should consider one more criterion regarding the suitability of a stock to be included in your watch list. Look again at the top left box (20) and check the Safety rating. Safety is a composite of the Financial Strength and the Price Stability Index, and this calculation is compared with the calculations of all other stocks in the 1700 that *Value Line* follows.[2] The Safety is rated between 1 and 5, with 1 being the highest rated. Conservative investors should consider only 1 and 2 Safety rated stocks, and investors that are more aggressive might want to consider 3 or even 4 rated stocks. The system that I recommend does not consider Safety rated stocks in the 4-5 range.

I have included a *Value Line* report on Emerson Electric (EMR) (Figure 2 on p. 196) to compare with Garmin regarding the points made above, particularly regarding a stock's price persistency and earnings growth. For practice, analyze and mark the page as I did for Garmin (GRMN), but also notice the difference between the two stocks regarding Price Stability, Earnings Predictability, and Annual Rates for Sales and Earnings. Now synthesize all this information and determine if Emerson should be included on your watch list.

Here is a hint: Different types of stocks serve different purposes in your portfolio. In chapter 9, I will explore this notion further in the strategy development section, as I attempt to synthesize all this basic information discussed in chapters 6-8.

If you are a subscriber to *Value Line*, another method of selecting stocks

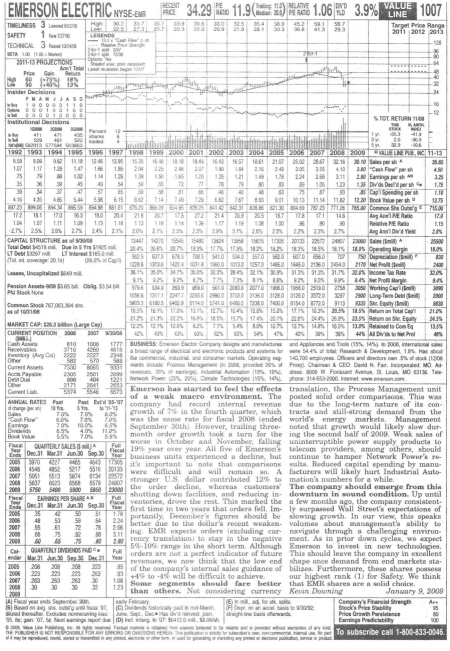

Used by permission of Value Line Publishing, Inc., New York, NY

Figure 2

196

for your watch list is to run a *Value Line* screen based on similar criteria as that discussed above. For example, if you want to emphasize growth stocks as you attempt to maximize price appreciation for your portfolio, you might set your screen as I did when writing this chapter. After you log on to ValueLine.com, click on Stock Screen in the left panel. Then set up the two main criteria as follows:

Value Line Ranks:
Timeliness: 1, 2, 3
Safety: 1, 2, 3
Technical: 1, 2, 3
Financial Strength: A++, A+, A, B++, B+

Additional Stock Information: (all are percentages)
Return on Equity (ROE): 15-100
Projected Earnings Per Share (EPS) Growth Rate: 10-100
Projected Sales Growth Rate: 10-100
Projected 3-5 Year % Annual Total Return: 10-100
Earnings Predictability: 70-100
Long-term Debt to Capital: 0-35

I ran the screen the first time without including Earnings Predictability and Long-term Debt to Capital, and the search reported 105 stocks. I added Earnings Predictability in the range of 70-100 percent, and the screen reported 54 stocks. You could narrow the search more by adding Price Stability and Growth Persistence, but the Earnings Predictability should be sufficient when screening for growth stocks.

Also, I added Long-term Debt to Capital in the range of 0-35 percent, and the screen reported 44 stocks. The Financial Strength rating probably is sufficient in developing the watch list, but you should consider the debt obligations of the company when you select your portfolio of stocks. I did not include a screen for Operating or Profit Margin because these measures are related to the industrial sector, so this is a step to exercise during the portfolio selection process.

I usually keep a stock on the watch list unless its financials collapse or some other calamity happens. We have to assume that companies flourish and flounder in sometimes inexplicable patterns, most often because of a lapse in the effectiveness of management. Therefore, keep your watch list information updated, but purging the list is not necessary because some companies are floundering. However, if you have a company that has a financial strength of A+ and you see its financial rating slip to C+, you probably should eliminate the stock from further consideration. Other issues may be negative, such as moral or ethical matters that come to your attention as you do further research. For the most part, I advise you to build your watch list and pare it only when you have too many stocks to follow or some calamity occurs, such as the financial stability of the company being destroyed.

Summary and Conclusions

Determining a plan for achieving wealth in stock investing is easy: simply buy low and sell high. However, very few investors ever really master that plan. Another chapter would be needed to discuss the multitude of reasons few people actually execute that simple plan. Far less time will be taken describing a system of education and implementation that will work in up and down markets and will help even the average investor make and retain money in stocks.

In this chapter, I have detailed a system whereby you can move from the general to the specific to determine the economic and investment conditions; analyze the universe of stocks based on a few key fundamentals; select a watch list of stocks; and measure your selections using uncomplicated technical indicators to determine when to buy and sell. In the next chapter, I will focus on the indicators and methods to use in developing and managing your portfolio.

I hope that I have not made this system appear to be just a mechanical process that is devoid of thinking and judgment. To the contrary, this system organizes your thinking and judgment. You should not fear that you cannot master this strategy. If you have read and studied this section, all you need is practice in working the system. Just remain focused on the method and try to ignore what the media pundits are saying about market conditions. Remember that the naysayers are part of your technical analysis, and their opinions sometimes are contra-indicators for what you should be doing with your portfolio. Also, ignore falling for stock tips without checking out any ideas with this system.

You are more than capable of earning great wealth in investing, but you just need to stay focused on a system. Most would-be investors think that they have to know everything about investing to be successful. Rather, you just have to master a system, adhere to that strategy in all market conditions, and be patient and persistent.

Chapter 8 gives you the tools to implement the investment strategy that will work for you and will be effective in all times and economic conditions. It held up for me very well in the 2008-2009 recession and bear market. These research and management tools are basically used by investment professionals, although the professionals may have proprietary models that cost infinitely more than what you will need to spend. Now let us move on to synthesizing all the foregone basic information as we discuss selecting and managing your portfolio and dealing with some of the barriers and common mistakes that can work against sound investment management.

CHAPTER NINE

Building Wealth on Main Street

The previous chapters set forth the tools for building wealth, and this chapter synthesizes these components into investment practices and an uncomplicated strategy that you can use with confidence. Of course, some work is required to set up the model and to monitor your stock selections, but no higher mathematics or other complicated methods are required.

You will just need to work through the steps that follow in this chapter and save your computer setups in order to select stocks and determine when to buy and sell like a Wall Street money manager. Furthermore, if you will follow this pattern to the letter, you should not lose any money over any five-year period, which is a typical market cycle, even in the worst of economic conditions.

I have developed this model over many years and as a results of several mistakes, some as recent as the 2008-09 bear market. Admitting the several mistakes is a bold disclosure, considering that I have said that this model will keep you from losing any money over any economic and market cycle. However, the bear market in 2000-02 got my attention about protecting on the downside. Furthermore, the 2007-09 bear market stamped indelibly on my game plan that using the technical indicators to get investors out of stocks at certain times is necessary. You will have to sell stocks eventually in order to preserve your profits and to build cash for another time to buy back stocks. In summary, the model will work for you over time if you follow the strategy exactly.

I need to tell you a story to illustrate the point of adhering to the method that I advocate. When I began investing for others, I did so for a college foundation in the early 1980s. I was an officer of the foundation, and two trustees were on the investment committee with me. I did the research and made recommendations to the committee for major strategy moves. We used no-load mutual funds mainly, and I found a simple thirty-nine-week moving average approach that I thought would work for investing the foundation money.

We used the system for several years and made money every year. Then I began teaching investment courses to adults, and a few members of the class each quarter asked me to manage their money for them. So I registered with the Securities and Exchange Commission and began using mutual funds to invest for my new clients. I used the thirty-nine-week moving average for each mutual fund and used the S & P 500 thirty-nine-week moving average to confirm the buy/ sell for each fund. I posted each closing price on Friday of each week, and made sure that each fund and the S & P Index closing prices were above each fund's thirty-nine-week average.

I made money for each client and for myself, and when stocks began to deteriorate in October 1987, I started posting daily the day-ending prices for the mutual funds and the Index. During the week of October 12, my mutual fund prices and the Index closing price fell below their thirty-nine-period moving averages. Therefore, I began selling the mutual funds. By the end of the week, I had sold every fund for every client. On Black Monday, October 19, the investments for every client and for my accounts were in cash, with most of the money in mutual fund money market accounts. Needless to say, my clients were pleased.

That is the good news, but the bad news is that I did not move the money back into stock mutual funds when the indicators rebounded in a very short time. Within a few months of the October 19, 1987 crash, stocks began to rebound, but the news and many economists and investment analysts were saying that the crash of the market in October would cause a worldwide recession like the US had not seen since the 1930s.

The news was bad, and I took my counsel from the experts and did not trust my indicators. Gradually, I did get back into the stock market, but I had missed the big move in the first few weeks of the rebound. To complete the story, after that experience and the fact that the mutual fund companies did not like the trading strategy, I did not use mutual funds any more. I began investing in stocks and in fact started my own stock mutual fund. I did not return to the technical indicators until 2008 when I began a long-term research project to determine the best technical indicators for long-term investors.

The point of this personal story is that you must trust your indicators and your strategy in general in all economic and market conditions. During the 1990s, you could have made money in stocks by buying and holding your positions, but with the volatility that began in the late 1990s and culminated in a horrific bear market during 2000-02, we have seen a sea-change in the nature of successful investing.

Technology and the trading mentality on Wall Street are dictating the investment strategies of professionals, and you should adapt to deal with the increased volatility and trading mentality. I am not suggesting that you become a trader, heaven forbid. However, you and I must be willing to sell: (1) stocks that are overpriced and in which other investors are taking profits and (2) stocks of companies and market sectors that are in deep trouble. Investing is likely to become more difficult, and we are not likely ever to return to the halcyon days when you could buy and hold any name brand company and make money over time. But you will be able to buy name brand companies and make money if you are willing to sell when stocks are at or near the top of their price range or their technical readings have deteriorated.

I hope that before you begin following this investment model, you work through the financial planning process as outlined in chapter 6 and write a clear vision statement. As I expressed before, defining your long-term investment goals will guide you in making asset allocation and other decisions as you implement your investment strategy. Also, I encourage you to review chapter 7 and make sure that you can use the vocabulary in addition to the ratios and concepts explained. As we work through this chapter, I will not define terms and ratios in the following text.

I have referred to components of my investment strategy in chapters 6-8, but now I will be more specific and develop an investment strategy that can guide us in an effort to build wealth over a lifetime. You should write your investment strategy as a guide to keep you on track in your investment process. The following paragraph is an example to guide you in writing your investment strategy, and it is compatible with the investment model that I outline under Organizing and Managing Investment Data.

My investment strategy shall be to grow my portfolio over time and protect capital in unfavorable economic and investment conditions by following asset allocation among stocks, bond, and cash equivalents. I need to realize an investment portfolio worth $_____ by the year 20___. I am prepared to invest $_____ each month; therefore, I need to realize an annual compounded return of _____ percent. My main growth investment will be common stocks of high quality companies, and I will buy stocks that project the highest total return for my portfolio. A high quality company evidences a strong balance sheet with low debt, strong management as evidenced by high return on equity and high profit margins, and consistent revenue and earnings growth. I will diversify my stock selections over numerous market sectors, and I will allocate no more than 5 percent to each stock.

I seek to identify a universe of stocks that meet my basis criteria of B+ or greater financial strength and 35 percent or less debt to capitalization, at least 10 percent revenue and earnings growth annually, 15 percent or greater Return on Equity, and operating margin that is at the top or near the top of a stock's industry. I seek to buy these companies at a 25 percent or greater discount to their intrinsic value. I will review the stocks in my portfolio at least weekly.

I will buy my stocks when each is improving in momentum and the broader market is improving in momentum, and I will sell my stocks when momentum deteriorates in both stock and index. Dividends will be a secondary consideration to improve total return for the portfolio, and bonds and cash will be used for defensive purposes when the overall market deteriorates.

Are you ready to move on now to organizing and managing your investment data and developing your own strategy for investing?

Organizing and Managing Investment Data

Let us assume that you will follow my recommendation that you look for growth stocks of high quality companies that are well-managed. You will find that some of these companies will pay a dividend, and there will be times, such as during the 2008-09 bear market, when stock prices are greatly reduced and even powerful growth companies pay a substantial dividend. Microsoft and Paychex are good examples of quality companies that are still growing and yet pay substantial dividends.

Now it is the time for you to begin working through the model; therefore, go to your computer and get ready to work. Just reading this section will do you very little good; you must work through the model step-by-step at your computer or within the pages of the *Value Line Investment Survey*, if you bought the paper edition. Let me remind you that you can buy a thirteen-week trial subscription for $65, so this valuable data is available to all who are serious investors.

In order to find, analyze and manage these growth companies in your watch list and portfolio, I recommend that you follow these seven steps.

Step 1: Run Value Line Screen for Watch List

Go online to www.ValueLine.com; select Investment Survey. Select Stock Screening on the left panel, click on Create a Saved Screen, name your screen WATCH LIST, and save your WATCH LIST. Go to Value Line Rank and then Additional Stock Information and enter the following, as listed also in chapter 8.

Value Line Rank:
   Timeliness: 1, 2, 3
   Safety: 1, 2, 3
   Technical: 1, 2, 3
   Financial Strength: A++, A+, A, B++, B+

Additional Stock Information: (all are percentages from Minimum Value to Maximum Value)
   Return on Equity (ROE): 15-100
   Projected Sales Growth Rate: 10-100
   Projected Earnings Per Share (EPS) Growth Rate: 10-100
   Projected 3-5 Year % Annual Total Return: 10-100
   Earnings Predictability: 70-100
   Long-Term Debt to Capitalization: 0-35

Practices: Select High Quality Companies with Excellent Growth Potential

This Value Line screen provides the best companies in the United States and a few foreign countries. These stocks will appreciate in value over a market cycle, and many will provide a good dividend. The companies are well-managed as reflected in their returns on equity (ROE), financial strength, and low debt to capitalization. When you screen for these stocks, you will be able to rank your selections according to any one of the selection criteria.

Since all of the companies in the selection pool are high quality, I recommend that you rank the companies according to the Projected 3-5 Year Percent Annual Total Return. If you have a lot of stocks to analyze, you might want to concentrate on the stocks with the highest total return potential. You definitely should read the analyst's summary for each stock and keep up with the warnings and reservations that any analyst might describe.

Print out the Value Line sheets for your stocks or use your weekly printed copy of *Value Line* to mark the page with the twenty or more items that I listed in chapter 8 under Figure 1. Also, note the position of the current price in relation to the Cash Flow Line in the chart on the Report page. This will give you a quick reference for determining if the stock is undervalued. Also, the Relative P/E Ratio gives you another quick determination of stock value.

Of course, you do not need to run a stock screen to benefit from Value Line's research. You can simply scan the pages of each week's copy of Ratings and Reports to garner the best stocks in each issue to follow. Then you can manually enter the data in the recommended research websites and software such as Morningstar Premium and Toolkit 6.

Step 2: Export Value Line Watch List to Microsoft Excel

After you have completed the stock screen in Value Line to identify the stocks that meet your criteria, click on **Export Results** at the top left of the screen page. Then click on Save the file, Name the file, and Save it on Excel. (See Appendix B for special instruction for navigating to Excel.)

Practices: Use Excel as Feeder for Other Operations

Excel provides a means of transitioning data from one source to another. Most software programs and websites import from and export to Excel. Therefore, if you have even an introductory knowledge of Excel, you can manage a variety of investment data and perform many operations and calculations. The first operation with Value Line data is to move the Watch List to Morningstar Premium (see Appendix B).

Morningstar Premium is reasonably priced at $250 annually, and of course, you will need a subscription in order to proceed through Step 3 below.

Step 3: Import Watch List into Morningstar Premium from Excel

A. Log in to www.Morningstar.com as a Premium subscriber. Click on Portfolio, Create a Portfolio, New Portfolio, Watch List, and Import Portfolio. Then follow the instructions in Morningstar to import your Watch List from your Excel files.

B. Set up your Watch List in Morningstar in the following sequence: Portfolio, My View, and Customize My Portfolio by adding the following entries to the box:
- Company Name
- Stock Symbol
- Current Price
- Fair Value
- Price to Fair Value
- Fair Value Uncertainty
- Stewardship Grade
- Morningstar Rating
- Economic Moat
- P E G
- Dividend Yield
- Percent Below 52-Week High
- Relative Strength vs. S & P 500: 1 Year, 3 Months, 1 Month
- Growth Grade
- Profit Grade
- Financial Health

Practices: Evaluate Each Stock's Intrinsic Value and Other Measures of Fundamental and Technical Analysis

The Morningstar Premium website provides an excellent means of evaluating each stock and reading analysts' reviews from another set of investment analysts. The first item to review is the intrinsic value of the stock or as Morningstar reports, the Fair Value. Also, Morningstar provides a measure of their faith in their Fair Value estimate with Fair Value

Uncertainty number. The Price to Fair Value and PEG ratios provide assessments of the current price in relation to benchmarks of value. If you find a stock that is significantly below its Fair Value and has a PEG of 1.00 or less, the current price of the stock provides a "margin of safety," which should provide some comfort that you are not overpaying for the stock if you buy it before its price appreciates. For a stock with a high Fair Value Uncertainty rating, I want a margin of safety of 40 percent, but for a stock with a Low FV Uncertainty rating, I accept a margin of safety of 25 percent if all other evaluation measures are acceptable. Morningstar Premium makes it easy for you because they provide a suggested Buy At Price for which the analysts calculate a margin-of-safety price.

The next set of items that I suggest you review is what I call Assessment of Management Grades and Ratings. Look at the Stewardship, Growth, Profit, and Financial Health Grades. These grades give you a measure of how well management is looking out for you as an investor. These grades are always important as you consider buying the stock or holding it in the case of analysts' downgrades, but these grades become even more important during tough economic periods like we experienced in 2008-09. Investors will sell off sharply poorly managed businesses during recessions.

The third set of items that you should consider are the Trading Indicators. After you have worked through the first two groups of indicators as discussed above, you likely will have pared your Watch List to a group of very special stocks. If you have money to invest, look at the Trading Indicators to see how they measure on these standards. Look at the Percent Below the 52-Week High and the Dividend Yield for the stock's current price relative to where the stock has traded in the recent past.

The basic assumption is that a stock sometimes during its 52-week cycle will establish a price range that can vary as much as 50 percent in a year. When the current price is at the low-end of its 52-week range, the dividend will increase to the top of its dividend yield range. Of course, some stocks do not pay a dividend, so you will have to rely only on the position of the current price in the 52-week price range. Try to buy the stock at the low end of the 52-week range and at the highest dividend yield that the stock has established in the last four quarters.

Next, review the Relative Strength Indicators. Try to buy the stock when its current price is trending higher than the performance of the S & P 500 Index for the last one- and three-month periods. The Moving Averages mentioned in the next Step 4 will provide confirming indicators as well.

The last item to review in Morningstar Premium is the analyst report for each stock. The analyst review may give you an improved perspective of some of the numbers that you see that are bad, for which the company may be in the process of improving or vice versa. This may give you an opportunity to buy a stock early that may not look good or to sell a stock that is performing well.

When you work through this Practice, you probably will have a short list of favorites that you would buy today, with all other factors being equal. However, take the next step to measure the strength of the stock in relation to its own history to see if investors favor the stock or still relegate the stock to unfavorable status. You want to buy the stocks that investors favor now and the stocks that show improving upward momentum.

Morningstar Premium also offers a sell-side advice that you should consider. The analysts provide a Consider Sell Price that reflects a suitable premium to the analysts' Fair Value assessment. When your stock reaches Morningstar's Consider Sell Price, consult the 200 DMA for the stock and begin selling about one-third of your position if the stock's current price is above its 200 DMA.

Sell half of the remaining shares in two additional increments if the price moves up or down. The Consider Sell Price is not infallible because sometimes stock prices move well beyond that price. However, in those cases of strong upward momentum, watch the slope of the 200 DMA and sell an increment as the slop begins to move down. If the slope accelerates downward or the price goes below the 200 DMA, sell the remaining shares in the position.

Step 4: Create Data File in Toolkit 6 with Watch List Stocks

A. Open Toolkit 6, click on File, Import Company, Import Several at Once, Other Data Files, My Documents, and Excel Folder.
B. Select from Two Options for Data Entry for Each Company:
    1. Electronic Transmission of NAIC Data Files using Standard & Poor's data, which requires an $79 membership with Better Investing. (Go to www.BetterInvesting.com to subscribe.)

     (a) Enter company symbol on Toolkit Home Page

     (b) Click on Retrieve for electronic transmission of data
        listed under B 2 (a) below.

2.   Manually Enter Value Line Data (my preference)

     (a) Enter stock symbol on Toolkit Home Page; click on File
     then on New Company; enter Basic Data, Annual Data,
     and Quarterly Data from Value Line Company Report.

     (b) Go back to Toolkit Home Page, enter stock symbol,
     and click on Retrieve to review company report.

Practices: Analyze Best Case and Worst Case Scenarios for Each Selected Stock

When you have your Watch List or portfolio of stocks set up in the Toolkit software, you are ready to determine the stocks that you want to buy now—or in the case of an existing portfolio—you have a tool to help you decide whether to sell or hold each stock. Toolkit will allow you to play "what if" with each stock to determine the best case scenario or the worst case scenario. The best case will usually be the numbers produced using the Value Line projected earnings per share or the S & P projected earnings per share if you are using the online retrieved data.

Let's assume that you are trying to decide on several stocks that are on your Watch List and passed the intrinsic value tests, and you want to focus on stocks with the greatest projected annual total return over the next five-year period. Here is an example of the analysis that you could do.

When you open Toolkit 6, update the prices of all your stocks and click on Portfolio/PERT. In the Select View box scroll to Summary and click on it, and in the Sort On box scroll to Total Run and click on it. You will see a report that provides a variety of data for each stock such as the Relative Value (based on current vs. historical P/E), recommended Buy Below Price, the Upside/Downside Ratio (U/D), the Projected Annual Total Return, and a Buy/Sell/Hold recommendation.

The B/S/H recommendation is based on the Price Range, U/D ratio, Relative Value, and Total Return. A buy rated stock must be within the calculated Buy Zone on the back of the SSG and have a U/D ratio of 3:1 or higher and a Relative Value of less than 100 percent.

Scroll through the report and note the Buy-rated stocks. Select several Buy-rated stocks that have high projected total returns, but make sure that each has at least a 3:1 U/D ratio. Work through your Buy-rated list by reviewing the Stock Selection Guide (SSG) for each stock. Enter a stock symbol in the Ticker box at the top left and click on Retrieve, and this will bring up the stock with the data that you entered from Value Line or the data that you retrieved with S & P data.

Look at the shape and slope of the three graph lines on the Front of the SSG for the sales, earnings, and profit numbers. Next, review the Back of the SSG and experiment with the numbers for PE's and Estimated High Earnings by entering worst-case scenario numbers. Calculate and enter numbers that will result if analysts' miss the earnings by 20 percent and investors sell off the stock to a much lower P E.

I did a worst-case scenario for AFLAC when it sold off to $12.57 a share (Figure 3). I used the lowest PE in the last five years (11.3) and reduced the Estimated High Earnings in five years to $3.31, which was the earnings per share in 2007. The projected price in five years with these revised numbers was $37.40. I used the Recent Severe Market Low Price of $10.80 as the Estimated Low Price and these numbers produced a U/D of 14.3:1 and the Estimated Compounded Annual Return of 25.8 percent. Therefore, AFLAC is a buy at even the worst-case scenario. Now I just have to wait until the stock begins to build momentum to buy it, and because the stock is so undervalued, I will buy when the current price exceeds the 50 DMA and plan to buy the full position in three increments. My last buying increment will be when the future price closes above its 200 DMA.

The best-case scenario will be produced by using the earnings and PE projections produced by the *Value Line* numbers or by the SSG calculations based on S & P data. With the best-case and worst-case scenarios you can get a feel for the range of possibilities for the stock; and of course, you will have to make the final decision based on your own reading and interpretation of the data composite.

Toolkit allows you to manage the data of a stock and to apply your own judgment regarding the future total return performance. Your objective to this point in the process is to focus on several stocks from different market sectors that project high annual total returns. With this small group of stocks, you are ready to zero in on how the market is treating these stocks by using a set of technical indicators.

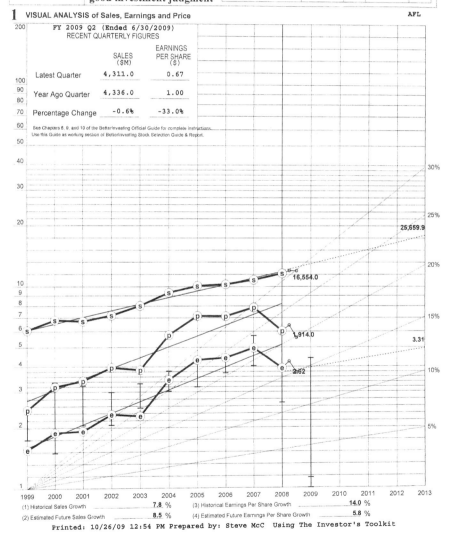

1 VISUAL ANALYSIS of Sales, Earnings and Price

Stock Selection Guide ®

NATIONAL ASSOCIATION OF INVESTORS CORPORATION

INVESTMENT EDUCATION FOR INDIVIDUALS AND CLUBS SINCE 1951

The most widely used aid to good investment judgment

Company	AFLAC		Date	10/23/09
Prepared by	Steve McC		Data taken from	NAIC Data
Where traded	NYSE	Major product/service	Life & Heal	

CAPITALIZATION --- Outstanding Amounts		Reference	1540	
Preferred ($M)	0.0	% Insiders	% Institution	
Common (M Shares)	467.5	0.0	0.0	
Debt ($M)	1,992.0	% to Tot.Cap.	23.0	% Potential Dil. None

AFL

FY 2009 Q2 (Ended 6/30/2009)
RECENT QUARTERLY FIGURES

	SALES ($M)	EARNINGS PER SHARE ($)
Latest Quarter	4,311.0	0.67
Year Ago Quarter	4,336.0	1.00
Percentage Change	-0.6%	-33.0%

See Chapters 8, 9, and 10 of the BetterInvesting Official Guide for complete instructions.
Use this Guide as working section of BetterInvesting Stock Selection Guide & Report.

25,659.9

16,554.0

6,914.0

3.31

2.62

(1) Historical Sales Growth 7.8 %
(2) Estimated Future Sales Growth 8.5 %
(3) Historical Earnings Per Share Growth 14.0 %
(4) Estimated Future Earnings Per Share Growth 5.8 %

Printed: 10/26/09 12:54 PM Prepared by: Steve McC Using The Investor's Toolkit

Figure 3

2 EVALUATING MANAGEMENT

Company **AFLAC** (AFL) 10/23/09

	1999	2000	2001	2002	2003	2004	2005	2006	2007	2008	LAST 5 YEAR AVG.	TREND UP	TREND DOWN
A % Pre-tax Profit on Sales (Net Before Taxes ÷ Sales)	9.0	10.4	11.3	12.3	10.7	13.8	15.8	15.5	16.2	11.6	14.6		DOWN
B % Earned on Equity (E/S ÷ Book Value)	14.2	14.2	12.3	12.5	11.7	15.2	18.1	17.4	18.3	18.4	17.5	UP	

3 PRICE-EARNINGS HISTORY as an indicator of the future

This shows how stock prices have fluctuated with earnings and dividends. It is a building block for translating earnings into future stock prices.

PRESENT PRICE **12.570**   HIGH THIS YEAR **49.360**   LOW THIS YEAR **10.830**

	Year	A PRICE HIGH	B PRICE LOW	C Earnings Per Share	D Price Earnings Ratio HIGH A ÷ C	E Price Earnings Ratio LOW B ÷ C	F Dividend Per Share	G % Payout F ÷ C X 100	H % High Yield F ÷ B X 100
1	2004	42.6	33.9	2.29	18.6	14.8	0.380	16.6	1.1
2	2005	49.7	35.5	2.88	17.3	12.3	0.440	15.3	1.2
3	2006	49.4	41.6	2.95	16.7	14.1	0.550	18.6	1.3
4	2007	63.9	45.2	3.31	19.3	13.7	0.800	24.2	1.8
5	2008	68.8	29.7	2.62	26.3	11.3	0.960	36.6	3.2
6	TOTAL	185.9			98.2	66.2		111.3	
7	AVERAGE	37.2			19.6	13.2		22.3	
8	AVERAGE PRICE EARNINGS RATIO		16.4		9 CURRENT PRICE EARNINGS RATIO		5.0		

Proj. P/E [4.75] Based on Next 4 qtr. EPS [2.64]   Current P/E Based on Last 4 qtr. EPS [2.50]

4 EVALUATING RISK and REWARD over the next 5 years
PEG=82

Assuming one recession and one business boom every 5 years, calculations are made of how high and how low the stock might sell. The upside-downside ratio is the key to evaluating risk and reward.

A HIGH PRICE -- NEXT 5 YEARS
Avg. High P/E 19.6 11.3 X Estimate High Earnings/Share 3.31 = Forecast High Price $ 37.4
(3D7 as adj.)   (4A1)

B LOW PRICE -- NEXT 5 YEARS
(a) Avg. Low P/E 13.2 5.0 X Estimated Low Earnings/Share 2.62 2.54 = $ 12.7
(3E7 as adj.)
(b) Avg. Low Price of Last 5 Years = 37.2
(3B7)
(c) Recent Severe Market Low Price = 10.8

(d) Price Dividend Will Support Present Divd. = 1.120 = 34.7
High Yield (H) 0.032
Selected Estimate Low Price = $ 10.8
(4B1)

C ZONING
37.4 High Forecast Price Minus 10.8 Low Forecast Price Equals 26.6 Range. 1/3 of Range = 6.6
(4A1)   (4B1)   (C)   (4CD)

(4C2) Lower 1/3 = (4B1) 10.8 to 17.4 (Buy) Note: Ranges changed to 25%/50%/25%
(4C3) Middle 1/3 = 17.4 to 30.8 (Maybe)
(4C4) Upper 1/3 = 30.8 to 37.4 (4A1) (Sell)

Present Market Price of 12.570 is in the **Buy** Range
(4C5)

D UP-SIDE DOWN-SIDE RATIO (Potential Gain vs. Risk of Loss)
High Price (4A1) 37.4 Minus Present Price 12.570
= 24.8 = 14.3 To 1
Present Price 12.570 Minus Low Price (4B1) 10.8   1.7   (4D)

E PRICE TARGET (Note: This shows the potential market price appreciation over the next five years in simple interest terms.)
High Price (4A1) 37.4
= (2.975) X 100 = (297.5) - 100 = 197.5 % Appreciation
Present Market Price 12.570   (4E)

Relative Value: 30.5%   Proj. Relative Value: 29.0%

5 5-YEAR POTENTIAL
This combines price appreciation with dividend yield to get an estimate of total return. It provides a standard for comparing income and growth stocks.

Note: Results are expressed as a simple rate; use the table below to convert to a compound rate.

A Present Full Year's Dividend $ 1.120
= 0.089 X 100 = 8.9 Present Yield or % Returned on Purchase Price
Present Price of Stock $ 12.570   (5A)

B AVERAGE YIELD OVER NEXT 5 YEARS
Avg. Earnings Per Share Next 5 Years 2.96 X Avg. % Payout (3G) 22.3 16.2 = 48.0 = 3.8 %
Present Price $ 12.570   (5B)

C ESTIMATED AVERAGE ANNUAL RETURN OVER NEXT FIVE YEARS

		P.A.R.	Tot. Ret.
5 Year Appreciation Potential (4E) 197.5			
5	= 39.5 %	Average Yield 2.0%	1.4%
Average Yield (5B)	3.8 %	Annual Appreciation 16.5%	24.4%
Average Total Annual Return Over the Next 5 Years (5C)	43.3 %	% Compd Ann Rate of Ret 18.5%	25.8%

© 1996, National Association of Investors Corporation; 711 West Thirteen Mile Road, Madison Hgts., Michigan 48071

Printed: 10/26/09 12:54 PM Prepared by: Steve McC Using The Investor's Toolkit

Step 5: Create Watch List Files in Finance.Yahoo.com

A. Log in to www.finance.yahoo.com. Click on My Portfolio,
    Create Portfolio, Create New Portfolio, Track a Symbol Watch List,
    Name Portfolio WATCH LIST, and Enter Ticker Symbols.

B. Highlight WATCH LIST Portfolio, click on New View, enter View
    Name WATCH LIST Review, scroll to View Fields, and click on the
    following fields:
    • Symbol
    • Name
    • Last Trade (Price Only)
    • Change & Percent
    • 50-day Moving Average
    • Percent Change from 50-day Moving Average
    • 200-day Moving Average
    • Percent Change from 200-day Moving Average
    • Percent Change from 52-week Low
    • Percent Change from 52-week High
    • P E G
    • Dividend Yield
    • 1-Year Target Price

Practices: Review Technical Indicators at Least Weekly

In addition to your Watch List setup, create a Preferred List with the stocks that you like from you analysis of intrinsic value and other indicators and your best-case and worst-case scenarios. The finance.yahoo.com setup will alert you to stocks that are beginning to move with green up-arrows and green price numbers. I like to stand on alert for stocks that have moved above their 50-day moving average, but I surely like to buy them when they move above their 200 DMA if most of the other numbers meet my criteria.

Unfortunately, sometimes a stock will "whip-saw" and reverse below the 200 DMA. I gave you a method in chapter 8 of dealing with this possibility; however, the chances are less that the 200-DMA reversal will occur than the 50-DMA reversal will happen. That is the main reason that I like the 200 DMA.

When you have an established portfolio, you should set up your portfolio to follow on the sell side. You should follow your portfolio at least weekly monitoring each stock until a stock or the S & P Index and/or other indexes that you follow fall below their 50 DMA. When the 50 DMA is violated for a stock or one or more of the indices that you follow, you will need to stand on alert and follow the moving averages daily.

Begin selling stocks that violate the 200 DMA if you have a short time to make up any lost value, but if you are young and want to be less conservative, you might want to wait on selling a stock until you see also that the S & P 500 Index falls below its 200 DMA.

In case you are reading this sell method and you are in the midst of a bear market and have already taken some losses, you might want to check your stocks against the 400 DMA or the 20-month moving average. If your stock is below its 400 DMA or 20-month MA, you should sell the stock because it is in a hopeless downtrend. Of course, if the bear market has been underway for many months, such as the downturn that we experienced beginning in November 2007, you will have to make a judgment about whether to take the loss.

In most cases with a taxable portfolio and stocks that you have held for the long-term capital gain period (12-months as a rule), you would be better off selling the stock in order to take a capital loss. You can buy it back in 31 days to avoid the "Wash Sale" rule of the IRS. During a bull market, you might have a stock that moves against the market for a while, but you might want to give it longer to allow the company to work out its problems. In these cases, you may want to ignore the 200 DMA and use the 400 DMA or 20-month MA. In any case, you will need to check the 400 DMA or 20-month MA on the Big Charts website (www.bigcharts.com) because at this writing, the Finance Yahoo website does not offer the 400-day MA or monthly moving averages.

Steadfast use of the 200 DMA for your stock and the indexes will keep you out of deep trouble with you stock portfolio. Furthermore, checking the fundamentals of your stocks periodically will assure that you are invested always in the best quality stocks in the market. Proper use of the fundamental and technical indicators is the reason that I say with great confidence that you will not lose money in any market cycle.

When you have determined the stocks on your Preferred List that are in favor with investors because their prices have moved above your designated MA, you are then ready to determine the percentage of your portfolio to devote to common stocks.

Step 6: Review HaysAdvisory.com for Economy and Market Direction

A. Check Model Condition: Psychology, Monetary, and Valuation
B. Check Asset Allocation: Stocks, Bonds, Cash
C. Review Charts
  1. Valuation
    (a) Market Valuation Model
    (b) S & P 500 12-Month Forward Earnings.
  2. Monetary
    (a) Yield Curve: 10-Year T Note vs. T Bill
    (b) MZM: 3-Year Growth Rate Annualized
    (c) Key Interest Rates
  3. Market Overbought/Oversold Indicators
    (a) NYSE Overbought/Oversold Indicators
    (b) NYSE McClellan vs. 21-Day Oscillator
    (c) NASDAQ McClellan vs. 21-Day Oscillator
    (d). Review Market Commentary

Practices: Determine Market Direction and Your Asset Allocation

The performance of your portfolio will be determined mainly by the mix of stocks, bonds, and cash that you own. For example, during the 2007-2009 bear market, if you had moved your money mainly into cash in late 2007, you would have outperformed all the stock indexes, and you probably would have outperformed most professional money managers.

Stated another way, if you had sold all your stocks that fell below their 200 DMA and kept the money in cash when the 200 DMA of the S & P 500 fell below its 200 DMA, you would have beaten all indexes, all stock mutual funds, and most professional money managers, not to mention the peace of mind that you would have had during the maelstrom of 2008-2009.

The charts and asset allocation recommendations on the Haysadvisory.com website certainly will provide you with sufficient data to make your own decisions. Haysadvisory.com provides an asset allocation model, but they missed the call in 2008-09, like almost everybody; but I do not expect a missed call again because of the adjustments that Hays Advisory made when they realized their mistakes and installed the Market Trend Indicator. Nevertheless, the three sets of indicators: Valuation,

Money, and Overbought/Oversold will provide you with all the data that you need to select entry and exit points for your stock allocation.

First, check the Market Valuation Model to determine if the market is undervalued or overvalued. Go to Charts and look under Valuation and click on Market Valuation Model, and you can see if stock prices are undervalued or overvalued. Then project the year-ahead value of the S & P 500 by multiplying its 12-Month Forward Earnings by the historic multiple of 15. Go to Charts and look for Valuation and scroll to S & P 500 12-Month Forward Earnings, and you will see the projected total earnings for the S & P 500.

Of course, you can then project the possible performance of the S & P 500 Index, which gives you a proxy for the broader market projected 12-month performance. For example, the projected 12-month earnings projection to July 2010 for the S & P 500 was $67.63. If you multiply $67.63 by a modest P E of 20, this calculation projects 1353 on the S & P 500 Index, which is a 103 percent increase in 15 months to July 2010 from the March 2009 low of 667. Even if the market realizes only half of that performance in 12 months, you still would be paid well to be heavily invested in stocks.

Second, keep up with the monetary indicators because when they change, the market direction is likely to change suddenly and significantly to follow the monetary trend. For example, when the yield curve inverts with the 3-month T-Bill rate moving higher than the 10-year T-Note rates, money growth measured by the MZM falls below 5 percent, and LIBOR is more than 1.00 percent higher than the 3-month T-Bill, you know that money is tight and eventually will affect businesses negatively and consequently hurt stock prices.

Third, check the market Overbought/Oversold indicators for an ideal time to invest. This is a short-term trading indicator, but it is useful if you are timing your trade for even a long-term holding period. Buy when the market is oversold and both the oscillator and the 21-day oscillator are at the bottom of the chart. Sell when both are at the top of the chart.

I recommend that you read the twice-weekly HaysAdvisory.com market commentary for the analysts' views on market directions. The analysts usually include charts that are very helpful as you decide on the market direction.

Step 7: Follow Your Portfolio in Portfolio Manager 5
A. Download Portfolio Manager 5 software from Better Investing
B. Set up Your Portfolio with Portfolio Setup Wizard
C. Import Your Portfolio from Toolkit 6 or Your Broker
   or Manually Enter Your Stocks at Enter Buy
D. Set up Various Reports
   1. Click on Reports and Graphs and Portfolio
   2. Click on Each Report and Set up Report: Appraisal, Holdings
      Summary, Transaction Activity, Upside/Downside, Portfolio
      Allocation, Portfolio Performance, and Sold Securities
E. Follow Several Reports Weekly
   1. Holdings Summary
   2. Appraisal
   3. Portfolio Performance
   4. Portfolio Allocation
F. Run End of Year Report for Income Tax Reporting:
   Securities Sold Report

Practices: Actively Review and Manage Your Account

This is the stage where you can demonstrate your good judgment and implement your unique investment strategy. You should become very familiar with all the reports and graphs of Portfolio Manager 5, and later you may need to add to the list of reports that I have suggested. In any case, study the report and management offerings of this powerful portfolio management software.

The Portfolio Holdings Summary Report will be your main working report. It provides the day-to-day data that you must have to manage your portfolio, although I have suggested that you only have to check it once a week. Check at least each week the gain/loss column that alerts you to how each stock is doing since you bought it.

Also, look at the Percentage of Portfolio column for each stock; I recommend that you keep your individual stock allocation to 5 percent or less. Of course, this allocation percentage would mean that you have at least twenty stocks if you have an all stock portfolio and are fully invested. The twenty stocks would provide ample diversification for your portfolio if you select stocks from many sectors.

If a stock loses more than 8 percent after you buy it and the market is stable or is trending higher, do more research on the company and see if something has happened that you did not anticipate. Of course, you need to check the 50 DMA and the 200 DMA. If both are trending lower, check the 400 DMA and the 20-month MA for confirmation that the equity is in a downtrend that could be prolonged.

From this and other data that you can find in *Value Line* and Morningstar Premium reports, you can make your own decision whether to Hold, Sell, or Buy additional shares. The percent of your portfolio devoted to this declining stock should hold weight in your decision, because an entry position of 1 percent might be treated as a hold or add, but a full position of 5 percent might dictate an outright sell signal.

The main function of your portfolio management software is to keep any sudden change in the value of your portfolio from surprising you. Also, another function is the income tax reporting feature of the Securities Sold Report for taxable portfolios.

Savvy individual investors can manage portfolios now in the same way only the professionals could do fifteen years ago. Technology provides a lot of information for our immediate use, and Portfolio Manager 5 is a very economical and powerful tool that competes favorably with the most comprehensive and expensive software for portfolio management on the market.

Portfolio Management Routine

Successful portfolio management is the end result of a disciplined approach to reviewing each stock in your portfolio and searching for new companies to follow. This disciplined approach should be done at least weekly, but more often if problems develop with any single company in your portfolio or in the stock market in general. Value Line updates its website on Tuesday of each week with a new issue from its 13-issue quarterly composite. Also, new information for stocks that appeared in previous issues is provided in a bulletin to keep you abreast of all corporate news. The paper issue of *Value Line* is normally mailed in time for you to receive it on Friday of each week. Therefore, set a day of your choice each week to conduct a review of your portfolio and the stocks on your Watch List.

The following outline is a routine that will enable you to keep current with your Watch Lists and portfolio and consequently avoid any sudden reversal in your portfolio value. Also, you will be able to identify additional stocks that are beginning to show signs of breakouts to the upside.

Weekly routine:

A. Run Value Line (VL) Screen in your saved setup.
B. Compare resulting screened stocks to your Watch Lists and portfolio of stocks.
    1. Delete stocks from Watch List that drop off VL screening.
    2. Consider selling stocks in portfolio that drop off VL screening.
        (a) View technicals for each of these stocks.
            (1) Hold if still above 50 DMA and 200 DMA.
            (2) Sell if below 50 DMA and 200 DMA.
        (b) Review Intrinsic Value (Fair Value) for each of these stocks.
            (1) Sell if 25 percent above intrinsic value (IV).
            (2) Hold if still below IV or at a slight premium above IV and above 50 DMA and 200 DMA.
C. Add new stocks from VL Screen to:
    1. Morningstar Premium Watch List
    2. SSG in Toolkit 6
    3. My Portfolios: finance.yahoo.com
D. Review your portfolio of stocks in Portfolio Manager 5
    1. Review any stocks with losses (G/L column)
        (a) Check 50 DMA and 200 DMA in finance.yahoo.com.
        (b) Review fundamentals in *Value Line*, Toolkit 6, and Morningstar Premium.
        (c) Develop sell watch list to follow daily.
    2. Review stocks with big gains
        (a) Determine if any exceed their intrinsic value (IV).
        (b) Sell one-half of the position if 25 percent above IV.
E. Review Watch List and My Portfolio in finance.yahoo.com.
    1. Watch List: Develop short watch list of stocks exceeding 50 DMA and 200 DMA for possible purchase.
    2. Portfolio: Develop short watch list of stocks falling below 50 DMA and 200 MA for possible sell.
F. Review short lists daily until disposition is made for each stock on lists.
G. Review Hays Charts for psychology, monetary and valuation.

Normally, this routine process should require only an hour to follow your current stocks in a 50 stock Watch List and 20 stocks in your portfolio. This time assessment is based on the fact that you probably will not have more than 6 to 8 stocks each week that *Value Line* updates.

Summary and Conclusions

This chapter provides all the information and practices that you need to be very successful in stock investing. Also, this system will allow you to sleep at night when the economy is in a deep recession and the stock market is in a gut-wrenching downtrend. You will be at peace during the maelstrom because for the most part, you will be out of stocks will have parked you money in a money market account that is invested in short-term government securities and has a stable $1.00 per share value.

The approach used in identifying stocks and managing a portfolio moves from the general to the specific with each step building on the former steps. The first step is to identify the universe of stocks that meet your criteria and then to expose each stock to a series of fundamental and technical tests to determine the best stocks for your portfolio. Also, the model has a selling practice that will help you preserve your gains.

The key to working the model is to follow steadfastly the sequential order of the steps and to work through the complete process at least once each week. The Buy/Sell short list should be checked more frequently than once a week.

The chapter also provides a recommended investment strategy statement, but as you get familiar with the system, you probably will make some modifications in your investment strategy. The only prerequisite for success is that you remain true to your strategy and methods.

I am sure that you will look at these steps and have some reservations about following this method. Of course, it will take some time to set up your strategy, but as you work the steps a few times, you will notice that the time you spend in following the routine will diminish each week. Like anything else that is worthwhile, investing takes study and practice, and the winners work at and master this craft. So, determine that you are going to devote the time to studying this system, and as you practice, you will become very proficient and efficient, and you will be rewarded accordingly.

Now I want to cover some of the common mistakes that investors make, even experienced investors, and the emotional battles that we all face in long bear markets. This may be more helpful than any chapter in the book.

CHAPTER TEN

Investment Faults and Fixes

The extremes in bull and bear markets bring out the worst in investors. During the froth of bull market tops, investor sentiment is too optimistic and investors often throw money at the market when even the stocks of the worst companies are going up, which is a signal that the market is topping. Conversely, when stocks have sold off unmercifully in a bear market, investors often sell stocks in a flourish at the bottom. Such was the case in the first quarter of 2009 when new lows were made in all three major stock indices. Savvy investors wait for these signs of tops and bottoms in markets to make their calculated moves, and that is the position that I want you to be in during the next market cycle.

I want you to reduce your exposure to stocks when the market is topping and keep the proceeds from your sold stocks in cash equivalents until the time is right to go back in at the bottom. Chapters 6-9 have related the investment system and method to accomplish that objective.

Investors often allow panic and poor judgment to override the best of intentions and the most sophisticated investment systems and methods. Professional investors are often guilty of these lapses in judgment and poor control of their emotions also. Therefore, the objectives of this chapter are to review the ten worst mistakes investors make, point out the emotional aspects of investing, and discuss seven rules of savvy investing.

Ten Worst Investor Mistakes

Investors could improve their performance in any market cycle if they would eliminate the following ten mistakes.

Under-diversification is the most crippling of all mistakes that investors make. The most notable signs of under-diversification in a portfolio are too few stocks and too large a percentage invested in one stock, insufficient industries represented in the portfolio, and limited asset classes composing the portfolio. Why is under-diversification such an egregious problem? Under-diversification compounds the unsystematic risk or the risk resulting from specific problems in an industry group or a single firm. For example, the credit problems and the credit default swaps impact on the financial services industry of 2007-2009 could have damaged a portfolio well beyond the broader market losses if that portfolio were filled with bank, insurance, and broker stocks and Real Estate Investment Trusts.

Typically, a portfolio should be set up along an asset allocation model of stocks, bonds, and cash with minor allocations in real estate and hard assets, such as gold. A minimum of eight stocks with equal value representing eight unrelated industries make an ideal entry-level diversified portfolio. The percent of the portfolio allocated to stocks is up to you, but my standard is simply to reduce the stock percentage in the portfolio as you get older.

I suggested a few guidelines regarding allocation in chapter 6. I normally do not like to see more than 5 percent of a portfolio devoted to one stock or to any single industry group. *Value Line* lists ninety-nine industries in the order of their timeliness, so finding sufficient industries to meet your diversification standards should not be difficult, even if you have 80-90 percent of your money invested in stocks.

Some very notable professional investors believe in finding the best stocks and overweighting (limited diversification) these stocks. The theory is that if you work hard to find these great bargains in good companies that you should structure your portfolio to maximize your return when these stocks run up in price. That is a very aggressive offensive strategy and can be very rewarding when it works, but my strategy is that investors need to play defense first and protect their portfolios from unsystematic risk because of the nature of the volatile markets in these days of technology-enhanced trading and the fast-money mentality.

If you are working full-time at another profession and you only have time to follow your portfolio in the evenings or on the weekend, you are not going to catch breaking news. Traders might trade your stock down 10-20 percent in a day based on some silly whim or other unwarranted reason. Diversification is one way to guard against total decimation of your portfolio. The downturn may provide you with an opportunity to add to your position in a stock that is destined to rebound eventually; but then again it may not rebound quickly, and the emotional stress in the meantime can be ameliorated by broad diversification.

In my investment management practice, our composite portfolio in 2008 was down about one-half of the loss in the S & P 500, and I owe our favored return, although still with some losses, to the fact that we were highly diversified. We held very small positions in banks, mainly regional banks, and even smaller positions in insurance, brokerage, and money management firms. All of these industries suffered the brunt of the market loss during the recent recession. No strategy has a more punitive effect than concentrated investing, and no strategy provides a greater reward than simple diversification.

Falling in love with a stock or an industry is an early symptom of an under-diversified portfolio. In Georgia and particularly the Atlanta metro area, Coca Cola has been historically one of the most favored stocks. In numerous families, this stock has been passed down to children for generations. Certainly, Coca Cola stock has sent many children to college or otherwise enriched a families' discretionary money, and I concede the stock did very well for decades. But a few years within the last ten years, Coca Cola has struggled, and families bemoaned the fortunes of their former benefactor.

Bank stocks are good representatives of an industry group that has held favored status for buy and hold investors for decades. The typical thinking has been, until 2007, that banking is a regulated industry, and hardly any major bank failures have occurred since the 1930s. The notion has been that banks are always going to make money and pay a good dividend. The financial industry problems of late have verified that banks certainly can lose money and banks can fail. Furthermore, banks are no less susceptible to bad management than any other industry.

I will have to acknowledge that some people who buy big positions in a particular stock like Coca Cola or a bank stock sometimes keep up with the news of their investment better than the average investor does. So they are able to feel more assured about their investment than the investor who has a small position in a bank and a fully diversified portfolio of stocks. However, these well-informed investors are in a position to trade the stock periodically to take advantage of the inevitable cyclical changes in stock prices. Just check the price range of a stock in any 12-month period and notice the price swings. It is not uncommon to see a trading range of 50 percent in any 12–month period. However, most of us are not short-term traders; therefore, we have to rely on other strategies to deal with possible wide swings in market prices.

I contend that any stock that is bought should be subject to being sold at the right time. If you hold a stock well beyond the price that its earnings will continue to support, your stock is susceptible to a sudden and vicious sell-off and even worse, to being relegated to an unfavored status that may restrict its attractiveness as an investment for many months or even years.

One of the reasons that some investors fall in love with a stock or industry is that they **will not sell because it cost too much in income taxes**. While an income tax strategy should be a major factor in your financial planning, risking huge losses in profits should not enter into your consideration. The current capital gains rate of 15 percent for assets held for 12 months or longer is a resounding bargain in view of the possible loss of profit and even losses in the principal investment cost.

I recommend that you ask yourself this question: *How much loss in my stock will it take to equal the income tax that I will pay on the stock if I sell it at a specified price?* You will be surprised at how small the loss will be to equal your capital gains liability.

For example, if you buy 1,000 shares of a stock at $25, and in 24 months the stock runs up to $50 a share, you will have made $25,000 in two years. That is an excellent return, but that kind of run-up is not unlikely if you buy your stock when it is well-undervalued and when it builds momentum as reflected in your technical indicators as described in chapters 8-9.

The fact that the stock has run up so far so fast is an indicator that you should consider selling a portion of your position and taking your profits. If you sell all shares, you will pay $3,750 in income taxes, and your stock would have to pull back only $3.75 (7.5 percent) to $46.25 to equal the loss that would equal your income tax liability. If you calculate what your stock could pull back to which would give it a more historically reasonable price/earnings ratio, you will discover that you might be in for a loss of at least half of your profit. Of course, this example is hypothetical. Extenuating circumstances may be a factor, but this is the mindset that you should adopt when you consider the next steps with your portfolio gains.

Sell a portion of the stock and pay the income taxes out of the capital gains, and you will not miss the income tax payment. If you like the stock, buy it back when it pulls back and repeat the process. Contrary to the income tax "wash sale" rule, there is no waiting period to buy back a stock that has been sold for a gain. You can even hold an eight-stock portfolio of the same stocks over a lifetime and make an enormous total return just by buying and selling the same stocks indefinitely.

You will get to where you know the companies so well that you know their flex points up and down. You might become so familiar with the patterns of these companies that you can even anticipate when the stock price will reach maximum optimism and when it will reach maximum pessimism. The key to this approach is your willingness to sell and pay the income taxes. As the old saying goes, "nobody ever went broke taking a profit"; and I add, paying the income taxes on profits is just a cost of doing business as an active investor.

You noticed that I suggested selling a portion of your shares of a stock to take profits. Incremental selling and buying is the more conservative approach to taking a profit and buying a position in a stock. **Investors commonly make only one trade to sell a position in a stock or to buy a stock.** Taking a full position on the buy side or selling out completely at one time assumes that you have all the information that is available on the company and that the stock price will behave in a perfectly orderly manner.

Unfortunately, stock prices do not move in perfect lockstep with the information that is publicly available. Many times traders and investors with huge cash or positions in a stock will speculate on future earnings or other events that are not already priced into the stock. Therefore, in the short-term of a few days or weeks, a stock price might gyrate considerably up or down. Also, during a bull-run by a stock, the stock can become outrageously overpriced before it pulls back to a more reasonable value.

In consideration of the possibility of short-to-intermediate term volatility and investor despair or exuberance, I like to take a position or sell a position in a stock in three increments. The first incremental size may vary from 50 percent to 33 1/3 percent of my total allocation, depending on how convinced I am that this is a good move. The later two increments will be from 25 percent each to 33 1/3 percent each.

You may wonder how it works if a stock price keeps rising after a buy. I just keep buying at a predetermined time period of usually two to three months, or I might buy on any weakness. Sometimes during a three-increment purchase period, I get a pull-back in the stock run-up, and then I buy more shares if I am still convinced the stock is a keeper. Every incremental buy is based on further assessment of the future value of the stock.

On the sell side, I might accelerate my second and third incremental sell orders if the stock has an above-average spike-up on any given day. This vigorous move up in an overpriced stock is usually indicative of topping action and is a good signal to sell more of your position. Also, if the technical indicators signal a sale based on moving averages, you may want to consider accelerating your selling process.

Now let us consider what happens if you make a mistake and buy a stock that looks undervalued, but it keeps plummeting. This is a condition in investing known as a *value trap*, and the stock could continue dropping in price. **Investors often say, "When it bounces back to where I bought it, I am going to sell it."** Hopefully, with the investment model that I have given you, you will have relied on the technical indicators of 50 DMA and 200 DMA to buy stocks that are attractive and on the move.

However, if the 50 DMA suddenly reverses, then stay alert to the 200 DMA, and be ready to bail out of the position as soon as possible. Of course, nobody likes to sell out of a position in which there is a loss. However, the fallacy of waiting until the stock bounces back is that it may not bounce back or if it does, you have wasted months or even years to realize a small psychological triumph. On the other hand, you could use the sale proceeds to invest in an appreciating stock that will make up your loss in a short-time if you get out of your losing position early enough.

During the bear market of 2000-2002, technology stocks took massive losses after the NASDAQ composite index reached just over 5,000. However, when the massive sell-off started, there were analysts who were advising investors to take the opportunity to buy into cheap stocks of growing companies. The stocks were cheap only in relationship to their past inflated prices, but their underlying fundamentals such as price/earnings ratios were sometimes over 100.

Also, the technical indicators early in the free fall signaled a sale was in order. These stocks have not recovered to their highs even after almost ten years, and they might not recover in the next ten years. The market pays you good money not to wait until a stock price bounces back to sell. Follow the sell discipline included in chapters 8-9, and you will avoid long periods of non-productivity in your portfolio.

The next two common mistakes that investors make should be discussed together because the root causes of the mistakes are the same:

buying on news and not on analysis. Investors who **jump into hot stocks or mutual funds** are listening to the news and not doing their homework. Typically, by the time that a stock or a mutual fund gets into the popular media, it is too late to buy because the best gains are past and indeed the popularity of the investment signals a topping process.

Technology and telecommunication stocks of the last decade and emerging markets mutual funds of the recent past are good examples of hot investments that were bought without any regard for the fundamentals of the underlying securities. I assume that often investors follow "free" advice because they do not know how to value a stock, but at other times, the arguments seem so logical that the message is the madness. However, the message usually is yesterday's story or information that is further back than you should even consider because it is looking at the stock in a rear view mirror. You want to look ahead and see how expected earnings per share relate to the current price.

For example, what kind of earnings growth will it take to sustain the historic growth rate and what P/E will it take if earnings slow down somewhat? Stocks have a historic P/E range that the market of investors is comfortable with, and when that range is violated, the stock price is in for a sell-off to a lower price that brings down the P/E. If you ask yourself some simple analytical questions, often you will pass up the "free" advice.

You can actually rely on this mantra of investing: there is no such thing as free advice. You may not pay an advisor, but you will sooner or later pay for the lack of analysis. *Money* magazine and CNBC have their places, but their positions are at best providing investment ideas that you should subject to your own thorough analysis. Remember, a class of momentum investors is out there who believe that you should buy stocks as long as they are going up. This is a trading mentality, which requires constant surveillance of your portfolio. Using fundamental analysis, and buying and selling when the technical trends change is still the best strategy for most investors.

The opposite of buying the hot stock and following a trading mentality is **hating a stock or industry that has burned you in the past**. Spurned love turns into eternal hate. Why? The reason is the same in stock selection as it is in the affairs of the heart: we feel rejected, embarrassed, and loss of our confidence.

Remember your high school love: skinny ninth grade boy falls for a fully-developed ninth grade girl. They date for a few times with a group and see each other at school. However, she soon gains confidence and is ready to test the junior and senior market and hooks up with a football player in the eleventh grade who has a car. The ninth grade boy is left out, and he does not forget that experience. By the time that he is a senior, he has a car, is the quarterback on the football team, and has early offers from major colleges. But he accepts no offer nor certainly makes no offer to his first love from the ninth grade because "once burned then twice cautious." However, he may be overlooking a real gem, someone who is perfect for him, and he might never realize it.

Stocks are as intriguing as youthful love. Company fortunes rise and fall, fortunately in long cycles of many decades, but just because an investor is burned, that does not mean it should leave a permanent scar. Good companies that sell-off savagely often go "back to the drawing board and re-tool" and come out of the process stronger, more efficient, and more viable in the marketplace. In fact, good companies that have sold off badly are good places to look for stocks with great potential. This is not investment advice, but for example, bank, brokerage, and insurance stocks smashed in the 2007-2009 crash may be the leading gainers in the early years of the next decade.

You remember that I cited Coca Cola as a stock that many Georgians fell in love with during the twentieth century. However, when the company started making a series of bad moves and saturated the marketable world with its products, leaving "no other worlds to conquer," the stock price crashed and many lovers of that beverage stock turned on the company and started selling it off. The P/E of the stock fell back in line with its historical average, and the company management began to "right the listing ship." However, there was not widespread love expressed for this world-class company with its very attractive price. Remember to let the company fundamentals and the technicals speak to you and guide your investment decisions and do not "shoot your toe off to make your shoe fit."

These last two common mistakes are typical of market bottoms and grieve me more than all the other mistakes combined: **selling at the bottom because you cannot take it any more, and freezing with fear during the best time to buy**. A typical scenario may be that your favorite stock has sold off unmercifully and you have grown sick of it. You want it out of your portfolio because it reminds you of what could have been and how lazy or blind that you have been. You did not know the fundamentals when you bought it, and you do not know its fundamentals now. You just bought it, and it did very well during its time. But now you are embarrassed, disappointed, and grim about the company's future. You tell your broker or you go online and sell at the market price at that very moment. You think, *Get this "dog" out of my sight.*

If you have waited to sell until this psychological nadir, you have waited too late to sell. I know that is a broad generalization and no doubt there are some mitigating circumstances, such as WorldCom in the 2000-2002 debacle. Certainly, if a company is going out of business, no time is too late to sell if you can get something for your stock. But in most cases of sell-offs at the bottom, the sale is made based on emotion and not sound judgment of the company's prospects for the future.

Too much attention is given to the news in the media, which of course is about past economic and market data. For example, investors sold a huge number of shares of Apple Computer (AAPL) just before it started taking off in 2004 when the iPod became a permanent establishment. Bank stocks got the axe in early 2009 as the news about the future of US banking went from worst to abysmal. The news is always the worst at the bottom of the market, but that is the best time to buy stocks, not to sell your holdings, regardless of how badly they have performed recently.

During the first week of March 2009, $22 billion were redeemed from stock mutual funds when the US Treasury Department announced plans to provide additional bailout money to AIG. As a result, the DJIA fell 4 percent to 6736, which was 50 percent below its high in October 2007. Let me repeat John Templeman's mantra: buy stocks at the point of maximum pessimism. However, too often even the best investors and the wisest financial counselors indicate their terror by sitting on their cash or even worse, as indicated above, selling at the bottom and putting their money in certificates of deposit.

When stocks go on sale, that is the time to buy, but it takes seasoning in the investment world to see or sense these glorious buying opportunities. The seasoning I am referring to is an emotional quality, an experience factor, and a learned response. I am going to address the emotional aspects of investing later in this chapter, but for now, I will explain the concept of capitulation.

Capitulation is the cumulative selling action of the mass of investors when they think that the economy is in permanent ruin and the stock market will never recover in "my lifetime." Seasoned investors look for signs of capitulation, but unseasoned investors freeze with fear during these times. You should know that many unsettling days will occur during the capitulation process as well as "fits and starts" before stocks take off in a new bull market. But this is not the time to freeze with fear and not get in the game. From these low points, the greatest stock gains are made.

In a concession to your emotions, the way to play these times is to use incremental investing that does not place all your money in stocks during this time of emotional despair. Set up an investment schedule over the next three to six months, seek the best stocks for investments, and put your money to work.

Dealing With Investor Emotions

Capitulation is the effect of panic by a major portion of investors, and this fear is the major cause of most of the mistakes investors make. Therefore, is it reasonable to conclude that if investors control their emotions, they can eliminate most of the mistakes that they make in investing? If you can eliminate the common mistakes, you should improve your total return significantly over a lifetime of investing. If you accept this simple premise, then how should you deal with your emotions in investing? Before we delve into that issue, I remind you that the emotional aspect of investing includes ebullience as well as despair. It is equally as important to follow investing fundamentals and technical indicators during powerful bull markets, when investor froth is rampant and not get swept up in ebullience, as it is to trust your investment methods and keep your emotions in check during a miserable recession and a menacing bear market.

During my formal education, I minored in psychology and counseling at the three degree levels. I served as a counselor for several years in my student personnel work and taught introductory psychology and mental health courses for a few years at Wofford College.

In all of this work, I had a special interest in studying the effects of fear on the physical body and on the reasoning process. This study and work do not make me an expert in psychology, but it does help me develop my own theory of fear that I can corroborate or discard after observing the actions of investors.

First, let me define fear as I observed it in college students. Fear is the anxiety that results from uncertainty about what is happening in one's life and how a culmination of events, circumstances, and situations will be resolved or fail to be resolved to one's satisfaction in the future. That definition may generate some debate, so let us approach the subject in another way. Is fear an emotion that we can control just by taking thought and determining to overcome it? My answer is no; we cannot control fear just by deciding to ride herd on the thoughts that creep into our minds and raise anxiety.

When we confront our anxieties, our fears go "underground." Our direct confrontation of fear causes our subconscious to program anxiety at an imperceptible level; if the anxiety is not resolved, it compounds or "layers" with anxiety upon anxiety. At some point, the anxiety controls our subconscious and begins to program abnormal reactions in our physical bodies and in our mental processing. In other words, we make ourselves sick and irrational. Usually, early in the deterioration process, we will do whatever it takes to relieve the anxiety, whether the relief mechanism is rational or not.

Investors have a way to deal with this anxiety (sell stocks), and quite often the relief mechanism is irrational, evidenced by sudden emotional reaction without a trace of sound judgment. The conscious decision to deal with anxiety is good in the sense that it works to motivate our developing a plan for dealing with our emotions. We should address three basic methods for dealing with fear. First, avoid the fear-producing stimuli; second, retrain our mind and subconscious to look for a positive outcome to our fear-invoking circumstances; and third, saturate our minds and subconscious with hope.

The best way to deal with situations that are likely to cause emotional upheaval, of course, is to avoid the circumstances that will provoke fear. In investment terms, this means being out of stocks when the economy is headed for a recession and stocks are selling off. If you follow the simple technical indicators that I recommended, the 50 DMA and the 200 DMA for your stocks and confirmed by the 200 DMA of the S & P 500 Index, this strategy will put you on the sidelines before the "bottom falls out of stocks."

Remember that I told you I was out of stocks on Black Monday, October 1987, for my clients and my own portfolio. I can tell you that on the day of the crash, I had no fear about the market. As the market gyrated for a few weeks, I was fine and needless to say, my clients were greatly relieved. Unfortunately, as I noted before, I did not reinvest back in stocks soon enough when my indicators turned positive after the crash because I listened to the fear-monger experts who said that the crash had set up conditions for a widespread and long-lasting economic recession. That did not happen. Nevertheless, I was at peace as the market tanked, but I had a lot of anxiety as the market rebounded because I did not have sufficient exposure to stocks. The point is, if you follow your indicators and move ahead of the broad-based market, you will avoid most of the fear-producing downdraft of the stock market.

During the 2000-2002 bear market, I did not deal with the fear very well. Technology and telecommunication stocks were absolutely killed, and significant fraud of several companies was devastating. I mentioned the analysts' positive reports about WorldCom right up to the point of the massive fraud that was revealed about the company. I cannot blame the analysts because they were not privy to accurate information, and I cannot blame myself. Nonetheless, it is not easy to see a client's money and my own small position in a stock destroyed because of the company lies about earnings that I had relied on for months.

Over the period of three years, my health suffered. My immune system did not work as it should, and I was gloomy frequently, particularly as the bear market lingered. Overall, diversification in our portfolios helped us to perform relatively well, but on an absolute basis, we all lost money. I had a dreadful time with my health and emotions. So I made up my mind to do something about this anguish that lies in wait as a potential for harm in the worst of times. I set about to condition myself spiritually and emotionally to deal with the emotions of a volatile and punishing stock market. The result is that during 2007-2009, I was at total peace with the conditions, unbelievably optimistic about the future of our country and the stock market, and used the low points in the market to invest new money for clients and my family.

Retraining the mind and renewing the human spirit to deal with emotional stress takes time, and the effectiveness of the process is relative to your intensity and perseverance in the task. Nevertheless, you can begin the process at any time, even though you might have neglected your fundamental and technical indicators and might be in the midst of a deep funk right now. In fact, despair is a mega-motivator for change, just as "necessity is the mother of invention." So let your deep funk motivate you instead of driving you to despair about your portfolio.

Education is the most important step in the change process because knowledge is powerful, and understanding helps us cope with dire forecasts. First, let us deal with the economy and stock market education. Study economic and stock market history. Learn about the great bear markets since 1900 and study the long-term charts of the Dow Jones Industrial Averages. As you will see on the Dow charts, even the horrible bear market of 1929-1938 is only a slight downward blip on the chart. If you do not know the dates of the downturn, you possibly could not actually pinpoint the appropriate wave in the chart.

Here is another story on that point. When the 2007-2009 bear market began in November 2007, and the subsequent recession followed soon afterward, I had an appointment with a health care provider. One of the people in the office of this provider asked me about the stock market news. Without giving much thought to the matter, I said that it was just a blip in our future. This later was a matter of some amusement for the assistant as the economic news grew worse, but this person did not have the perspective of the long-term history of markets. Granted, if you are in the market with less than five years to go before retirement, your asset allocation should take care of your loss protection. Otherwise, you need a working knowledge of how markets fluctuate and how increasing earnings over a decade drive up stock prices to keep pace with corporate growth and inflation.

Read everything that you can about the great bear markets and also learn how bull markets eventually sold off when overzealous investors began throwing money at poor quality companies and their overpriced stock. Google the bear markets of 1980-82, 1987, 1990, 1993-94, 2000-2002, and 2007-2009 and read the doomsday predictions in the midst of those bear markets. You will see that in every recession and every leading bear market, dire predictions were made by the experts about the future of stocks.

Furthermore, with the immediacy and graphics of television and with the talk-show formats that are so popular, the drama of a sell-off in any day in stocks can be turned into an unwarranted media-made calamity. Remember the media thrives on bad news, and if its hosts can riveted your attention during their market "sweeps" season, you are a statistic that can help boost their viewer ratings and improve their advertising fee structure. Not all media is so driven, but many reporters are journalists first and investment counselors without portfolios next. For your own peace of mind, analyze the media treatment of the financial news; and be skeptical of everything that you read, see, and hear. Analyze the analyzers, think for yourself, and allow your judgment and experience to precondition your emotions.

Basically, you can retrain your mind to react to bad economic and stock market news by going immediately to historical lessons that demonstrate that the US economy has always recovered, and stock markets always have rebounded vigorously. Focus on the fact that economists and market strategists always say that this time it is different from past recessions and market crashes. You can train yourself to focus on a better day by looking beyond the veil of these dark days and envisioning a vigorous economy and thriving stock market, which is your goal for the future.

As you absorb these historical facts, you will become optimistic, and this optimism actually will draw people to you. Some will argue with you, but the weight of the evidence is overwhelmingly in your favor. I had a friend ask me in the recent bear market how I could be so optimistic. My response was, "Why should I not be? I know the history of the stock market, and this is a good time to buy." You should keep your goals in mind to persevere in tough times.

This story about great long-distance swimmer Florence Chadwick's swim of the Catalina Channel is a good example of the power of seeing your goal. She attempted to swim the twenty-six miles from Catalina Island to the California mainland on July 4, 1952. A vast fog enshrouded her and her attendants during the swim, and all she could see was the dense fog, the lifeboat, and the gunners who were firing shots to scare away the sharks. After almost sixteen hours in the water, she gave up the swim; she did not know that she was less than a mile from the coast. She said that if she had been able to see the coast that she probably could have made it. The fog kept her from seeing her goal and victory. Two months later when she made the swim again, she controlled her emotions by keeping a mental image of the shoreline in her mind when the fog arrived. [1]

Your research and study will help you see your goal, and your vision will tell you not to worry about the future of your investments. Use the downturn to invest more money in high quality companies, and look forward to the compounding effect of your investments in more shares at lower prices as they produce excellent returns.

I have saved the best advice for the last: realize who you are as a Christian and practice the biblical deterrents to fear. Jesus said do not be anxious about anything. Do not fear the unknown or any circumstances that surround you. Instead, pray and rely on the Lord God for your strength and your future, and thank Him for the peace that He will give you (Phil. 4:6-7 TLB). He said only to fear the Lord in order to control our greed and other carnal desires. If we take care of our indiscretions, He will take care of our fears and anxiety.

In Isaiah 8:11-14 (NLT), God spoke to the prophet:

The Lord has given me a strong warning not to think like everyone else does. He said, "Don't call everything a conspiracy, like they do, and don't live in dread of what frightens them. Make the Lord of Heaven's Armies holy in your life. He is the one you should fear. He is the one who should make you tremble. He will keep you safe."

As Christians, we can deal with our anxiety by invoking Scriptures like Paul's admonition to the Philippians and these words to Isaiah. Of course, we must shore up our lives to be consistent with His expectations of us as good stewards and obey His commands such as taking care of the poor and spreading His gospel.

Remember the story of the three servants whom the Master entrusted with different talents [money] while he was on a business trip. When he returned, he called each servant in to give an account of how each handled his money. The first two who received the most grew the money, but the third servant reported that he feared the Master and hid his money to keep it safe. The Master was furious and took the money from the slothful servant and gave it to the productive servants (Matt.25:14-30). God expects us to see things through and not to be anxious or otherwise bound by fear. We are to rely on Him and to continue being productive during the worst of circumstances.

If we hide the money entrusted to us and quake in fear, it marks us as unfaithful to the Lord, who makes it possible for us to prosper. As the admonition to Isaiah says, we are not to think as everyone else does when we are surrounded by the worst of circumstances; we are to look beyond the circumstances and see the hand of the Lord God Almighty moving on our behalf.

The inspired advice that Paul the apostle gave his ward, Timothy, gives us a clue about how to treat our wealth and what to do to deal with any future concerns.

> *Tell those who are rich not to be proud and not to trust in their money, which will soon be gone [when Jesus returns], but their pride and trust should be in the living God who always richly gives us all we need for our enjoyment. Tell them to use their money to do good. They should be rich in good works and should give happily to those in need, always being ready to share with others whatever God has given them. By doing this they will be storing up real treasure for themselves in heaven—it is only the safe investment for eternity! And they will be living a fruitful Christian life down here as well* (1 Tim. 6:17-19 TLB).

Based on this Scripture from 1 Timothy, I have a suggestion for you if you have a panic attack about the reduced value in your 401(k) and the economy is scaring you. Find a family that is destitute and minister to their needs. For example, find a family where the husband is out of work, the mother stays at home with three small children, and their heat and electricity services have been disconnected. Pay their utility bills, buy them some food, and give the husband and father some work around your house. Offer encouragement and instruction for this wage-earner and help him present himself at his best in any job interviews that you might help him arrange.

Get other people in your church or circle of friends to help you with this family. Dip into your investments if necessary. Spend time with them and give them hugs every day during their ordeal. Seek other families in your city who are in great need at this time. You will be amazed at what divinely happens to you as the joy of giving takes over your life, and you do not feel any anxiety with your investments. You will understand the principle of sowing seed in a comparable field (financial), and you will want more of what God offers in eternal treasures.

If you will reach out financially to others in need during a recession and stock market crash, I guarantee you that your fear of the economy or your worry about your portfolio loss will disappear. You will be amazed how calm you will be when you receive your monthly portfolio statement. If you help others in distress, you store up spiritual capital that is lending to the Lord, and He will then supply all your needs (Prov.19:17). The immediate fulfillment of this promise is to give you the "peace that passeth all understanding" (Phil.4:7 KJV).

I lived through the 2007-2009 recession and market crash with almost no anxiety, but I could not perceive in my mind or feel in my spirit an end to the market downturn. I was calm but not powerfully optimistic. I believe that during this time, God gave me a lesson about the powerful effect of putting others first and the blessing that results from giving in an area of my need.

In late 2008, I answered a newspaper ad from a man who was looking for work. I had some jobs around the house, and I felt that I should give the work to someone who had a critical need. I called the man and invited him to come by the house to appraise my first job. We struck a deal, and he told me later in our conversation that he was fifty-five years old and was a physics graduate of a major university. He wanted to talk, and he told me more about himself and the important jobs that he had held. I made no further inquiry, but I did compliment him on his record at a certain company. He was very pleasant and was a good worker; therefore, when he finished a job, I offered him another job. Finally, I asked him to cut down several trees and thin out some shrubs and underbrush on the property.

Halfway into the project, he said that he had underestimated the job and needed to double the price. I was shocked, but I did not really protest because he needed the money, and he had already worked more hours than the estimated price would have produced on an hourly basis. I paid him and he was satisfied, and he came back later and brought us a bird feeder that he had made. He said that we had helped him out in his time of need. That meant more to me than anything that he could have done.

I noticed that my optimism improved dramatically about the economy and the stock market after that, although the economic news was still grim. Two weeks later, the stock market rebounded, and the news about the economy improved. I believe that God gave me an indication of what was immediately ahead as fulfillment of his promise to lift our spirits if we help those in need.

Fear can bash us over the head unless we are proactive in exercising our faith. By invoking applicable Scriptures and practicing good deeds toward those in need, obedient Christians can deal successfully with anxiety.

Seven Cardinal Rules of Investing

This section concludes my recommendations of principles and practices for building wealth in a business and stock investments. Here are seven basic rules, in no particular order, that I recommend for your consideration, some of which you will not read about anywhere else.

1. Keep Good Investment Records. You need good investment records to be able to evaluate you management results, such as the performance of each stock, and to establish a credible tax basis for any stock sale for taxable accounts. If you use comprehensive portfolio management software, like Portfolio Manager 5, the software will keep your records if you download data regularly. Also, archive any past sales because these records will be useful in later years as you study your investment performance and do other research.

2. Read Widely About Your Stocks. Study about your stocks in each weekly *Value Line* issue. Scan your newspaper and surf the Internet for stories about your stocks. Keep up with earnings reports and key developments with your companies. MSN.com/Money has good sections labeled Key Developments, Recent News, and Earnings Estimates. Review your 50 DMA and 200 DMA.

Some of the items to look for in the news: company or competitor reduces sales and/or earnings forecasts; company makes a major purchase that increases the debt to capitalization ratio; company announces an earnings restatement, SEC investigation, or company official is terminated for nefarious conduct; same store sales drop; and profit margins drop for two or more consecutive quarters. You can probably add to this list.

3. Sell Companies Reporting Fraud or SEC Sanctions: When you learn about an investigation, probably it will take a long time for the story to play out. Sell your stock because this initial news is likely just "the tip of the iceberg," and the stock price may stay under pressure longer than you want to tie up your money. If you use the 50 DMA and the 200 DMA, this process should get you out of the stock, even thought you may not initially know about the details. You know something bad is causing the sell-off, so you might sell before you know the entire story.

4. Let the Market Dictate Your Plan of Action. Sometimes the economic news might be good, and the stock indexes start going down. To the contrary, sometimes the investment conditions look grim, and stocks start appreciating in price. As I have expressed before, the market is a discounting mechanism, and investors anticipate the next big move in stocks. Watch your 50 DMA and 200 DMA of the major indexes and the sector averages, and you will get an early alert about how to shift your asset allocation. Sometimes the index price will reverse after a brief time and will move above its 200 DMA, but you can get back into the market with little effort. These "whipsaws" are just the price that you pay for protecting on the downside, but this process is very rewarding when you avoid a major calamity like happened in 2000-2002 and 2007-2009. When you preserve your capital, you have more resources to invest in the banner years.

5. Analyze the Earnings Impact of a Company's Product or Service. If you buy a stock because of a new product or service, make sure that the revenue and earnings from the product or service will be a substantial portion of the total company revenue and earnings. The company needs a big return per product or service to move the stock. This rule assumes that the stock has met all the criteria for a high quality company that is selling at a price well below its intrinsic value.

The Apple iPod is a good example of a powerful product. Product or service analysis can work for you also when the market has sold off a stock because a small-sales product is not doing well. You can buy at a good price before the market realizes that the product does not reduce sufficiently the bottom line to warrant a sell-off.

6. Be Wary of Investment Gurus. High profile market analysts, investment advisors, and investment research gurus usually overstay their calls. The typical pattern includes the analyst making a correct bullish or bearish call when the market is going in the opposite direction. The media elevate him or her to superstar status with frequent interviews. The analyst is predisposed to retain this status and goes further out on a limb, and wham, the market or a stock goes in the opposite direction from that individual's prediction. I have seen too many newsletters and individuals going back to the 1960s go down in flames after a correct call that was layered with pomp and circumstance. I could authenticate this observation by calling names, but that is not my policy. But the Adulation and Arrogance Indicator mentioned in chapter 8 works, so be wary of high-profile gurus.

7. Study Investor Sentiment and Federal Reserve Policy. This is the most important rule for you to master. If you are successful in working this rule, you will be well ahead of the average investor. Investor sentiment identifies market bottoms and Federal Reserve monetary tightening determines market tops. Watch the American Association of Individual Investors (AAII) Bull/Bear sentiment ratios for calling market bottoms. Also, follow the yield curve to predict when stocks will come under selling pressure. An inverted yield curve (higher Fed Funds than 10-year T Note) signals that the Federal Reserve has tightened interest rates to the point of affecting stocks.

The AAII indicator set a record 70.27 percent bears in early March 2009, which called a market bottom, and the market soon responded with a significant rally. The previous low of 67 percent in October 1990 marked the absolute bottom of that bear market. Furthermore, interest rates peaked during the 2000-2003 period before starting to come down in June 2004, but the damage had been done by Federal Reserve policy. The result of this tight money policy by the Federal Reserve was that during the ten-year period from 2000-2009, the S & P 500 Index showed almost no gain.

Summary and Conclusion

I have suggested ten common investor mistakes, reviewed the emotional aspects of investing, and recommended seven commonsense rules of investing. If you will eliminate the mistakes I've outlined; retrain your mind to see first a historical perspective to the stock market; acquire an emotional discipline based on biblical principles; and master the rules of investing, you will enhance your prospect for successful investing, and you will be at peace during the most difficult of economic and investment conditions.

EPILOGUE

Dear Austin,

Granddad is writing to you on this clear autumn day from the porch of the mountain house. As I soak up the freshness of the autumn spectacle, I am in awe of the natural grandeur that the Great Creator has boldly stroked for our inspiration and restoration. I am counting my blessings, among them the joy of welcoming you just over three years ago. Shakespeare said it best: "For thy sweet love remembered such wealth brings, that I would scorn to change my state with Kings." [1]

Soon after you were born, I started writing to leave you with my system for building wealth over a lifetime and the righteous use of wealth. This system starts with positioning yourself to receive God's blessings. Basically, I have written about God's plan for you and your money, and recommended a simple investing plan intended to help you prosper. This path that I am recommending is for the glory of God, the benefit of your fellowman, and your peace and prosperity. Of course, your mom and dad will continue to guide you and provide for you until you mature to adulthood.

I have taken the liberty of sharing these ideas in a book format for others who might be seeking direction for their lives, with particular reference to their finances. You, Austin, are also a proxy as I summarize these ideas for my readers who will study this plan with you over the years.

First and foremost, I urge you to give your heart and soul to Jesus at an early age and follow Him the rest of your life. Read and study your Bible and be obedient to God's commandments and to your parents' directions. Join a church and actively follow the Great Commission that Christ gave His disciples. Be generous, loving, and caring; and seek to be of service always to those less fortunate than you. Early in life, seek God's direction for your life. Ask Him for a vision of what He has for you in life.

When you feel that you have His direction, pursue the vision with all your might. He may call you to start a business. In any event, get a job early in life and learn to work with your brain as well as your back. Learn to think and to write well, which can be enhanced by reading good literature and joining a debate team. Be thorough in your work, whether for yourself or your employer. Be totally honest even when it hurts. Picture yourself as working for the Lord and not for yourself or your employer. Give God back a tenth of all He provides for you. Make sure that you know who you are as a child of God. Trust His guidance and be open to hearing the "still small voice" in your decision-making.

Save your money and invest a portion in a diversified portfolio of stocks and bonds. Consider starting a business; and if you do, seek divine guidance. Set up a thorough system of investing such as I have outlined for you. Establish a complete research program that provides the basic information that you will need to conduct fundamental analysis of the economy and each company that you choose.

Follow your research procedure without deviation or compromise. Buy stocks that are undervalued relative to their intrinsic value, are financially strong, project double-digit total returns, and have established a strong price uptrend. Sell stocks that become overpriced, project weak future total returns, and begin to lose momentum in price appreciation. Next, train yourself to be unemotional in your investment program. Trust your economic and investment indicators.

Learn about economic and market history and understand how trends reverse at the top of bull markets and the bottoms of bear markets. Train yourself to be optimistic. Based on a thorough understanding of economic and market history, and your natural optimistic outlook, you will be in a good position emotionally to take advantage of markets that have sold off unmercifully and risen ebulliently.

As you grow your wealth, remember your obligation to contribute into the kingdom, maintain your humility, and be discrete in mind and action in your stewardship.

Grandmama and I look forward to watching you grow and mature for as long as the Good Lord gives us days. Let eternity guide you, and remember that your mission in life is to hear at your end, "Well done, Austin, you have been a good and faithful servant. Enter into the joy of the Lord."

Love,
Granddad

ENDNOTES

Chapter 1

[1] Wilkinson, Bruce. *The Prayer of Jabez*. Sisters, Oregon: Multnomah Publishers, 2000, p.76.

[2] Prince, Derek. *God's Plan for Your Money*. New Kensington, Pennsylvania: Whitaker House, 1995.

Chapter 2

[1] Hoffman, Susan. *Conversations*. Atlanta/Athens: Georgia Public Broadcasting, July 17, 2007.

[2] Mannes, George. "The Price of Faith." *Money*. New York: Time, Inc. June, 2009. pp. 88-95.

[3] Bevere, John. *Driven By Eternity*. New York: Faith Words, 2006. p. 226.

[4] Davis, M. Steve. "Seeking God in a SUV Society" (Sermon). Carrollton, GA: First Baptist Church, October 4, 2009, pp. 1-2.

[5] "I Have Been Blessed," *The Atlanta Journal Constitution*, August 18, 2007, Section A, page 1.

[6] Crowell, Henry Parsons. "The Crowell Trust." Retrieved from www.CrowellTrust.com. October 2009.

[7] Selina Shirley Hastings. "Silina Hastings, Countess of Huntingdon." Retrieved from http://en.wikifedia.org. October, 2009

[8] Wilkinson, Bruce. *The Prayer of Jabez*. Sisters, Oregon: Multnomah Publishers, 2000, pp.79-82.

Chapter 3

[1] Jones, W. Randall. *The Richest Man In Town*. New York: Business Plus, 2009, p.26

[2] Ibid, p. 125

[3] Ibid, p. 122

[4] Jones, W. Randall. *The Richest Man in Town* . p. 95-103.

[5] *The Atlanta Journal Constitution*, December 13, 2007, Section B, p. 4.

[6] Shakespeare, William. *Henry V*. Retrieved from www.Shakespear-Literature.com. October 13, 2007.

[7] *Atlanta Journal Constitution*, November 4, 2007, Section E, pp. 1, 6.

[8] *He Touched Me: The Gospel Music of Elvis Presley* (DVD). Anderson, Indiana: Spring House Music Group, 2002.

[9] Stanley, Thomas J. and Danko, William D. *The Millionaire Next Door*. New York: Pocket Books, 1996, pp. 30-34.

Chapter 5

[1] Wolfe, Thomas. *You Can't Go Home Again*. New York: Harper & Brothers, 1940.

[2] Anderson, Johathan R. (ed.). *Entrepreneurs of West Georgia: Selected Cases.* Carrollton, GA: University of West Georgia Press, 2007. p. 132.

[3] High, David. *Kings & Priests.* North Bryant, OK: Children of the World, 1993, pp. 7-8, 12.

[4] Davis, M. Steve. "Seeking God in a SUV Society" (Sermon). Carrollton, Georgia: First Baptist Church, October 4, 2009, p. 3.

Chapter 6

[1] Stanley, Thomas J. and Danko, William D. *The Millionaire Next Door.* New York: Pocket Books, 1996, pp. 11-14.

[2] Ibid, pp. 13-14.

[3] Ibid.

[4] Ibid.

[5] Ibid, pp. 30-34, 67-69.

[6] Stowers, James E. with Jonathan, Jack. *Yes, You Can Achieve Financial Independence.* Kansas City, MO: Stowers Innovations, 2000. pp. 197-198.

[7] Blue, Ron. *Master Your Money.* Nashville, TN: Thomas Nelson, 1991, pp. 102-103

[8] Ibid, p. 104.

[9] Ibbotson Associates. *Stocks, Bonds, Bills, and Inflation 2006 Yearbook.* Chicago: Ibbotson Associates, 2006. p. 25-26.

Chapter 7

[1] Evins, Karlen. *I Didn't Know That.* New York: Scribner, 2007, p. 14.

Chapter 8

[1] *How To Invest In Common Stocks.* New York: Value Line Publishing, 1999, p. 29.

[2] Ibid. p. 11.

Chapter 10

[1] Spencer, Chris. *Florence Chadwick: Keeping Your Goals in Sight.* Retrieved from www.thestorytellers.com, September 15, 2009

Epilogue

[1] Shakespeare, William. "Sonnet XXIX." Retrieved from www.Shakespears-Sonnets.com. October 20, 2009.

APPENDIX A

1. **The Law of Reciprocity** says that we will benefit from our own generosity. In Luke 6:38, Jesus says, "If you give, you will receive. Your gift will return to you in full measure, pressed down, shaken together to make room for more, and running over." *Also 1 Chron. 29:12,14; Ps. 37:10-11,25; Mal. 3:7-10; Matt. 6:33, 7:1, 22:39; Luke 6:31; 2 Cor. 9:6-8,11; James 4:7.*

2. **The Law of Use** says that we must use what the Lord has given us, putting it to work and building on it. This is illustrated in Matthew 25:14-30, when Jesus tells the parable of the talents. *Also Ex. 25:9; Lev. 25:4,8-10; Deut. 15:6, 23:19; Matt. 4:8-9, 13:31; Mark 4:26-29; John 12:31, 14:30.*

3. **The Law of Perseverance** tells us to keep pressing on despite our circumstances. Jesus teaches this law in Matthew 7:7-10, when He says, "Keep on asking, and you will be given what you ask for. Keep on looking, and you will find. Keep on knocking, and the door will be opened." *Also 1 Kings 19:4; Luke 11:5-8, 18:1-8; Acts 14:22; Rom. 8:37; Phil. 4:6-7,13.*

4. **The Law of Responsibility** teaches us to rise to the level of our giftedness. Jesus says, "much is required from those to whom much is given, and much more is required from those to whom much more is given" (Luke 12:48). *Also Isaiah 58:1-11; Mark 4:11; Luke 12:46-47; Rom. 1:14; 1 Tim. 3:1-7, 3:10,15; James 1:22-25, 3:1.*

5. **The Law of Greatness** tells us that we become great by being humble. In Luke 22:26, Jesus says, "But among you, those who are the greatest should take the lowest rank, and the leader should be like a servant." *Also Prov. 22:4; Matt. 23:11-12, 18:2-4; Luke 22:25-27.*

6. **The Law of Unity** states that God's power is released where there is harmony. In Matthew 18:19-20, Jesus says, "If two of you agree down here on earth concerning anything you ask, my Father in heaven will do it for you. For where two or three gather together because they are mine, I am there among them." *Also Gen. 3:22-23, 11:6-8; Matt. 6:24, 12:25; John 17:20-23: Acts 4:32-35; 1 Cor. 12:4-7.*

7.   **The Law of Fidelity** teaches that if we are faithful in the small things, then we will be entrusted with greater things. But the reverse is also true, for "unless you are faithful in small matters, you won't be faithful in larger ones" (Luke 16:10). *Also Matt. 25:21; Luke 12:47, 16:10-12; 2 Cor. 5:10.*

8.   **The Law of Change** says that God's plan never changes, but His methods sometimes do. And the greatest change of all must occur in the hearts of His people: "those who become Christians become new persons. They are not the same anymore, for the old life is gone. A new life has begun!" (2 Cor. 5:17). *Also 1 Kings 8:47; Eccl. 1:9; Mal. 3:6; Matt. 9:17; Luke 5:36-38; Rom. 12:2.*

9.   **The Law of Miracles** shows that God is willing to disrupt the natural order to accomplish His purpose. But we must be willing to take our eyes off the circumstances and look to God, because He makes the impossible possible. *Also Num. 13,14; Mark 10:27; John 11:43; Acts 2:4, 24:49; 1 Cor. 12:8-10.*

10. **The Law of Dominion** teaches us that God wants people to rule the earth the way we were created to rule—with humility, discipline, partnership, and not arrogance. Man was created to have dominion on the earth (Gen. 1:26). *Also Gen. 1:29; Matt. 28:19-20; Luke 9:1-2; Rom. 15:19; Phil. 4:13; 2 Tim. 1:7; Heb. 2:14-15.*

APPENDIX B

Value Line to Excel to Morningstar—Stock Transfer

1. At the stock screening results page in Value Line, click the "Export Results" hyperlink above the company name(s). A new dialog window will open stating, "Do you want to open or save this file"—click "Open." The result will be an Excel file requiring minor adjustments before use in Morningstar.

2. If the Excel file does not contain the following headers, and only these headers, in order from left to right beginning in cell A1 (results most likely do not), make the following column adjustments: (A) Name, (B) Symbol, (C) Action, (D) Shares, (E) Price, (F) Commission, and (G) Date. (Delete all other headings and columns.) It is not necessary to dwell on inputing accurate data beneath the Action, Shares, Price, Commission, and Date headings. Your selection(s) will transfer to a Morningstar portfolio regardless. See Example 1-1 on next page for reference.

3. After making the Excel adjustments, click "File" in the upper left-hand corner of the Excel spreadsheet.

4. Click "Save As." A new window will open.

5. In the "File Name" drop down box, name the file something you will remember. In the "Save as Type" drop down box, select "*.csv (comma deliminated)" file. Then click "Save."

6. Open Morningstar.com.

7. Click "Log In" at the top of the home page.

8. Enter your e-mail address and password then click "Log In."

9. Once logged in, click the "Portfolio" tab on the Morningstar home-page.

10. Locate the "Create a Portfolio" label on quarter of the way down the page. Click the middle icon, "Import." A new window will open.

11. Select the Excel "bubble" beneath the Microsoft Excel File heading. Then click "Continue."

12. Locate the Excel file you saved in step 5 by clicking the "Browse" tab. Highlight the file by selecting it, and then click "Open."

13. The file appears in the once blank browse box. Notice above the file name there is a hyperlink stating, *View Export Portfolio Instructions.* If you should encounter problems, use this link as a resource. When the

file appears in the box, click "Continue." A new window appears.

14. Select "Watchlist Portfolio" and click "Continue."
15. In the new window, a "Found Holdings" box appears. Highlight the holdings as they should correspond with the screened Value Line holdings. Click the right-hand arrow next to the "Found Holdings" box to transfer the holdings to "Holdings to Import." When the desired holdings appear in the "Holdings to Import" box, click "Continue." A new window appears showing the holdings.
16. Click "Save" in the bottom right-hand corner of the dialog box.
17. Your holdings should now appear in a Morningstar portfolio.

Example 1-1

Name	Symbol	Action	Shares	Price	Commission	Date
Cognizant Tech	CTSH	Buy	1	1.00	0.1	21-Jul-09
Infosys Tech	INFY	Buy	1	1.00	0.1	21-Jul-09
St. Jude Medical	STJ	Buy	1	1.00	0.1	21-Jul-09
Gildan Activewear	GIL	Buy	1	1.00	0.1	21-Jul-09

Instructions provided by David King, SCM Associates, Inc. summer intern from the University of West Georgia Richards College of Business, Carrollton, Georgia.

About the Author

Steve McCutcheon is an entrepreneur, investment manager, and former university administrator. He holds a doctorate from Indiana University and bachelors and masters from Auburn and Florida State universities respectively. Early in his career he taught psychology and was assistant dean of students at Wofford College, research assistant at Indiana University, and assistant to the president of West Georgia College, later University of West Georgia.

Dr. McCutcheon also served as executive director of the West Georgia College Foundation, where he later began his investment career. He founded his money management firm, SCM Associates, Inc., in 1986, and founded and managed a broker/dealer (1988), Southern Capital Management Company, and a SEC-registered mutual fund (1989), SCM Portfolio Fund, Inc. Currently he serves as chairman and president of SCM Associates, Inc., which manages investment portfolios for individuals, trust and estates, foundations, and corporate retirement plans.

He has written extensively on investment management, including a stock analysis column for 50 issues of *Georgia Trend*, a monthly journal covering business and politics. He also has taught investment analysis professional education courses and interned finance majors from the University of West Georgia.

He served six years in the U. S. Army Reserves. Steve is an avid golfer and fan of Auburn football and I U basketball.

The awards and recognition that he has received include: Outstanding Adult Educator in Georgia (1989), Who's Who in the South and Southeast (20th edition), and Vocational Practices and Ethics Award, his most-prized award, from his Rotary Club in 2007.

You may visit Dr. McCutcheon at www.scm-invest.com and contact him at buildingwealth@scm-invest.com/